CW01023965

Imagining Transatlantic Slavery

Imagining Transatlantic Slavery

Edited by

Cora Kaplan

and

John Oldfield

palgrave
macmillan

First published 2010 by
PALGRAVE MACMILLAN

Palgrave Macmillan in the UK is an imprint of Macmillan Publishers Limited, registered in England, company number 785998, of Houndmills, Basingstoke, Hampshire RG21 6XS.

Palgrave Macmillan in the US is a division of St Martin's Press LLC, 175 Fifth Avenue, New York, NY 10010.

Palgrave Macmillan is the global academic imprint of the above companies and has companies and representatives throughout the world.

Palgrave® and Macmillan® are registered trademarks in the United States, the United Kingdom, Europe and other countries.

ISBN-13: 978-0-230-57820-3   hardback

This book is printed on paper suitable for recycling and made from fully managed and sustained forest sources. Logging, pulping and manufacturing processes are expected to conform to the environmental regulations of the country of origin.

A catalogue record for this book is available from the British Library.

A catalog record for this book is available from the Library of Congress.

10 9 8 7 6 5 4 3 2 1
19 18 17 16 15 14 13 12 11 10

Printed and bound in Great Britain by
CPI Antony Rowe, Chippenham and Eastbourne

Contents

List of Illustrations

List of Contributors

Brycchan Carey is Reader in English Literature at Kingston University. He is the author of *British Abolitionism and the Rhetoric of Sensibility: Writing, Sentiment, and Slavery, 1760–1807* (2005), and has edited (with Markman Ellis and Sara Salih) *Discourses of Slavery and Abolition: Britain and its Colonies, 1760–1838* (2004) and (with Peter Kitson) *Slavery and the Cultures of Abolition: Essays Marking the British Abolition Act of 1807* (2007). His essay, '"Accounts of Savage Nations": *The Spectator* and the Americas' won the Society of Early Americanists' Annual Essay Prize in 2004.

Vincent Carretta is Professor of English at the University of Maryland. His books include *Equiano the African: Biography of a Self-Made Man* (2005), *George III and the Satirists from Hogarth to Byron* (1990) and scholarly editions: *Olaudah Equiano* (1999 and 2003) and *Letters of the Late Ignatius Sancho, an African* (1998). His biography of Equiano was co-winner 2004–06 of the Annibel Jenkins Prize for Best Biography of the Year, American Society for Eighteenth-Century Studies.

Lisa Maria Crisafulli is Professor of English Literature at the University of Bologna and Director of the Centro Interdisciplinare di Studi Romantici. Her books include *P. B. Shelley fra '800 e '900: La Fortuna Critica* (1990) and *La Realita del Desiderio: Saggi Morali, Teoria Estetica e Prosa Politica di P. B. Shelley* (1999). Her edited books include *Itineraries in British Romanticism* (2002) and *Poetesse Romantiche Inglesi, Antologia*, 2 vols. (2003).

Eileen Razzari Elrod is Associate Professor of English and Women's and Gender Studies at Santa Clara University. She is the author of *Piety and Dissent: Race, Gender, and Biblical Rhetoric in Early American Autobiography* (2008). Her articles have appeared in *African American Review*, *Prospects: An Annual Review of American Cultural Studies*, *Legacy: A Journal of American Women Writers* and *The Journal of the American Academy of Religion*.

Catherine Hall is Professor of History at University College London. Her most recent book is *Civilising Subjects: Metropole and Colony in the English Imagination, 1830–1867* (2002), awarded the Morris D. Forkosch Prize by the American Historical Association. With Keith McClelland

and Jane Randall she has written *Defining the Victorian Nation: Class, Race, Gender and the Reform Act of 1867* (2000). She has also edited with Sonya O. Rose *At Home with the Empire: Metropolitan Culture and the Imperial World* (2006).

Douglas Hamilton is RCUK Fellow and Lecturer in History at the Wilberforce Institute for the study of Slavery and Emancipation (WISE) at the University of Hull. He is a visiting fellow at the Centre for Imperial and Maritime Studies at the National Maritime Museum, where he was Curator of Eighteenth-Century Maritime and Imperial History. He is the author of *Scotland, the Caribbean and the Atlantic World, 1750–1820* (2005) and joint editor of *Representing Slavery: Art, Artefacts and Archives in the Collections of the National Maritime Museum* (2007).

Cora Kaplan has held Chairs of English at Rutgers University and at the University of Southampton. Most recently she has been Visiting Professor of English at Queen Mary, University of London. A feminist critic with strong interests in both race and class, her work has had a particular focus on the long nineteenth century in Britain and on politics, culture and theory from the 1960s onwards. Her most recent book is *Victoriana: Histories, Fictions, Criticism* (2007).

Elizabeth Kowaleski Wallace is Professor of English at Boston College. Her books include *The British Slave Trade and Public Memory* (2006), *Consuming Subjects: Women, Shopping and Business in the Eighteenth Century* (1997) and *Their Fathers' Daughters: Hannah More, Maria Edgeworth and Patriarchal Complicity* (1990).

Jessie Morgan-Owens did her PhD in American Literature at New York University. Her essay in this collection comes from her dissertation, 'Black and White: Photographic Writing in the Literature of Abolition', which studies the influence of photography in the campaign to abolish slavery in the United States. She currently holds the position of assistant professor in the Division of English at Nanyang Technological University, Singapore. Jessie Morgan-Owens is also a professional photographer.

HollyGale Millette is completing her PhD in Cultural History at Royal Holloway, University of London. Her dissertation explores the trade and traffic in popular culture between the United States and Britain in the long nineteenth century. Her research interests include transatlantic popular culture and entertainments between 1850 and 1950.

John Oldfield is Professor of Modern History at the University of Southampton. He is the author of *Popular Politics and British Anti-Slavery: The Mobilisation of Public Opinion against the Slave Trade, 1787–1807* (1995) and *'Chords of Freedom': Commemoration, Ritual and British Transatlantic Slavery* (2007). He is the editor of *The British Atlantic Slave Trade*, vol. 3, *The Abolitionist Struggle: Opponents of the Slave Trade* (2003) and has written extensively on the American South, US race relations and slavery and abolition in the Atlantic World.

Marcus Wood is Professor of English and American Studies at the University of Sussex. His books include *Blind Memory: Visual Representations of Slavery in England and America, 1780–1865* (2000) and *Slavery, Empathy and Pornography* (2002). He has written extensively on slavery and abolition in the Atlantic World. His new book, *The Horrible Gift of Freedom: Marketing the Emancipation Moment from 1807 to 2007*, is forthcoming from Georgia University Press. Marcus Wood is also an artist and filmmaker.

Acknowledgements

With two exceptions, all of the essays in this volume began life as papers that were delivered at the 'Imagining Transatlantic Slavery' conference held at Chawton House Library, Alton, Hampshire, in March 2007. We are extremely grateful to Chawton House Library and its then director, Heather Shearer, for agreeing to host the conference, and to Dr Gillian Dow and the library's excellent staff for making the conference such a success. We could not have done it without you.

Various people helped to pull the volume together, but special thanks must go to Duncan Barrett and to Sandy White, who has been a tower of strength. We would also like to thank everyone at Palgrave and the press's anonymous reviewer, who helped to iron out a number of inconsistencies. Financial assistance came from the School of Humanities, University of Southampton. We were also fortunate enough to receive a grant from the British Academy (Conference Awards) to support 'Imagining Transatlantic Slavery'. We are extremely grateful for their assistance.

Cora Kaplan
John Oldfield

Introduction

Cora Kaplan and John Oldfield

The enormous variety of commemorative events surrounding the sequential bicentenary anniversaries, in 2007 and 2008, of the abolition of the British and United States' slave trade has revived public interest in the history of transatlantic slavery and its abolition, and renewed as well a debate that Catherine Hall has likened to a 'war of representation' – visual as much as verbal – surrounding abolitionist discourse from the late eighteenth century onwards. Many of the formal, public events of 2007/8 have centred around celebrations of such iconic figures as William Wilberforce. But the bicentenary has also provoked a more critical response to the ways in which this complex history both of enslavement and enfranchisement have been imagined, told and taught – a response that challenges official accounts and invites us to look again at the paradoxes embedded in national histories that have first enslaved and then liberated persons of African descent, and continued to discriminate against them at home and abroad.

To understand how those histories have been and are told, we need to understand the troubled and troubling ethics and aesthetics of the representation of enslaved persons and the institution of slavery. Questions of inclusion, emphasis and appropriation are still relevant – and the use and misuse of sentiment and melodrama in depicting the trauma of transatlantic slavery remain paramount. Scholars, as well as curators, authors and filmmakers, argue about who the changing target audiences for new histories, fictions, films and exhibitions are and should be. Acts of the imagination reciprocally shared by the makers of narrative, and their readers and viewers, are key to how we think about the implication of Anglophone nations in the transnational history of slavery. Nor is this an abstract academic question, as the conflicting narratives of memorialisation have made clear. Rather, it asks what sort of modern

1

political subjects, with what sense of their own agency to change the present bitter legacies of slavery, are constructed and informed by the still unfolding story of transatlantic slavery.

In the interdisciplinary essays in *Imagining Transatlantic Slavery* historians, art historians and literary scholars take a critical view of the histories leading up to the defining decisions of 1807–08 and reflect on their complex legacies over the last two centuries. The first two sections trace the development of these debates, marking the shifting terms through which Europeans and ex-slaves characterised the injustice and trauma of slavery from its inception through to its abolition in Britain and the United States, while the third section, and an Afterword by Catherine Hall, focus on representation from the last decade up to and through the recent commemorative events, which come under particular scrutiny.

Abolitionists were among the first people to grapple with the problem of representing or 'imagining' transatlantic slavery. It was one thing to condemn slavery on philosophical or moral grounds, quite another to convey its potential to dehumanise Africans. This struggle to comprehend, literally to describe the horrors of slavery, led Thomas Clarkson to include in his *Essay on the Slavery and Commerce of the Human Species* (1786) an imaginary interview with a 'melancholy African'.[1] Clarkson turned to this literary device almost in desperation, for want of information and direct, first-hand experience of what he was describing. For this very reason, collecting and publishing evidence about slavery and the slave trade would become a preoccupation of British abolitionists throughout the 1780s and 1790s. Clarkson himself conducted hundreds of interviews with slave captains, merchants, sailors, doctors and military and naval personnel. Others, like the former slave Olaudah Equiano, volunteered their services, or else agreed to speak before the bar of the House of Commons. In each case, these witnesses contributed to an ever-increasing pool of information that, in turn, helped to shape popular perceptions of transatlantic slavery. Scenes of depredation on the West Coast of Africa, the unmitigated horrors of the Middle Passage, the brutality and oppression of slavery in the Americas; all of these would become familiar abolitionist tropes during the late eighteenth century.

Just how familiar is only now becoming fully apparent. In recent years, scholars have devoted a lot of time to mapping the contours of abolitionist discourse and, in particular, the growth of what we might call 'cultures of abolition'. Eighteenth-century drama and poetry have been successfully mined for evidence of abolitionist sentiments, as has eighteenth-century fiction. Thanks to the work of Vincent Carretta, Helen Thomas, Moira Ferguson and Felicity Nussbaum (among others), we now know much more than we ever did about slave narratives and the relationship between abolitionism and women's writing.[2] Similarly, historians and cultural critics alike have paid increasing attention to the representation of slaves and slavery in art.[3] What this painstaking research has shown is that abolitionism penetrated deeply into British and American culture during the eighteenth and nineteenth centuries, interacting with (and sometimes helping to shape) literary and cultural forms like sentimentalism and Romanticism.

Part I of *Imagining Transatlantic Slavery* offers important new insights into this culture of abolition. In the opening chapter Brycchan Carey revisits the Germantown (Pennsylvania) Protest of 1688, a remarkable document that was seemingly lost and then rediscovered in 1844. Carey's interest in the Protest is, in part, genealogical. So far from being forgotten, he argues, the Protest should be seen as an important factor 'in the subsequent development of Quaker antislavery thought'. At the same time, Carey highlights the explicit radicalism of the Protest and, in particular, its insistence that the Golden Rule ('do unto others as you would have done unto you') extended to all men, regardless of 'descent or Colour'. Here, perhaps, we can discern the origins of the abolitionists' motto, 'Am I not a Man and a Brother?'. The Germantown Protest was also remarkable for condemning Quaker slave traders and owners as 'robbers', emotive language that compromised seventeenth-century beliefs in the sanctity of property. Equally striking is the willingness of the authors of the Protest to contemplate the possibility, even the legitimacy, of slave resistance. In doing so, they highlighted not only the violence of the master–slave relationship, but also its potential to subvert Quaker beliefs, not least their commitment to peace.

In Chapter 2 John Oldfield excavates a different but complementary worldview, that of radical Dissent, represented here by Benjamin Flower, editor of the *Cambridge Intelligencer* (1793–1803). Employing language rich in Old Testament images of sin and retribution, Flower attacked slavery as a national sin and one that, if left unchecked, would result only in the ruin of Britain and her empire. As Oldfield makes clear, Flower's stance was typically uncompromising, leading him into direct conflict with Wilberforce and the 'Saints', whose private and public conduct he viewed with increasing distaste. As such, Flower highlights a significant fissure in abolitionist discourse of the 1790s, that between radical Dissent, on the one hand, and Evangelical Protestantism, on the other. No less significant was Flower's success in turning the *Cambridge*

Intelligencer into a national newspaper, thereby enabling him to keep abolition (and his own distinctive views on the subject) before the British public during a difficult period in the movement's history. Flower's importance is therefore twofold: not only did his intemperate attacks on figures like Wilberforce highlight the increasing alienation of some grass-roots activists; they also confirmed the strength and vibrancy of alternative (radical) cultures of abolition.

Turning once again to the American movement, Jessie Morgan-Owens examines the role of daguerreotypes in shaping late abolitionist rhetoric. Daguerreotypes were an important innovation, not least because they gave the black body its own individuality. They were also highly malleable. To illustrate this, Morgan-Owens focuses on the sensational daguerreotype of Mary Botts, a light skinned mulatto who had been purchased and manumitted by Massachusetts Senator Charles Sumner. Significantly, Northern abolitionists re-inscribed Botts' slave body as white; and to emphasise this point they juxtaposed her image with the story of Ida May, the fictional white heroine of Mary Langdon's novel of the same name, who is kidnapped from her family in Pennsylvania and sold into slavery in the South. As Morgan-Owens stresses, the plight of white slaves was a highly effective rhetorical device, and one that was calculated to elicit the sympathies of white viewers/readers, many of whom were unmoved by representations of black suffering. But its success also depended on disavowing the fact of sexual slavery. Even radical abolitionists fought shy of addressing the vexed issue of miscegenation, or, if you will, Mary Botts' origins, preferring instead to use white slaves to challenge racially defined slavery, that is, slavery based on 'unmistakable' differences between the races.

Ironically, some blacks were also able to exploit the indeterminacy of 'race', as in the case of William and Ellen Craft, who escaped from slavery in 1848, Ellen disguising herself as a Southern white gentleman, William filling in as 'his' black slave. Making their way first to Philadelphia, the Crafts subsequently moved to Boston and then, following the passage of the Fugitive Slave Act (1850), to London. Britain would become an important haven for black Americans in the years immediately preceding the Civil War. Estimates vary, but something like 80 of them crossed the Atlantic between 1830 and 1865.[4] Many of these men and women were fugitives or else had some other direct experience of slavery, and in Britain they found willing friends, as well as a home away from home. Alexander Crummell, who visited Britain in 1848, spoke for many when he told an audience in Liverpool: 'When I was in America I THOUGHT I was a man. In England I FEEL – I KNOW that

I am.' Frederick Douglass also remarked upon the absence of colour prejudice in Britain. On his initial visit to Ireland in 1845 he told William Lloyd Garrison that 'one of the most pleasing features of my visit here thus far has been a total absence of all manifestations of prejudice against me, on account of my color'.[5]

As HollyGale Millette shows in her essay, the Crafts insinuated themselves into British society with consummate ease. The couple were hugely popular on the abolitionist circuit, already well established by 1850, and won the support and admiration of influential British reformers, among them John Estlin and Harriet Martineau. But, as Millette argues, this success involved yet another form of disguise. Thus, while Ellen Craft appeared at public meetings she never spoke, preferring to let her husband (re)tell their story. Millette's essay sheds important light on transatlantic abolitionist cultures. Ellen Craft's willingness to acculturate, in effect to become a domesticated woman, reinforced white cultural expectations (as Henry 'Box' Brown was to discover, Britons had no time for showmen, or for those who overstepped the bounds of taste and decency). Put another way, the essentialising whiteness of abolitionist cultures demanded that black visitors conform; hence the emphasis on 'respectability', an important word in the abolitionists' vocabulary.

'Authenticity' was another key word associated with slave testimony. A favourable review of *The Interesting Narrative of the Life of Olaudah Equiano* in the *Monthly Review* of June 1789 opened with the assertion that 'We entertain no doubt of the general authenticity of this very intelligent African's interesting story'. The quality of the writing itself raised an important related issue: because the reviewer thought it 'sufficiently well written' he thought it 'not improbable that some English writer has assisted him in the compilement, or, at least, the correction of his book'.[6] Authenticity and mediation, in relation to both story and style, were central questions in the reception of slave narratives at the time of publication, and ever since. When, in the 1970s, historians of slavery and literary critics began applying narrative analysis to the body of transatlantic slave narratives, they granted them a new and 'higher' status as a literary genre. Nevertheless, there has been a preference for simplicity of language and reference in slave narratives: literary embellishment has often been seen as evidence of the controlling, interfering hand of amanuensis, editor, 'mentor' or publisher, a judgement that has been true in the twentieth-century reception of both Mary Prince and Harriet Jacobs's narratives.[7] The dubious ideal of a single-authored, factually accurate, uncensored slave narrative, whose rhetoric and even narrative shape remained uninfluenced by contemporary fashions in prose or verse has haunted slave testimony from its inception. Like all impossible demands for 'purity', whether racial or discursive, it creates new and unhelpful categories of difference. At least now the politics, aesthetics and ethics of the writing of the once enslaved is the subject of heated and interesting scholarly engagement.

Part II, from which the collection takes its name, explores the complicated aesthetic and political questions at stake in abolitionist discourse, whether written by ex-slaves or about them. As the latest and most definitive editor of Equiano's *Interesting Narrative* as well as his biographer, Vincent Carretta has been at the sharp end of these debates for some years. In the opening essay of this section Carretta turns to Equiano's subtle use of literary intertextuality in his argument against the slave trade. Drawing on Earl Wasserman's suggestive study of allusion in eighteenth-century writing, Carretta emphasises the crucial role elliptical allusion – where what is not directly cited is called up as a silent referent for the knowing reader – can play in making a more daring and radical case against slavery itself. Carretta rightly characterises Equiano's fat volume as multi-generic, appealing to 'original subscribers and subsequent readers as a spiritual autobiography, captivity narrative, slave narrative, argument against the slave trade, adventure tale, travel book, economic treatise and *apologia.*' Allusion is used, in Chapter 5, to universalise: Equiano uses Thomas Day and John Bicknell's *The Dying Negro*, a poem published in London 1773 about a retaken slave who commits suicide, to highlight the perfidy of his own master, Pascal, who seemed to promise freedom but sold Equiano back into slavery. Representing himself, as Day and Bicknell do their fictitious 'Negro', Equiano cites the lines that describe the miseries of slavery but leaves out the later invocation in the poem of Africa as a personified 'avenger' of the race. Milton's *Paradise Lost* is also a rich resource adapted to move the 'lamentable lot' of the slave from the first to the third person. Reference to Moses in Exodus 2:11–15 provides perhaps one of the most effective allusions, one that Equiano can be sure his readers are familiar with. These sources combine in a last invocation in Beelzebub's voice from *Paradise Lost* explicitly asking on behalf of the injured and repressed 'what peace can we return?' and warning of 'revenge, tho' slow.' The political thrust of such intertextual reference is, Carretta reminds us, tricky to assess – indeed, it is crafted to be so. Yet at the very least, he argues, Equiano's use of allusion leaves 'open the option of violent resistance' for the attentive contemporary reader.

The black poet Phillis Wheatley, like her contemporary Equiano, was writing in the originary moment of 'abolitionist discourse'. Reading her complex poetry and her letters for their overt and covert anti-slavery sentiments has been a challenging interpretative enterprise; her life part of her modern rehabilitation. An exemplary figure in the debate about human difference in her lifetime, she has, in the last two hundred years and more, been reinvented and re-imagined to suit the changing political and aesthetic agendas of social movements and cultural histories. Henry Louis Gates' *The Trials of Phillis Wheatley* traces the suspicions that circulated around questions of authorship and authenticity in her work in the eighteenth century and the late twentieth and twenty first century.[8] Eileen Razzari Elrod's important essay on the 1834 edition of her work published by George W. Light in Boston with a memoir by Margaretta Matilda Odell helps to flesh out a forgotten nineteenth-century history of Wheatley's reception and appropriation. Directed to, and assuming, an abolitionist reading for this 'African genius', Odell's biographical sketch remained a key source for later writers, her errors repeated through the nineteenth century. Elrod argues that the contours of Odell's depiction of Wheatley dictated not only how she was to be understood, but shaped the identities of her readers, through their sympathetic response to her story. At the same time William Lloyd Garrison was republishing Wheatley's poetry in *The Liberator*. Indeed, Wheatley reappears as a subject for abolitionism in the 1830s through an uneasy conjunction of Garrisonian abolitionism, with its radical anti-racist emphasis on political equality, the conventionally gendered, sentimental Christian piety of Light's wider list and Odell's soothing, domestically orientated memoir. Interestingly, the memoir excludes both Wheatley's conversion and her manumission, a manumission that she may have actively pursued. More in tune with the sentimental domestic fiction of the day, Odell's memoir may have been a reassuring counterpoint to sensational accounts of violent male slave revolts, notably Thomas Gray's *Confessions of Nat Turner*.

For all its abolitionist fervour, Odell's memoir, in which the exceptional Phillis is a figure of humility, invites the reader to identify with the liberal kindness of the slaveholding Wheatleys, rather than with any form of black agency. How abolitionist discourse addresses and constructs the sympathetic white reader and potential anti-slavery activist has been a subject of much critical and historical debate in recent years. The 'sentimental anti-slavery' poetry and prose of the late eighteenth and early nineteenth century by both men and women imagine the slave as victim rather than agent; it is this tradition that

lies behind Odell's later characterisation of Wheatley. Both the affect
and the politics associated with the tradition of white-authored 'sentimental' anti-slavery writing have received much critical attention
in the last few decades.[9] This is particularly true of British women's
anti-slavery poetry, a genre that extends from Hannah More's *Slavery:
A Poem* and Ann Yearsley's *A Poem on the Inhumanity of the Slave Trade*,
both published in 1788, through to Elizabeth Barrett Browning's *The
Runaway Slave at Pilgrim's Point* (1848). Marcus Wood, among others, contrasts the piety as well as the racial and social conservatism
of More's abolition verse with that of her idiosyncratic protégé, the
working-class Yearsley, who, he argues, makes 'an obsessive assault on
the hypocrisy of state religion.'[10]

Ann Stott's brilliant biography of More, *Hannah More: the First
Victorian* (2003) led the way in reviving interest in More as a 'complex
and contradictory figure' whose life seemed to belie her conventional
views of women's place. Indeed, she has become a fascinating if always
controversial figure for late twentieth and early twenty-first century
feminism.[11] Lilla Crisafulli, writing about More and Yearsley in this
volume, mounts a stout defence of the boldness of women's anti-slavery
stance, emphasising the ways in which both poets challenged the
authority and integrity of parliament, and 'adumbrated a demystification of the money nexus' that underpinned slavery. Her analysis
highlights the ways in which 'British sons of murder' – from traders
to the ship's 'tars' in their different roles – are seen to be engaged in a
brutal and 'savage' activity. Crisafulli argues through careful close readings that the language of *Slavery: A Poem* and 'The Sorrows of Yamba' is
never simply complicit with colonialist discourse as some critics have
suggested, but constructs 'an uncompromising counter-discourse that is
not only, and powerfully, humanitarian but also stringently political'.
Linking Yearsley's invitation that slave traders bring their own 'daughters to this market' (together with their wives, aged mothers and 'ruddy
boys') to Swift's *A Modest Proposal*, these poets, Crisafulli suggests, used
their rhetorical skills on behalf of the slave's humanity and against the
'greed' of the commercial nature to critique and to refeminise Britannia.
If this meant contributing to a formulation of women and domesticity
as key to the nation as family, at this moment and on this issue, the
challenge was radical on several fronts.

How we choose to remember slavery is neither haphazard nor unme-
diated. On the contrary, when a society creates or modifies its traditions
(its ways of remembering), it does so to 'satisfy rational needs, and at
the very moment in which they appear'.[12] In Britain's case, adjustment

to the reality of an empire without slaves necessitated a reordering of priorities. In practice, this meant absolving themselves of responsibility for transatlantic slavery and, instead, highlighting the role that the British had played in bringing slavery to an end. Emancipation (1834/38) marked the nation out. Such selfless actions, it was argued, legitimised Britain's role in the world, the country's stewardship over countless millions in Africa, India and the Caribbean, and, no less important, its particular claim to speak for those who were too weak to speak for themselves. Put another way, Britons became used to viewing slavery through the moral triumph of abolition. Wilberforce was a key figure here. Wilberforce's high idealism, and his reputation as a 'statesman-saint', came to embody a certain type of British philanthropy and, just as important, a certain type of Britishness. As *The Times* put it in 1933, in a typically glowing tribute: 'He, if any man, was worthy to establish the Victorian faith in a continuous progress of humanity in and to freedom, and to vindicate for politics the sublimity that they possessed in the eyes of PLATO.'[13]

For the most part, historical writing on slavery (really 'abolition') tended to reflect this emphasis on Wilberforce and, by extension, Britain's tradition of humanitarian interventionism. By the 1980s, however, if not before, such interpretations had begun to lose salience and, indeed, relevance. Trends in academic discourse that highlighted black agency, not least through forms of resistance, together with a growing political awareness of Britain's multicultural heritage, led, in turn, to a reappraisal of slavery and abolition. We now tend to think of abolitionism less as a campaign conducted in Parliament, than as a popular movement depending on the efforts (and money) of thousands of local activists who were willing to distribute books and pamphlets, organise local committees and sign petitions against the slave trade. One of the best examples of this shift towards a more inclusive or 'popular' view of abolition, was the 2007 exhibition at the Palace of Westminster, where the organisers put on display the 1806 Manchester petition against the slave trade, linking it to a searchable database ('The Big Conversation') containing the names of all of those who signed the petition. In the same spirit, in 2007 Birmingham Museums and Art Gallery launched 'The Equiano Project', a multi-tiered heritage project that commemorates Equiano's visit to Birmingham in 1790.[14]

Running alongside this more inclusive view of abolition, and sometimes in competition with it, has been a growing emphasis on the human indignity of the transatlantic slave trade. As Gary Streeter, Conservative MP for South-West Devon, told the House of Commons ahead of the bicentenary; 'there must be an acknowledgement of the part that the country played in this appalling atrocity; that what we did was wrong; that it is a scar on our history, and is only partially redeemed by the fact that we led the way in the abolition of the trade and then the abolition of slavery'.[15] Streeter's comments reflected a widespread sense that 2007 was an opportunity not simply to 'do justice' to transatlantic slavery but also to ensure that Britons 'learnt the lessons of the past'. Hence the demands for an apology of some kind (an issue that, for the most part, the British government has managed to dodge). Hence, too, the calls for reparations, a highly emotive issue that continues to divide opinion on both sides of the Atlantic, and for a national slavery remembrance day (23 August), a permanent commemoration that, in MP Louise Ellman's words, would recognise the inhumanity of transatlantic slavery, 'celebrate' slaves' resistance and emphasise the links between slavery and racism, 'much of which still persists'.[16]

Part III of *Imagining Transatlantic Slavery* offers three meditations on contemporary efforts to commemorate slavery within the context of the 2007 bicentenary. In the first of these, Douglas Hamilton discusses the detailed planning behind the National Maritime Museum's new 'Atlantic Worlds Gallery', opened in November 2007. Since the 1980s museums have been at the forefront of 'new' representations of transatlantic slavery, offering visitors fresh perspectives and experiences (for example, mock-ups of the interiors of slave ships). But mounting these displays involves a delicate balancing act, not simply between different types of audiences but also between different narrative strategies, the weight given to black agency being an obvious case in point. Given the intense pressures, mistakes are easy to make, as the NMM discovered with its 'Trade and Empire Gallery'. Yet, as Hamilton argues, what is at issue here is our ability to arrive at a new consensus, one that recognises (and applauds) the specific, British roots of abolition, but at the same time also acknowledges the true horror and enormity of transatlantic slavery, and its role in transforming Britain into a major mercantile and military power.

The particularity of each Atlantic nation's experience of slavery and abolition becomes manifest not only in the themes highlighted by museum and exhibition halls, but also in the modern rewriting of that history in fiction, drama and film. Elizabeth Kowaleski Wallace's *The British Slave Trade & Public Memory* (2006) explored the fin-de-siècle representations of slavery and its legacies through a range of genres that provided sites for its re-representation, from the exhibitions in Bristol and Liverpool to Rozema's controversial film version of Jane Austen's

Mansfield Park, which puts back into the text the conversation on Britain's implication in slavery that the novel, through its naïve heroine Fanny, raises as a question that cannot be answered at the genteel dinner table. Discussing films and docudrama as diverse as the BBC's brief treatment of Equiano, *A Son of Africa*, to Mike Leigh's *Secrets and Lies* about the taboos still surrounding mixed race relationships and their children in today's cosmopolitan London, Kowaleski Wallace emphasises the paradoxes that face British writers and audiences as they attempt to situate that imagined history and its many mutations at the end of the twentieth century, so marked throughout, as W. E. B. DuBois prophetically said at its opening, by the problem of the colour line.

Enlarging on her argument in her essay for this volume, Kowaleski Wallace explores the ways in which this 'problem' is understood differently in the United States and in Britain. The success in London of the play *Coram Boy*, with its highly theatrical presentation of an eighteenth-century story of interracial adoption, is linked to the theatrical tradition of depicting slavery on the British stage, from the many adaptations of Aphra Behn's *Oroonoko* from 1695 onwards. These representations come with a health warning: the theatricalisation of slavery, its literal rendering as melodrama and trauma, engage the viewers' scopophilia – their pleasure in viewing – but not perhaps their moral sense. *Coram Boy* uses visually stunning pieces of theatre to make its political point about the horrors of slavery – the black orphan Toby jumping from a ship into the ocean to avoid being enslaved – but the thrilling spectacle coupled with the play's very traditional liberal humanist closure, which invokes the family of man, repeats some of the more suspect elements of abolition discourse in the first half of the long nineteenth century – its dramatic visual panoramas and its sentimental evocation of the family – in this case the white family who graciously and sympathetically take Toby in. The success of the piece in London and its critical and financial failure in New York raise interesting questions about the divergent representational history of slavery in Britain and the United States. Is the appreciation of British audiences for such history replayed as melodrama a sign of their lack of political and aesthetic sophistication? Is the rejection of American theatregoers a lack of affective attachment to the national story of *Coram Boy*, or is it a more nuanced resistance to 'race' narratives as sentimental entertainment? Further issues arise. In its oblique and partial reference to a history still largely absent in Britain's 'public memory', *Coram Boy* suggests that the politics of an audience's sympathetic identification with the spectacle of enslavement remains problematic.

In the concluding chapter Marcus Wood revisits some of the issues raised in Hamilton's essay. But, in doing so, he pushes the argument further. Wood's point is straightforward, that while public officials and institutions paid lip service to the idea of black agency in commemorating 1807, the visual culture surrounding the bicentenary was curiously unadventurous, particularly in the way in which it perpetuated black passivity. One of the most familiar of these images was the plan and description of the slave ship *Brookes*, produced by abolitionists in the late eighteenth century and produced and (re)produced countless times since. Indeed, Wood argues that this single image has been used so much that it has lost its power to shock, or even to surprise. The same might be said of Wedgwood's famous cameo of the kneeling slave, together with the motto 'Am I Not a Man and a Brother?' In each case, such motifs were strangely reassuring, offering viewers a familiar 'history' of slavery and abolition, and one that prioritised 'slave inactivity, slave suffering and slave anonymity'. Wood, however, is dissatisfied with such safe solutions, challenging us to re-imagine the boundaries of transatlantic slavery, not least by paying more attention to an alternative tradition of slave resistance.

Yet, at the same time, the use and re-use of familiar images reveals the complex and often contradictory ways in which each generation interprets its past. At an official level, at least, what the 2007 commemorations were at pains to emphasise was a more popular or inclusive interpretation of abolition – one that remembered 'the commitment and energy of a group of abolitionists, black and white, male and female, who gave much and risked much to end the cruelty of the transatlantic trade in slaves'.[17] As Catherine Hall argues in her Afterword, this attempt to re-imagine abolition as the people's abolition should be seen in the context of a growing political emphasis on 'social cohesion', the implication here being that multiculturalism had led to 'social fracturing and increased separation'. But it may be that what happened in Westminster Abbey on 25 March 2007, or what was represented on our postage stamps, was less important than reforms to the National Curriculum, or initiatives like the Wilberforce Institute for the study of Slavery and Emancipation (WISE), jointly funded by Yorkshire Forward and Hull City Council.[18] One thing is certain. The old consensus, the one that traditionally focused almost exclusively on Britain's tradition of humanitarianism, has broken down. It may be too early to predict what will take its place but, as Hall concludes, we should not underestimate the extent to which 2007 shifted perceptions and created new paradigms.

Fifty or even forty years ago, it was still possible for Britons to view transatlantic slavery through the moral triumph of abolition. Today, such 'histories' are likely to provoke alarm and consternation. As the essays in this volume demonstrate, we now recognise slavery for the 'foul iniquity' that it was. We also recognise its power to excite passions, to spark creative endeavour and to shape thought and action. If the 2007 bicentenary of the abolition of the British slave trade proved anything, it was the continued relevance of and interest in all aspects of slavery and abolition. Just as important, that interest was not confined to centres like Liverpool, London and Bristol; indeed, one of the features of 2007 was the number of exhibitions and events put on in places not usually associated with transatlantic slavery: Guernsey, East Anglia, Derbyshire, Stroud, Fulham, Enfield. The public's thirst to understand, to imagine transatlantic slavery, is a potent reminder of how each generation re-writes the past, not least as a way of making sense of the present. In this sense, we are all bound up in the same enterprise that fascinated and tormented Thomas Clarkson, and led him in frustration to imagine an interview with 'a melancholy African'.

Notes

1. Thomas Clarkson, *An Essay on the Slavery and Commerce of the Human Species* (London: Longman, Hurst, Rees and Orme, 1786), pp. 117–18.
2. See Vincent Carretta, ed., *The Interesting Narrative and Other Writings*, by Olaudah Equiano (London: Penguin Books, 2003); Helen Thomas, *Romanticism and Slave Narratives: Transatlantic Testimonies* (Cambridge: Cambridge University Press, 2000); Moira Ferguson, *Subject to Others: British Women Writers and Colonial Slavery, 1670–1834* (London: Routledge, 1992); Felicity Nussbaum, *The Limits of the Human: Fictions of Anomaly, Race and Gender in the Long Eighteenth Century* (Cambridge: Cambridge University Press, 2003).
3. See, in particular, Albert Boime, *The Art of Exclusion: Representing Blacks in the Nineteenth Century* (Washington, D.C.: Smithsonian Institution Press, 1990); Emma Nogrady Kaplan and Sidney Kaplan, *The Black Presence in the Era of the American Revolution*, second revised edition (Amherst: University of Massachusetts Press, 1989); Marcus Wood, *Blind Memory: Visual Representations of Slavery in England and America, 1780–1865* (Manchester: Manchester University Press, 2000).
4. Peter Ripley, ed., *The Black Abolitionist Papers, vol. 1, The British Isles, 1830–1865* (Chapel Hill: University of North Carolina Press, 1985,), pp. 571–3.
5. J. R. Oldfield, *Alexander Crummell (1819–1898) and the Creation of an African-American Church in Liberia* (Lewiston, New York: Edwin Mellen Press, 1990), pp. 28, 37; Waldo Martin, *The Mind of Frederick Douglass* (Chapel Hill: University of North Carolina Press, 1984), p. 114.
6. Quoted in Charles T. Davis and Henry Louis Gates, Jr., eds., *The Slave's Narrative* (New York: Oxford University Press, 1985), p. 5.

7. For an excellent overview, see Davis and Gates, *The Slave's Narrative*. See also John W. Blassingame, 'Using the Testimony of Ex-Slaves: Approaches and Problems', *Journal of Southern History*, 41 (November 1975), pp. 473–92; C. Vann Woodward, 'History from Slave Sources', *American Historical Review*, 79 (April 1974), pp. 470–81; Eugene D. Genovese, *Roll, Jordan, Roll: The World The Slaves Made* (New York: Pantheon Books, 1974).

8. Henry Louis Gates, Jr., *The Trials of Phillis Wheatley: America's First Black Poet and Encounters with the Founding Fathers* (New York: Civitas, 2003).

9. See, for instance, Ferguson, *Subject to Others: British Women Writers and Colonial Slavery*, and Nussbaum, *The Limits of the Human*.

10. Marcus Wood, ed., *The Poetry of Slavery: An Anglo-American Anthology 1764–1865* (Oxford: Oxford University Press, 2003), p. 120.

11. See, for example, Harriet Guest, 'Hannah More and Conservative Feminism', in Jennie Batchelor and Cora Kaplan, eds., *British Women's Writing in the Long Eighteenth Century: Authorship, Politics and History* (Basingstoke: Palgrave Macmillan, 2005).

12. Maurice Halbwachs, *On Collective Memory*, edited, translated and with an Introduction by Lewis A. Closer (Chicago: Chicago University Press, 1992), p. 183.

13. Quoted in J. R. Oldfield, *'Chords of Freedom': Commemoration, Ritual and British Transatlantic Slavery* (Manchester: Manchester University Press, 2007), p. 102.

14. For the Palace of Westminster exhibition, see http://www.slavetrade.parliament.uk/slavetrade/index.html (accessed 9 April 2009) and the accompanying collection of essays, *The British Slave Trade: Abolition, Parliament and People*, edited by Stephen Farrell, Melanie Unwin and James Walvin, and published by Edinburgh University Press, 2007. For the Equiano Project, see http://www.equiano.org (accessed 9 April 2009).

15. *Hansard*, sixth series, vol. 425, col. 149WH.

16. Ibid., col. 159–62WH

17. The words are those of the Very Reverend John Hall at the commemorative service held in Westminster Abbey on 25 March 2007. See http://www.anglicancommunion.org/acns/news.cfm (accessed 8 April 2009).

18. For changes to the National Curriculum, see Hall, 'Afterword', in this book and http://www.understandingslavery.com/teachingslavetrade/teaching_tools/national_curr (accessed 9 April 2009). For WISE, see www.hull.ac.uk/wise (accessed 9 April 2009).

Part I Cultures of Abolition

1

Inventing a Culture of Anti-Slavery: Pennsylvanian Quakers and the Germantown Protest of 1688

Brycchan Carey

In the spring of 1688, in Germantown, a Pennsylvania village that was just five years old, a small group of Dutch and German settlers, Francis Daniel Pastorius, Gerrit Hendricks, Derick op den Graeff and Abraham op den Graeff, put their name to a now celebrated statement of anti-slavery that has become variously known as the Germantown 'Protest', 'Declaration' or 'Petition'. The statement, outlining the reasons why the four were 'against the traffick of men-body', was read out in their meeting in Germantown, then passed upwards through the colony's Quaker hierarchy for consideration, before being discussed, noted and dismissed by the Philadelphia Yearly Meeting – the highest Quaker body in Pennsylvania. It was then, according to historical orthodoxy, lost and entirely forgotten until 1844, when it was rediscovered, reprinted and distributed further than its original authors could possibly have imagined. Hailed in 1844 and afterwards as the first formal statement of antislavery thought in territories that would later become the United States (although this is not in fact true), it is nevertheless generally agreed that before 1844 the document had no impact or influence at all on whatever conversations Quakers – or Americans more generally – were having about slavery and the slave trade. Thus, Lery T. Hopkins argues that 'the Germantown Protest can only be considered a manifestation of internal discussion since there is no evidence that anyone outside of the Monthly and yearly Meetings was aware of it'.[1] For the same reason, David Brion Davis maintains that the Protest cannot be seen as part of 'a continuous and progressive evolution of antislavery doctrine'.[2] For these historians, the Germantown Protest, however inspiring subsequent generations might have found it, was a dead end, quickly forgotten, without influence or impact.

This approach mirrors a wider assessment of early Quaker writing about slavery. In the main, historians pass quickly through the first century of Quaker anti-slavery literature, discussing each text for a few lines or, at the very most, a few paragraphs. In addition to brevity, historians' discussions have one thing in common: at the end of their reading of any text, they almost invariably conclude with a phrase such as 'the book went largely unread' or 'the book had little impact'. Essentially, what the historians of early Quaker anti-slavery present us with is a narrative of failure; a story about heroic but disconnected Quakers calling out as 'lone voices' in the darkness until, miraculously, in the 1750s the Quaker community shifted en masse to an anti-slavery position, a position that took on an international and ecumenical flavour, arguably providing the impetus for the British and American abolition movements.[3]

A central problem with this analysis is that it rests on very narrow definitions of 'impact' or 'influence'. If by 'influence' we mean 'legislation', then clearly the Germantown Protest (with other early Quaker writings on slavery) lacked influence in that it did not lead immediately to colonial or national laws outlawing slaveholding or slave trading. Likewise, there is no evidence that the Protest led directly to the formation of anti-slavery societies of the sort that would be founded in the late eighteenth century. Nevertheless, even without such measurable indicators of impact, a text might still be influential, and even though manuscript copies of the document may not have circulated in colonial Pennsylvania, the ideas themselves may well have been current. Indeed, while it is of course impossible to know what private conversations about the morality of slavery might have taken place in the early years of the colony, that those conversations must have taken place is evident from the fact that the colony's first formal statement of anti-slavery thought comes from a group of men, and not from an individual. I choose, therefore, to read early Quaker anti-slavery writing as discourse – as a network of interrelated texts – and the Germantown Protest as a node in that network. Instead of emphasising its failures and its disconnectedness, as the historians have done, I thus view the Protest as a connected moment in a developing conversation about slavery; a conversation that leads ultimately to the decision taken by Pennsylvanian Quakers in the 1750s to outlaw slaveholding within their community. In this essay, therefore, I will read the Germantown Protest first in its historical context, second as a literary document amenable to critical analysis, and finally as part of a discourse of anti-slavery that extended far beyond a seventeenth-century colonial village hall and that continues to resonate in our own historical period.

Every British colony in North America and the Caribbean either permitted or encouraged slaveholding during the seventeenth century, and Pennsylvania, founded in 1681 by the aristocratic Quaker William Penn, was no exception. Initially, the colony comprised the city of Philadelphia and some outlying villages of which Germantown, founded in 1683, was one. The colony grew rapidly in its early years as settlers, often attracted by its policy of religious toleration, and just as often attracted by the opportunity for economic advancement, arrived from across northern Europe. By 1700, Philadelphia had a population of approximately 2,500 and was prospering, although despite having ample natural resources and being surrounded by high-quality agricultural land, it had few cash crops to sell to Europe. It solved that problem by developing a system of trade with the British Caribbean colonies. In return for Pennsylvanian forestry and agricultural products, the Caribbean islands provided the hard cash, or the saleable goods such as sugar, that allowed Philadelphia to buy manufactured goods from England. Thus, although not itself primarily a slave-plantation colony, Philadelphia's economy increasingly depended on the wealth generated by slaves. Moreover, despite advocating tolerance and brotherly love, William Penn did not outlaw slavery in his colony. Slaveholding was common in early Pennsylvania, although never on the scale of Virginia, Carolina and the Caribbean colonies. Members of all religious denominations held slaves and, in the early years at least, Quakers were no exception. Most of the enslaved in Pennsylvania were brought to Philadelphia in small groups on ships trading with the Caribbean and the southern American colonies, and once in Philadelphia would be set to work on a wide range of projects including, but not confined to, agricultural labour, domestic service and the construction of new buildings in the growing town. Slaves, as well as free Africans, were not invited to join in the civic culture of the new town although some Quakers did encourage segregated Quaker Meetings for the enslaved. As with all slaveholding societies, discipline was harsh and could be brutal and slave mobility was severely constrained.[4]

Few studies have investigated personal and private responses to slavery and the slave trade in the early modern period, but it is clear from a great many disparate texts that from the early years of European involvement in the Atlantic slave trade some individuals questioned either its extent, its particular brutality or even its actual existence.

Expressions of disquiet about slavery – whether directed towards those in power or not – were written by people of all nations, of all faiths and at all times in the early colonial period, and it might be argued that those Quakers who articulated anti-slavery sentiment in the seventeenth and early eighteenth centuries were essentially no different to the many other disconnected voices that expressed concern over this burgeoning branch of colonial trade. Unlike the London Anglicans and Boston Puritans who questioned slavery, however, the Quakers would eventually go on to make a commitment to anti-slavery part of their corporate identity; indeed, they were the first organisation to do so. Historians do not agree precisely on the reasons why, but the roots of Quaker anti-slavery undoubtedly extend back into the seventeenth century. In the first place, it is certainly significant that Quakers were pacifists, having developed their 'peace testimony' against the backdrop of the English Civil War. By the 1680s, it must have been apparent to many Quakers that there was a contradiction between the demands of the peace testimony and the violence inherent in slavery. It was also significant that two of the founders of the movement, George Fox and William Edmundson, had openly questioned the morality of slaveholding while visiting the British colony of Barbados in the 1670s. Both of them had since made their views known more widely, Edmundson in open letters sent around the American colonies, and Fox in a number of pamphlets issued in London.[5] By 1688, therefore, both precedent and ideology were combining to make Quakerism fertile ground for the first stirrings of anti-slavery thought.

Most freely available versions of the Germantown Protest available in print or on the Internet are based on nineteenth-century transcriptions made before the document was apparently lost in 1874.[6] In most cases, the editors of these transcriptions corrected what they perceived as mistakes of grammar and spelling, and most of them modernised the spelling as well.[7] Although few of these 'corrections' materially change the sense of the argument, with the rediscovery of the manuscript in 2006 the original orthography has again become apparent. Accordingly, since the text is short enough to reproduce in full, I here offer my own transcript of the document, which is written in a reasonably clear hand, covering both sides of a single sheet of paper.

This is to ye Monthly Meeting held at Richard Warrells.
    These are the reasons why we are against the traffick of men-body, as followeth: Is there any that would be done or handled at this manner? viz., to be sold or made a slave for all the time of his

life? How fearful & fainthearted are many on sea, when they see a strange vessel. being afraid it should be a Turck, and they should be tacken, and sold for Slaves into Turckey. Now what is this better done as Turcks doe? yea, rather is it worse for them, wch say they are Christians for we hear that ye most part of such negers are brought heither against their will & consent, and that many of them are stollen. Now tho' they are Black; we can not conceive, there is more Liberty to have them slaves, as it is to have other white ones. There is a saying, that we shall doe to all men, licke as we will be done our selves; macking no difference of what generation, descent or Colour they are. and those who steal or robb men, and those who buy or purchase them, are they not a licke? Here is liberty of Conscience, wch is right & reasonable; here ought to be lickewise liberty of ye body, except of evildoers, wch is an other case. But to bring men hither, or to robb and sell them against their will, we stand against. In Europe there are many oppressed for Conscience sacke; and here there are those oppressed, wch are of a black colour. And we who know that men must not committ adultery, some doe committ adultery in others, separating wifes from their husbands and giving them to others, and some sell the children of these poor Creatures to other men. Ah! doe consider well this things, you who doe it, if you would be done at this manner? And if it is done according Christianity? you surpass Holland & Germany in this thing. This mackes an ill report in all those Countries of Europe, where they hear off, that ye Quackers doe here handel men, Licke they handel there ye cattel. And for that reason some have no mind or inclination to come hither. And who shall maintaine this your cause, or plaid for it? Truely we can not do so, except you shall inform us better hereoff, viz: that christians have Liberty to practise this things. Pray! What thing in the world can be done worse towards us, then if men should robb or steal us away, & sell us for slaves to strange Countries, separating housbands from their wifes & children. Being now this is not done at that manner we will be done at, therefore we contradict & are against this traffick of menbody. And we who professe that it is not lawfull to steal must lickewise avoid to purchase such things as are stollan, but rather help to stop this robbing and stealing if possibel. And such men ought to be delivered out of ye hands of ye Robbers & made free as well as in Europe. Then is Pennsilvania to have a good report, in stead it hath now a bad one for this sacke in other countries. Especially whereas ye Europeans are desirous to know in what manner y^e

Quackers doe rule in their Province., & most of them doe loock upon us with an envious eye. But if this is done well, what shall we say is done evill?

If once these Slaves; (: wch they say are so wicked and stubbern men should joint themselves, fight for their freedom and handel their masters & mastrisses, as they did handel them before; will these masters & mastrisses, tacke the sword at hand & warr against these poor slaves, licke we are able to believe, some will not refuse to doe? Or have these negers not as much right to fight for their freedom, as you have to keep them slaves?

Now consider well this thing, if it is good or bad? and in case you find it to be good to handel these blacks at that manner, we desire & require you hereby lovingly that you may informe us here in, which at this time never was done, viz., that christians have such a Liberty to do so. To the end we shall be satisfied in this point, & satisfie lickewise our good friends & acquaintances in our natif Country, to whose it is a terrour or fairful thing that men should be handeld so in Pennsilvania.

This is from our meeting at Germantown, hold ye 18. of the 2. month 1688. to be delivered to the monthly meeting at Richard Warrell's.

garret hendericks

derick up de graeff

Francis daniell Pastorius

Abraham up Den graef

Two handwritten notes at the bottom of page, in a different hand from the main text, recount the Protest's journey through the Pennsylvania Quaker hierarchy, noting its progress from the nearby Dublin Meeting, where the matter was considered too 'weighty' for that meeting, to the Philadelphia Quarterly Meeting, who likewise found it 'a thing of too great A wayt for this meeting to determine'. It reached its zenith at the Philadelphia Yearly Meeting in October 1688 (which in fact was held across the river at Burlington, West Jersey) where, according to the minutes of that meeting, 'it was adjudged not to be so proper for this Meeting to give a Positive Judgement in the Case, It having so General a Relation to many Other Parts, & therefore at present they Forbear It.'[8] Thus, no ruling was made on the issues articulated in the Germantown Protest and, while Quakers would discuss slavery many times over the coming years, the Protest itself was never again referred to in the minutes of Quaker Meetings.

Writing in 1941, Hildegard Binder-Johnson observed that, 'generally speaking the anti-slavery Protest of 1688 has received more admiration and praise than critical investigation'.[9] Nearly seventy years on, there is little reason to revise this observation. Accordingly, I here attempt to rectify this lack with a critical reading of the text of the Protest, before making an assessment of its influence and impact. Such critical readings must begin by noting that the Protest's opening sentences go to the heart of Christian theology since they invoke the Golden Rule; the rule that tells us to treat others as we would wish to be treated ourselves, in similar circumstances. In a pattern repeated by dozens of Quaker anti-slavery writers, the Protesters state quite bluntly that 'we are against the traffick of men-body' because 'is there any that would be done or handled at this manner? viz., to be sold or made a slave for all the time of his life?' This is forthright enough, in its condemnation of perpetual slavery as opposed to temporary indentured servitude, but it is not original. In the 1670s, George Fox had urged all Quakers to emancipate their slaves after a period of time varying from seven years to thirty years.[10] Whether this aspect of the Germantown Protesters' argument derived directly from Fox is uncertain, and it is not known whether they had access to any of Fox's writing on the topic. It seems unlikely, however. Ten years after the Protest, the Philadelphia Monthly Meeting gave Pastorius, the best known of the Protesters, the duty of 'Collecting of all George Fox's books & writings in these parts', a request that might suggest that he had access to Fox's writings and was to bring them to one place, but that probably indicates instead that none of Fox's works were to be found locally and that they were thus to be procured from elsewhere.[11] In either case, if the Protesters did have access to Fox's writing on slavery, they do not allude to the fact, nor do they make much use of his particular arguments – although in their repeated application of the Golden Rule they, like Fox before them, draw attention to what would become the most central Quaker argument against slavery.

What the Germantown Protesters write next certainly is original, and is the first articulation of a trope that was later to be familiar in abolitionist literature. Recognising that general principles, even important ones such as the Golden Rule, are not enough to persuade, they provide an example. 'How fearful & fainthearted are many on sea, when they see a strange vessel', they argue, 'being afraid it should be a Turck, and they should be tacken, and sold for Slaves into Turckey'. As Linda Colley has shown, fear of enslavement in the Islamic world was widespread among travellers in the period, and melancholy accounts of such incidents provided popular reading.[12] Later abolitionists would sometimes flag up Islamic slavery to point out the hypocrisy of Christian slavery. Christianity, they argued, was inherently a more merciful system than Islam and so Christians should behave likewise – although clearly many did not. 'I do not believe in my Soul', wrote the anti-slavery Quaker Benjamin Lay in 1737, 'the *Turks* are so cruel to their Slaves, as many Christians, so called, are to theirs'.[13]

This message is present in the Germantown Protest, but the Protesters use the occasion of the comparison between Christianity and Islam to go further; restating the Golden Rule in terms that explicitly reject justifications for slavery based on race. Part of the argument is that most slaves are kidnapped and that kidnapping is both illegal, in the everyday sense, and that it is against Quaker precepts of non-violence: quite in addition to the moral problem that we ourselves would not wish to be kidnapped, as demonstrated by our fear when Turkish ships approach. These might appear to be incontestable arguments, but the Protesters recognised the existence of a double standard in which the same notions of law and non-violence were not applied equally to Africans and Europeans. Realising that the Golden Rule had thus become racialised, while not being able to 'conceive' of any justification for that racialisation, the Protesters call attention to the form of the Golden Rule – calling it 'a saying' – and having thus foregrounded its status as dictum, they embellish it in important ways. The saying says 'that we shall doe to all men, licke as we will be done our selves'. This is the Biblical injunction. The Protesters add: 'macking no difference of what generation, descent or Colour they are'. These sentiments can be found in the Bible, and are implicit in the 'Parable of the Good Samaritan', Christ's explication of the Golden Rule, but the form of words is new – newer even than the words written by George Fox a few years earlier where he had argued that 'did not Christ dye for the *Blacks* and the *Taunies*, as well for the *Whites*?'[14] Here, the Protesters explicitly deny any 'difference' in the application of the Rule, regardless of 'generation, descent or Colour', and this refutation of the application of racial ideology to the Golden Rule is in itself an important reflection of the racial ideology of late seventeenth-century Pennsylvania. The triplet of words, encompassing all objections, is legalistic in register and this type of forensic rhetoric no doubt echoes the legal quibblings that accompanied the buying and selling of chattel. 'And those who steal or robb men, and those who buy or purchase them', the Protesters continue, conflating the questions of legal and illegal commerce; 'are they not a licke?'

The Protest continues in a similar vein for a few lines before being punctuated by a heartfelt expostulation: 'Ah! doe consider well this things, you who doe it, if you would be done at this manner?' Once again, the Golden Rule is the final authority, both intellectual and emotional. But the puncture is brief and the document swiftly returns to more material considerations. Knowing well that the colony of Pennsylvania was a commercial enterprise that depended on a steady influx of colonists for its success, the Protesters consider the effect that slavery might have on the perception of potential immigrants that the colony was a place of universal toleration and brotherly love. News about slavery, they argue, 'mackes an ill report in all those Countries of Europe, where they hear off, that ye Quackers doe here handel men, Licke they handel there ye cattel. And for that reason some have no mind or inclination to come hither'. The Germantown settlers were clearly under no illusions about the Friends' commercial objectives in the colony, hence this hard-headed counterbalance to the more theoretical and/or emotional discussion of the Golden Rule. In fact, the question of Pennsylvania's reputation in Europe dominates the central section of the Protest, and as the document progresses the Protesters' thinking grows more radical. Quakers should oppose the slave trade since to own a slave is to receive stolen goods. 'We who professe that it is not lawfull to steal' they reason, 'must lickewise avoid to purchase such things as are stollan, but rather help to stop this robbing and stealing if possibel'. Such statements, using the language of avoidance, ask merely that Friends exclude themselves from the slave trade, and may have received a sympathetic hearing from many Quakers. But when they state that slaves 'ought to be delivered out of ye hands of ye Robbers & made free as well as in Europe' they push their argument further, demonstrating that they seek not merely to put an end to future slave trading, but to emancipate all existing slaves.

The uncompromising tone of this argument, no less than its unimpeachable morality, no doubt helped to secure the Protest's short-term demise. Rather than suggesting that future slave owning and trading be regulated and eventually phased out, the Protest implied that otherwise honest and godly Friends were 'robbers' and that it was the duty of all other Friends to immediately emancipate the slaves of those slaveholding Quakers' against the will of their owners. Of course, this was a highly principled stand, and one that later generations would applaud. At the time, however, it would have seemed to many as little more than a call for the colonial authorities to alienate the legally held property of some colonists. Neither English law, emerging colonial practice, or

Quaker notions about private property could countenance such a course of action. Indeed, it could quite plausibly have been argued by those present that alienating the property of colonists would have sent a far worse message to potential colonists in Europe than the presumably widespread knowledge that Africans were being sold into slavery.

In either case, the Protesters probably overplayed their hand in the following paragraph where they invoked the spectre of a slave uprising, but questioned whether such an uprising would automatically be unjust. What if the slaves 'fight for their freedom and handel their masters & mastrisses, as they did handel them before', they ask. 'Will these masters & mastrisses, tacke the sword at hand & warr against these poor slaves, licke we are able to believe, some will not refuse to doe? Or have these negers not as much right to fight for their freedom, as you have to keep them slaves?' With this statement, the Protesters conflate two serious objections to Quaker slaveholding, both of which draw attention to the violence implicit in the master-slave relationship. If enslaved people 'fight for their freedom', they ask, will Quakers abandon their commitment to the peace testimony and take up the sword against them? This was not merely a hypothetical question. Slave rebellions were not unheard of, and while colonial Pennsylvania did not have the same ratio of slaves to slaveholders as did the plantation colonies of Barbados and Virginia, the possibility of an uprising of the enslaved that threatened the community as a whole was nonetheless a frightening idea. But the reality was that most acts of resistance did not involve the gathering together of hundreds or thousands of enslaved people or the necessity to resort to calling out the troops. Instead, slaves daily registered their protest against slavery as individuals by absconding, by refusing to work, by working inefficiently or by directly challenging, verbally or violently, their immediate overseers. Throughout the colonies, such acts of resistance were usually met with an immediate violent response, which slaveholders justified as necessary to maintain discipline and to prevent major uprisings. Pennsylvania was not a classic plantation colony, and the likelihood of a major slave uprising taking place along the lines suggested by the Germantown Protesters were clearly exaggerated, but nonetheless enslaved people in Pennsylvania were not exempt from forceful coercion, even if Fox had exhorted Quaker slaveholders to show restraint. By drawing attention to the possibility of a general slave uprising, the Germantown Protesters are in fact drawing attention to the violence implicit in slaveholding, the prospect of a coordinated violent response to a single mass rebellion metonymically representing the many daily acts of violence by which slavery was maintained.

Hyperbole can be a dangerous rhetorical strategy, and metonymic hyperbole especially so. If the exaggerated threat of a general slave rebellion represents the inherently violent nature of slavery, then dismissing the possibility of that rebellion is also to dismiss the central rhetorical thrust of the argument. It would not have been difficult for those present in the Quaker Meetings where the Protest was read to argue that there was little likelihood of a general uprising in Pennsylvania at that time, and thus the danger of Quakers needing to take up arms was correspondingly overstated. The Protesters overplay their hand in other ways as well, not least in that they question whether a slave rebellion would actually be unjust: 'have these negers not as much right to fight for their freedom', they ask, 'as you have to keep them slaves?' By asserting an equivalence between slaveholding and rebellion, the Protesters would probably win the approval of most twenty-first-century readers. By contrast, their contemporaries, some of whom were slaveholders and most of whom believed in the inviolability of private property, may well have greeted this rhetorical manoeuvre with dismay. Like many protesters, the Germantown Protesters undercut their own arguments with a rhetoric that was more radical than its audience could bear. It should not surprise us, therefore, that the Monthly Meeting at which it was read decided that it was 'not expedient for us to meddle with it', and promptly passed the buck. As we have seen, the Protest passed up through the Quaker hierarchy and ultimately failed to secure the support of enough Friends for a ruling to be made on the matter.

According to the often told story, the manuscript was lost and forgotten for a century and a half, and had no bearing or influence on the direction of subsequent Quaker thinking on slavery. Then, in 1844, the Philadelphia based Quaker journal *The Friend*, in a somewhat excitable tone, announced that 'the testimony of the Friends at Germantown against slavery, sent up to the Yearly Meeting of 1688, has, within the last few days, been discovered'.[15] That an antiquarian discovery should be hurried so quickly into press is a clear indication of the importance attached to it by contemporary Quakers, and the author, Nathan Kite, is quick both to praise the sentiments expressed, while also careful to distance himself from the language of the Protest. He writes:

> It is certainly a strong document; and whilst it bears evidence that the writers had an incompetent knowledge of the English language, it plainly demonstrates that they were well acquainted with the inalienable rights of man, and with the spirit of the gospel. We publish it as it is in the original, and doubt not that our readers will

find sufficient clearness in the argument, notwithstanding some confusion in the use of prepositions.

In fact, Kite had 'corrected' the document to some extent, and other commentators would also see the language as problematic. Marion Dexter Learned, the biographer of one of the signatories, Francis Daniel Pastorius, noted in 1908 that when reading the Protest 'it is easy to detect the earmarks of [Pastorius's] style and manner of thought in the quaint Germanisms of the document. The handwriting also is his'.[16] Allegations of quaintness and linguistic incompetence somewhat mask the fact that Pastorius, as Learned herself shows, was a noted intellectual who was a published author, a lawyer and a schoolmaster and the founder and first citizen of Germantown.[17] The 'quaint Germanisms' might also have been more strategic than Learned acknowledges. The repeated use of the verb 'handel', for example, is no doubt an intended macaronic pun combining English meanings of the word with the German meaning: 'to trade'. But, as Kite's article makes clear, to mid-nineteenth-century observers the Protestors' language was of secondary importance to the seemingly self-evident truth that the Protesters 'were well acquainted with the inalienable rights of man, and with the spirit of the gospel'. In 1844, the document was thus hailed as an early statement of anti-slavery in the New World, and proof that the abolition movement, at that time gathering in strength, had a long history in America.

Despite its alleged loss and sensational rediscovery, I argue that the Protest of 1688 was nevertheless an influential document in its own time, with a discursive afterlife in the seventeenth and eighteenth centuries, since much of its rhetoric resurfaces in later Quaker writing on slavery. Indeed, it cannot even be said to have been lost, since a copy of the Protest is set down in the minutes of the Philadelphia Yearly Meeting for 1688, and the text of the document, if not the original piece of paper, was thus available to anyone who cared to look into the minutes.[18] Few may actually have done so, but it is nevertheless clear that the Germantown Quakers' position on slavery was well known throughout the eighteenth century and beyond. In 1715, the anti-slavery Quaker John Hepburn speaks of 'the *German Quakers*, who live in *German Town* near *Philadelphia*, Who (to their renowned Praise be it spoken) have above all other Sects in America, kept their Hands clean from that *vile Oppression* and *inriching Sin* of making Slaves of the their fellow Creatures, the Negros, as I was credibly informed by one of themselves'.[19] The Protest itself was well enough known for Thomas Clarkson to allude to it in his important *History of the Rise, Progress, and Accomplishment of the Abolition of the African Slave Trade*, published in London in 1808. This book includes a 'map' of the abolitionist movement from its beginnings with George Fox to its accomplishment with Thomas Clarkson. Portraying the progress of the abolition movement as a network of rivers and tributaries, Clarkson clearly marks the first 'tributary' as 'Qua. Pennsylvania 1688'. In the text of the book he notes that 'so early as in the year 1688, some emigrants from Krieshiem in Germany, who had adopted the principles of William Penn, and followed him into Pennsylvania, urged in the yearly meeting of the Society there, the inconsistency of buying, selling, and holding men in slavery, with the principles of the Christian religion'.[20] While the text of the Germantown Protest may have been unavailable to Clarkson, the fact that the Protest took place clearly did not require rediscovery.

It is also a mistake to argue that the Protest was without influence or, in the words of David Brion Davis, that it cannot be seen as part of 'a continuous and progressive evolution of antislavery doctrine'.[21] On the contrary, sufficient evidence survives to show that it was indeed a factor in the development of subsequent Quaker anti-slavery thought. In the first place, later Quaker anti-slavery writers, including John Hepburn, either knew of it or used its arguments – we have already seen how Benjamin Lay contrasted Christian and Turkish slavery, for example. But there are more direct lines of connection than the merely discursive. The minutes of the Philadelphia Yearly Meeting for 1688 show that it was 'Agreed that an Epistle be sent from this Meeting to that at London'. While the contents of this letter make no reference to the Germantown Protest, its authorship is significant.[22] A committee of eight Friends, all of whom were present at the meeting, was formed to send the letter, headed by George Keith, whose schismatic followers would five years later publish the first important anti-slavery pamphlet in the English language, *An exhortation and caution to Friends concerning buying or keeping of Negroes*. Keith was clearly present when the Germantown Protest was read and discussed and, as a senior – and famously outspoken – member of that Meeting, it is inconceivable that he played no part in the debate that followed.

Keith may not have written the 1693 pamphlet, but it was clearly published with his blessing. It contains many arguments against slavery, several of which are plainly inspired by the Germantown Protest. In the introduction, for example, the pamphleteers argue that 'in some places in *Europe* Negroes cannot be bought and sold for Money, or detained to be Slaves, because it suits not with the Mercy, Love & Clemency that is essential to *Christianity'*. With this, the Keithians are making essentially the same point that the Germantown Protesters did when they argued that European Quakers would see Pennsylvanian slavery as a cruel oppression. Moreover, as the slave trade 'is occasion of much War, Violence, Cruelty and Oppression' it infringes the peace testimony. And like the Germantown Protesters, they argue that 'to buy such is the way to continue these evil Practices of Man-stealing, and transgresseth that Golden Rule and Law, *To do to others what we would have other do to us'*.[23] The main body of the pamphlet is equally indebted to Germantown. The first of several itemised arguments against slavery is 'because it is contrary to the Principles and Practice of the *Christian Quakers* to buy Prize or Stollen Goods', an argument central to the Germantown Protesters. The second argument is the invocation of the Golden Rule, which the Germantown Protesters had put first. As in the Germantown Protest, which objected to a person being 'sold or made a slave for all the time of his life', the Keithian Pamphleteers single out 'perpetual Bondage and Slavery' as unacceptable, not slavery limited by a term of years.[24] These, and other correspondences, indicate that the authors had Germantown in mind when they composed their pamphlet.

In of itself, the Keithian pamphlet of 1693 was not the end either of slavery or the slave trade, but it too went on to have a discursive afterlife, being referred to or echoed by many Quaker anti-slavery writers over the coming years. Indeed, the ideas first expressed by the Germantown Protesters surface repeatedly in Quaker writing about slavery throughout the seventeenth, eighteenth and nineteenth centuries, albeit often in a disguised or developed form. But such is the nature of public discourse; once articulated, the arguments made by the Protesters could neither be unsaid nor could they be controlled or contained in the future. The slavery issue arises repeatedly in records of Quaker Meetings in the 1690s and beyond, as well as in published pamphlets and books in Pennsylvania and – increasingly as the eighteenth century progresses – further afield. Although many of these discussions and texts owed much to George Fox's writings derived from his experience in Barbados, Germantown is also a rhetorical and discursive presence. Thus, though not immediately convincing the Quaker hierarchy to formally condemn slavery, the Germantown Protest clearly initiated a public discourse of anti-slavery in Pennsylvania, and I therefore argue that it was ultimately neither a failure nor a missed opportunity but, instead, a key moment in the development of a public rhetoric of anti-slavery.

Notes

1. Lery T. Hopkins, 'The Germantown Protest: Origins of Abolitionism among the German Residents of Southeastern Pennsylvania', *Yearbook of German-American Studies*, 23 (1988), pp. 19–29, 22.
2. David Brion Davis, *The Problem of Slavery in Western Culture* (Ithaca and London: Cornell University Press, 1966), p. 309.
3. Brief discussion of Quaker anti-slavery before 1750 appears in many historical surveys, but most derive wholly or in part from one or more of the following seven texts, given here in chronological order: Edward Raymond Turner, *The Negro in Pennsylvania: Slavery–Servitude–Freedom, 1639–1861* (Washington: American Historical Association, 1911); Thomas E. Drake, *Quakers and Slavery in America* (New Haven: Yale University Press, 1950); Sydney V. James, *A People Among Peoples: Quaker Benevolence in Eighteenth-Century America* (Cambridge, MA: Harvard University Press, 1963); Davis, *The Problem of Slavery in Western Culture*; J. William Frost, ed, *The Quaker Origins of Antislavery* (Norwood, PA: Norwood Editions, 1980); Jean Soderlund, *Quakers and Slavery: A Divided Spirit* (Princeton: Princeton University Press, 1985); Gary Nash and Jean Soderlund, *Freedom by Degrees: Emancipation in Pennsylvania and its Aftermath* (Oxford: Oxford University Press, 1991).
4. For a detailed general history of Philadelphia, see Russell F. Weigley, ed., *Philadelphia: A 300-Year History* (New York, W.W. Norton, 1982). A recent work, challenging many traditional approaches, is Gary Nash, *First City: Philadelphia and the Forging of Historical Memory* (Philadelphia: University of Pennsylvania Press, 2002). For William Penn, see Jean R. Soderlund, ed., *William Penn and the Founding of Pennsylvania, 1680–1684: A Documentary History* (Philadelphia: University of Pennsylvania Press, 1983), which combines cogent commentary and analysis with generous extracts from Penn's writing, and Edwin B. Bronner, *William Penn's 'Holy Experiment': the Founding of Pennsylvania, 1681–1701* (New York: Temple University Publications, 1962). For the history of Germantown, see Margaret B. Tinkcom, *Germantown and its Founders* (Germantown: Germantown Historical Society, 1983).
5. For detailed discussion, see Brycchan Carey, 'The Barbadian Origins of Quaker Antislavery', in *ARIEL: A Review of International English Literature*, 38/1 (January 2007), pp. 27–47.
6. Martha Crary Halpern, in 'Background and Circumstances of the 1688 Protest Against Slavery, Part II', *Germantown Cryer*, 40 (Summer 1988), pp. 53–61, writes that 'It seems clear that the original Protest remained in the archives of the Philadelphia Meeting at Arch Street. A footnote (p. 12) in Thomas Drake's *Quakers and Slavery in America*, published in 1950, located the document in the Records of Philadelphia Yearly Meeting (Orthodox), vol. N24. But in 1982, when Mark Frazier Lloyd, Director of the Germantown Society, made a search, it was found missing. In 1874 the records of the Arch Street Meeting were divided between the Quaker historical libraries at Swarthmore and Haverford. It is thought that in this subdivision the document was somehow misfiled and its location is, as of this writing, still unknown.' (p. 60). A further search in the Arch Street records was conducted in 2006, and the misfiled document was again located. It is now housed in the Quaker Collection at Haverford College Library, Pennsylvania.

7. In addition to the original manuscript, the Protest was also recorded in the Philadelphia Yearly Meeting (PYM) minutes, 5/7M/1688. It has, however, been reprinted several times. The first reprint was as 'The German Friends', in *The Friend: A Religious and Literary Journal*, 17 (1844), pp. 125–6. The article is signed 'N' (Nathan Kite). It was then distributed widely as a pamphlet, and printed in many places. A photographic facsimile and a reliable transcript can be found in Marion Dexter Learned, *The Life of Francis Daniel Pastorius: The Founder of Germantown* (Philadelphia: William J. Campbell, 1908), pp. 260–3. More recent copies, all based on nineteenth-century transcriptions, can be found in *The Journal of Negro History*, 18 (1933), pp. 99–101, in Frost, *Quaker Origins of Antislavery*, p. 69, and, now, in many locations on the Internet.

8. PYM minutes, 5/7M/1688.

9. Hildegard Binder-Johnson, 'The Germantown Protest of 1688 Against Negro Slavery', *Pennsylvania Magazine of History and Biography*, 65 (1941), pp. 145–56, 145.

10. Carey, 'Barbadian Origins of Quaker Antislavery', pp. 42–3.

11. Philadelphia Monthly Meeting minutes, 29/2M/1698.

12. Linda Colley, *Captives: Britain, Empire and the World, 1600–1850* (London: Jonathan Cape, 2002), pp. 23–134.

13. Benjamin Lay, *All Slave-Keepers That keep the Innocent in Bondage, Apostates...* (Philadelphia, 1737), pp. 15–16.

14. 'The Addition' to 'For the Governour and his Council', in George Fox, *To the ministers, teachers, and priests, (so called, and so stileing your selves) in Barbadoes* (London: 1672), pp. 71–9, 77.

15. Kite, 'The German Friends', pp. 125–6.

16. Learned, *Life of Daniel Pastorius*, p. 260.

17. As well as Learned, see the much shorter but useful biography in Craig W. Horle, et al., eds, *Lawmaking and Legislators in Pennsylvania: A Biographical Dictionary. Volume One, 1682–1709* (Philadelphia, University of Pennsylvania Press, 1991), pp. 586–90.

18. While it is conceivable that the text was added to the minutes after 1844, the writing is on the original paper, is contiguous with the rest of the minutes, and appears to be in a seventeenth-century rather than a nineteenth-century hand. However, there is a blank page following the Protest, which is unusual.

19. John Hepburn, *The American defence of the Christian Golden Rule, or an essay to prove the unlawfulness of making slaves of men* (1715), p. 18.

20. Thomas Clarkson, *The History of the Rise, Progress, and Accomplishment of the Abolition of the African Slave Trade*, 2 vols (London: Longman, Hurst, Rees, and Orme, 1808), I, p. 136.

21. Davis, *The Problem of Slavery in Western Culture*, p. 309.

22. London Yearly Meeting, *Epistles Received*, vol. 1, pp. 69–72; PYM minutes, 5/7M/1688.

23. *An exhortation and caution to Friends concerning buying or keeping of Negroes* (n.p., 1693), p. 2.

24. *An exhortation and caution*, p. 3.

2
(Re)mapping Abolitionist Discourse during the 1790s: The Case of Benjamin Flower and the *Cambridge Intelligencer*

John Oldfield

In recent years we have become accustomed to thinking of abolition, and specifically the campaign against the transatlantic slave trade, as a grass roots movement.[1] Narrating the history of the early abolitionist movement from below is problematic, however. Ideally, one would want the story to end in 1792 when the House of Commons resolved to abolish the British slave trade, albeit gradually, following a massive petitioning campaign throughout the length and breadth of the British Isles. But, as we know, 1792 proved something of a false dawn. Instead of following the Commons' lead, the House of Lords insisted on hearing its own evidence for and against the slave trade, a delaying measure that left abolitionists playing a dangerous waiting game. Success finally came in 1807 in the shape of the Abolition Act, which outlawed the British transatlantic slave trade *tout court*. The intervening years are generally seen as a period of retrenchment, even retreat, on the part of British abolitionists. Thomas Clarkson's retirement in 1796 is one element of this, but so too is the climate of fear generated by the French Revolutionary wars and the successful prosecution of radicals like Thomas Walker of Manchester, who had been key figures in galvanising popular support for abolition between 1787 and 1792.[2]

If abolitionism took a battering in the 1790s, however, it still functioned, and by way of illustrating this I want to consider the case of Benjamin Flower and the *Cambridge Intelligencer*, which was launched in 1793, ostensibly to fill the gap left by the destruction of the opposition press in London, and finally ceased publication in 1803. The *Intelligencer* is perhaps best known among literary scholars, largely because of Flower's patronage of Samuel Taylor Coleridge, then still an undergraduate at Cambridge University. In all, Flower published four of Coleridge's early poems, among them 'Absence' and 'Maid of my Love, sweet Genevieve.'[3] The *Intelligencer* has also attracted the attention of bibliographers and historians of the British press. As John Feather has pointed out, by 1790 most provincial newspapers tended to have 'compact circulation areas which they covered very thoroughly'. By contrast, the *Intelligencer* could rightly claim to be a national newspaper with agents in towns as far apart as York, Dartmouth, Camarthen and Glasgow. By 1797, when circulation had reached 2,800 copies, Flower's newspaper was available 'throughout East Anglia, the south and east midlands, most of Yorkshire, parts of Durham, Hampshire, the west country, London, South Wales and central and eastern Scotland'.[4] The other unusual feature of the *Intelligencer* was that it always carried a weekly editorial, in which Flower set forth his political and social views, an innovation in British journalism usually credited to William Cobbett.[5]

As Feather argues, the success of the *Intelligencer* needs to be set in the context of increasing government repression, particularly after 1792, and, with it, the virtual silencing of radical opinion. Flower survived, he suggests, in part because the *Intelligencer* was nominally a country newspaper and therefore considered of little national importance, in part because he followed the usual (country) practice of distributing his paper through newsmen and agents, thereby avoiding the Post Office and the threat of government censorship.[6] But politics played a part, too. Fiercely independent – he liked to say that he belonged to no political party – Flower was in favour of parliamentary reform, religious toleration and peace with France. Yet, at the same time, he distanced himself from groups like the London Corresponding Society, which he considered too extreme, and believed that 'the true spirit of liberty [was] a spirit of order, a strict observance of the laws and a peaceable conduct.'[7] For obvious reasons, this was a delicate balancing act, but one that seems to have paid dividends. Significantly, only once did Flower fall foul of the authorities, and that was in 1799 when he was sentenced to six months imprisonment in Newgate for calling Richard Watson, Bishop of Llandaff, 'an apostate and timeserver.'[8]

Flower seems to have found his way into journalism almost by accident. The second son of a wealthy London stationer and importer of linen rags, he was brought up in a Dissenting household (the family were nominally Unitarians), though by his own admission 'the regulation of the heart, the temper and the disposition was somewhat overlooked.' 'I had indeed deep impressions of the evil nature of sin, the importance of salvation, the danger of neglecting it, the terror of the judgment day, and the horror of future punishment,' he later confessed, 'but these ideas were of too general a nature.'[9] Lacking any real sense of purpose, he joined his father's business at sixteen but then picked up a taste for speculation, quickly running up huge debts and dragging down his widowed mother and elder sister with him. Practically destitute, in 1785 he resolved to go abroad, eventually accepting a job as the European representative of a merchant house in Devon, which allowed him to travel on the continent for six months of the year. This arrangement seems to have come to an end in 1791, but Flower decided to spend a further six months in France before finally returning to England in 1792, whereupon he agreed to become editor of the *Intelligencer*, which was then being established in Cambridge by, among others, his younger brother Richard, who was 'a farmer, brewer and staunch liberal.'[10]

Flower never made any secret of his 'criminal' past. What sustained him through these years, he said, was his religious faith, 'the peculiar glory of the gospel, as displayed in the offer of free pardon to the truly penitent of all descriptions.'[11] Flower returned to England chastened and keen to make amends. His aim, clearly, was to establish the *Intelligencer* as an opposition newspaper whose content reflected his own belief that 'liberty of the press [was] the palladium of all the civil, political and religious Rights of Freemen.'[12] Reconciled to his past and to his God (he obviously went through some kind of spiritual rebirth between 1785 and 1792), Flower fixed his sights on the political excesses of the 1790s with an unforgiving and sometimes frightening intensity. He was no respecter of wealth or status and, as will become apparent, was unrelenting in his attacks on the government, William Pitt and politicians in general. Just as important, Flower returned to England with a deep respect for the French constitution, the subject of his first book, published in 1792, and, conversely, a keen sense of the defects of the British political system.[13] This was a heady mix and one that helped to give the *Intelligencer* its own distinctive character, although Flower was not a republican (he was adamant on this point) and stopped short of recommending the introduction of republicanism in Britain.[14]

A lot of this will be familiar to historians of the 1790s. Less well known or appreciated, however, is Flower's role in keeping the abolition of the slave trade before the British public during these critical years in the movement's history. Like many Dissenters, Flower was an ardent abolitionist. The *Intelligencer* regularly carried reports of the parliamentary debates on the slave trade, as well as abolitionist poems, news stories and editorials connected with transatlantic slavery. At a rough estimate, between 1793 and 1803 Flower wrote over thirty major editorials on the slave trade, some of them one or even two columns in length. Many other editorials either refer to the subject, usually in the context of 'national sins,' or deal with slavery-related themes (the Maroon Wars, for instance). So, in reality, we are dealing here with a much larger body of material. Equally striking is the consistency of Flower's attacks on the British Atlantic slave trade. For ten years he pursued abolition with a dogged determination, pushing and prodding his readers, pouring scorn on the inactivity of both houses of Parliament, and reserving some of his bitterest criticisms, significantly, for figures like William Wilberforce.

As one might expect, Flower's abolitionism was typically uncompromising. His attacks on the slave trade were not conceived in terms of equity or human rights (Flower was not interested in political economy). Rather, slavery was for him a religious question, as it was for many rational Dissenters, among them figures like Joseph Priestley and Gilbert Wakefield. 'This subject has been so fully discussed,' he wrote in March 1795, 'that it is unnecessary to say anything to convince any man of the extreme – of the unparalleled wickedness of this traffic in the flesh and blood of our fellow-creatures.'[15] In language that evoked William Fox's pamphlet against the consumption of slave-grown sugar (1791) and that anticipated Garrisonian rhetoric of the 1830s, Flower consistently dismissed slave merchants as 'blood suckers,' 'murderers' and 'flesh dealers.'[16] Similarly, in his view the hands of those members of the House of Commons who resisted calls for abolition were 'crimsoned with blood.' Flower would return time and time again to these Old Testament images of sin and retribution. Condemning the inactivity of the House of Lords in 1794, he cited the 'awful address of the Almighty Avenger of the oppressed [Genesis 4:10] – What hast thou done? The voice of thy brother's blood crieth unto me from the ground! Though ye make many prayers, I will not hear you – Your hands are full of blood!'[17]

Flower was convinced that if left unchecked such 'villainy' would only end in national ruin. Crises in the Caribbean – the delay of the West India fleet in the 1796, the ongoing struggles in Saint Domingue – were all seen as signs of impending disaster. 'Calamities thicken in the West Indies,' Flower told his readers in July 1795, 'and till the infernal SLAVE TRADE is abolished, we can hardly wish them to cease. Desperate measures require desperate remedies.'[18] As this language suggests, Flower was not above encouraging or looking forward to such disasters. More controversially, he also invoked the possibility of slave revolution and resistance. 'Rather than that the system of slavery should continue as it has done, both in the French and the English West India islands for centuries past, we confess we had much rather the whole system were completely revolutionised,' he wrote gloomily in December 1801. 'And if statesmen are resolved to persevere in their infernal system of slavery we most sincerely hope that the Almighty Avenger will enable the oppressed "to break their chains over the heads of their oppressors"!'[19]

What was at stake here was not only Britain's national well being but also the fate of her empire. Reflecting in December 1798 on the 'crimes' committed by Britons in Africa and the West Indies, as well as 'the numerous millions massacred and famished in the East Indies,' Flower concluded that 'perseverance in such a course must end in destruction, such an empire must fall, to the astonishment and warning of surrounding empires contemplating the MIGHTY RUIN!'[20] Interestingly, Flower returned to this same theme in one of the last editorials he wrote for the *Intelligencer* in April 1803. His mood was characteristically downbeat. But decline, he seemed to suggest, was not inevitable. 'In the present moral state of the nation,' he lamented, 'we have little hopes of national prosperity: should even the clouds which now hang over our political hemisphere be dispersed, we have little doubt but that fresh clouds will soon arise; we have at present all the marks of a falling empire upon us, and unless effectual reformation takes place, we may rest assured that the doom of all the corrupt nations of antiquity will be ours!'[21]

For Flower, in other words, slavery was inextricably linked to debates surrounding the morality and purpose of empire, and his apocalyptic visions were clearly intended to rouse Britons, or, at least, their political masters, into action. But here again he was disappointed. 'Thus is the Public trifled with, and thus is Heaven insulted, by our perseverance in a trade, which no one ought to vindicate, but a *devil incarnate!*' he wrote in February 1794, following another defeat for Wilberforce and his supporters. 'If any thing can add to our national guilt, it must be our *fasting* and *praying*, while we continue in this course of villainy.'[22] For Flower, fast days were important dates in the religious calendar, moments of reflection and quiet contemplation. But fasting was only meaningful if it led to something positive, preferably acts of atonement.[23] This is why Flower was so intemperate in his attacks on what he saw as the hypocrisy of both houses of Parliament. As he pointed out in March 1795, after the House of Commons had rejected Wilberforce's motion to introduce a slave trade bill, 'this was the *first* vote of the House after

the day of *public fasting and humiliation*! The members returned as they
went, with their hands full of blood, and immediately set Heaven in
defiance, and dared its vengeance!' It was the same thing in 1796. 'The
impious aggravation of last year's vote has been repeated,' he complained bitterly, barely disguising his frustration. 'A fresh sanction has
been given to the trade just after the day of fasting and prayer. We have
again defied heaven, and insulted the Almighty to his face!'[24]

Impatient for success, Flower was frankly bemused by the inactivity
of the imperial Parliament. If the House of Lords proceeded 'as expedi-
tiously as hitherto in the examination of evidence on the Slave Trade,' he
observed in 1794, 'they will *only* be TEN YEARS longer before they have
finished, when it is expected they will be able to determine whether the
trade is *unjust, cruel,* and *murderous,* or *just, benevolent,* and *humane!*'[25]
Similarly, as time went on, Flower came to regard Wilberforce's annual
motions against the slave trade as 'tragic-comic farces' whose various
acts followed an all too predictable path. 'The bill will, between its
lukewarm friends, and determined opponents, by some means or other
be lost,' he wrote in April 1799, 'injustice, oppression, villainy, and
cruelty the most atrocious will complete her triumph; while the house
of Commons, and the nation at large, are too much engaged fighting
for religion to attend to the subject.'[26] Yet, Flower always gave space
to Wilberforce's motions in the Commons, just as he always took the
trouble to remind his readers of the decision taken by the House in 1792
gradually to abolish the slave trade (that is, by 1796). In these and other
ways, he kept the subject before the British public, repeatedly drawing
attention to the massive popular support for abolition, as evidenced by
the five hundred petitions presented to the Commons in 1792.

Unsparing in his criticism of both houses of Parliament, Flower took
particular delight in mocking the pretensions of Pitt and Wilberforce.
Flower was in no doubt that Pitt had deserted his former principles, or
that he simply refused to put his full weight behind abolition of the
slave trade. 'What a minister has most at heart he will use his utmost
endeavours to accomplish,' Flower observed in March 1796.

> Mr Pitt since he has been in the Cabinet, has [had] his party squabbles
> for power and patronage, and on one of these occasions (his quarrel
> with the late Lord Chancellor it was generally understood) he had
> adopted the resolution – Aut Caesar, aut nullat. The consequence
> was, Lord Thurlow was turned out. But, respecting the Slave Trade,
> the abolition of which has always been 'the grand object nearest the
> heart' of this *virtuous, patriotic, sincere, consistent* minister, he has gone

on from year to year, suffering his 'righteous soul to be vexed' at the constant rejection of every measure brought into the house for the purpose.[27]

Flower struggled to comprehend Pitt's actions on the abolition question, just as he struggled to comprehend Pitt's domestic and foreign policies; indeed, it was perhaps inevitable that he should have viewed Pitt's record on abolition through the prism of his (Pitt's) war with France. As Flower put it: 'The indisputable truth is – if Mr Pitt had felt a small part of that sincerity, which has accompanied his endeavours to kindle Europe into a blaze, and to vitiate the spirit, and destroy the liberties of his countrymen, the Slave Trade would have been long abolished.'[28]

In short, Flower viewed Pitt as an apostate or, worse, as a hypocrite. 'This wretch was for a long time thought sincere in his wishes for its abolition,' he wrote in January 1798. 'He once declared that, "He had rather all our West India possessions were buried in the ocean, than that they should be preserved by such a traffic".'[29] Flower, of course, knew better. It was not just that he thought Pitt was unsound on abolition. He also believed that 'the GRAND APOSTATE' connived at the conduct of his minions in the House of Commons and was guilty of encouraging foreigners, 'although at war with us,' to continue the slave trade. 'Thus this infernal traffic, this scandal on the nation is to be continued, without even an effort on the part of the minister, who has so frequently and so solemnly professed himself the champion of justice and humanity, for its abolition,' Flower observed in June 1800, after Pitt had, at the last minute, decided against introducing a motion on the slave trade. 'Let us however do the minister justice,' he added contemptuously. 'We believe him equally sincere in his professions respecting the abolition of the slave trade, as in those respecting the interests of religion, social order, and parliamentary reform!'[30]

Flower's responses to Wilberforce were more complex, but no less damning. On the one hand, Flower condemned Wilberforce because he was too close to Pitt, and, by extension, the government. As he put it in 1797, 'the close attachment shewn by Mr Wilberforce to an abandoned apostate, on account of early friendship, affords an awful lesson to more respectable characters, how they suffer themselves to be deluded, or to place confidence and panegyrise men whose public conduct they cannot but condemn.'[31] It was this same delusion, Flower surmised, that had led Wilberforce to support Pitt's scheme of oppression at home, what Flower pointedly referred to as 'Mr Pitt's SLAVE BILLS' (that is, the treason and sedition bills of 1795). To Flower, such conduct naturally smacked of hypocrisy, and he lost no opportunity in reminding Wilberforce of the fact. 'Must we call it affectation, or a wish for popularity, that induces Mr Wilberforce to plead the cause of the Africans, while he forges chains and fetters for his own Countrymen,' he demanded in February 1796. 'Such persons deserve no support: such inconsistency unfits them for being the Champions of Liberty, nor can its sacred cause thrive in such hands!'[32]

This might not have mattered quite so much, save for Wilberforce's professed piety. This was the real sticking point. For Flower, living a Christian life meant being consistent in thought as well as action. Wilberforce, by contrast, struck him as being flighty and insincere. Flower took particular delight in comparing Wilberforce's record in the House of Commons, where he had not only supported Pitt's 'Slave Bills' but also war with France, with the principles set out in his *Practical Christianity*, published in 1797.[33] Flower went further, claiming that Wilberforce's 'practical conduct' had done 'more towards the DAMNATION OF MILLIONS OF IMMORTALS! – than his book on practical Christianity can do towards saving them, were it to pass through not only five, but five hundred editions.' Even Wilberforce's hands, it seems, were 'crimsoned with blood.' 'Let men talk or write about VITAL CHRISTIANITY as much as they please,' Flower wrote in January 1799. 'While their conduct as legislators, for a long series of years, proclaims them persecutors, enemies to the rights of mankind, friends to corruption, offensive war, and to the destruction of the human species, we will never cease to affirm they are either hypocrites, or deplorably ignorant of the nature and the spirit of true Christianity.'[34]

Flower, therefore, was prepared to engage with Wilberforce on his own terms, questioning his sincerity, a key concept for Evangelicals, and exposing what he saw as Wilberforce's lack of conviction (Flower had little time for the 'art' of politics or for political bargaining). Flower instinctively came to think the worst of Wilberforce. 'Whatever he professes,' Flower wrote in 1797, 'his [Wilberforce's] uniform support of war, bloodshed, and corruption, too evidently shews, that his religion is not the pure and peaceable religion of Jesus.'[35] In saying this, Flower contested Wilberforce's claims to be regarded as a Christian statesman; on the contrary, he dismissed Wilberforce's Christianity as 'not worth mentioning'. Flower was equally critical of the other members of the Clapham Sect, noting bitterly that 'nothing is more common than for Saints of a certain class, to practice those liberties which they deny to every one but themselves, and to raise a most dismal outcry when any one follows their example.' 'When we consider the conduct of these gentlemen,' he echoed in November 1795, 'who have with their pretension to superior piety, supported almost every species of corruption and wickedness for years past, we cannot help exclaiming with the poet, "Curse on their virtues, they've undone their country!"'[36]

Wilberforce, of course, was hardly immune to criticism. In the popular prints of the period he is invariably portrayed as being inconsistent ('Bewilderforce'), supine and even devious.[37] To give an obvious example, in Isaac Cruikshank's *The Victorious Procession to St Paul's; or, Billy's Grand Triumphal Entry* (1797) Wilberforce walks with his head in the air and a 'Book of Common Prayer' in his hands, but with a cocked pistol behind his back, possibly a reference to his alleged involvement in the Spithead naval mutiny of that year.[38] In other words, Flower's attacks on Wilberforce can be located within a distinctly anti-ministerial, or, at least, an anti-Pittite discourse. Very few polemicists, however, subjected Wilberforce's conduct, his every word and deed, to this level of scrutiny; indeed, Flower's editorials in the *Intelligencer* represent one of the most sustained critiques we have of Wilberforce's political conduct between 1793 and 1803. Influenced in large part by his sons' eulogistic biography, we have become accustomed to viewing Wilberforce as a saintly figure, seemingly beyond reproach (and, as the recent commemorations of the bicentenary of the abolition of the slave trade attest, this view of Wilberforce still has considerable purchase). Flower, by contrast, saw Wilberforce as a more deeply flawed and contradictory figure, and in this he anticipated the attacks of radicals like William Hazlitt, who viewed Wilberforce with similar distaste and suspicion.[39]

Disillusioned with Pitt, Wilberforce and both houses of Parliament, Flower looked to the British people to set an example by boycotting slave-produced goods. This was not a new idea; in fact, it had been around since 1791, if not before, and Flower himself had endorsed it in his *French Constitution* (1792).[40] But, characteristically, Flower was not satisfied with the non-committal declarations issued by the Society for Effecting the Abolition of the Slave Trade. Why, he wanted to know, had they not 'resolved on a non-consumption agreement themselves'? To his mind, 'an association with the names of Wilberforce, Fox, William Smith and the Thorntons at the head of it, would do more towards abolishing the trade than all their eloquence, powerful and convincing as it is to every one deserving the name of man'.[41] Here again, Flower could not help pointing an accusing finger at Wilberforce. Reflecting on the high price of West Indian sugar, particularly during the second half of 1799, he concluded that 'NOW is the time for our countrymen to abolish *themselves* the infernal traffic: let them enter into non-consumption agreements respecting West India produce; let them at least resolve to relinquish, except for medicinal purposes, the use of SUGAR, as long as the slave trade is continued. This would certainly accomplish the benevolent end proposed.'[42]

Consistent with his religious principles, Flower advocated non-consumption because he believed that self-denial reflected genuine benevolence. 'The subduing a single inclination, is in the sight of God a greater proof of our sincerity than all our professions,' he wrote in 1798. 'Let our actions display our sensibility; and if we should remain singular, we shall have the reward, and a rich reward it will be to those who justly appreciate it – the approbation of our conscience and of our GOD.'[43] Flower was particularly strenuous in his appeals to 'those whose influence in society can effect any thing they wish to accomplish – the LADIES who preside at our tea-tables.' 'We hear much in the present day of refined sensibility,' he observed testily, flinging down a challenge to his female readers. 'Is this exalted virtue to be met with in novels only?'[44] Increasingly after 1798 Flower came to view the boycotting of slave-produced goods, and specifically the boycotting of West India sugar, as the only practical means of effecting the abolition of the slave trade; perhaps just as important, he believed strongly that if 'properly encouraged and persevered in' such a campaign could and would succeed. 'We may on this subject be called enthusiasts,' he acknowledged in September 1799, 'but we are, when pleading the grand cause of humanity, regardless of the application of any term, however opprobrious.'[45]

In the summer of 1803 Flower and his partners decided to wind up the *Intelligencer*.[46] By this date, circulation had dropped to about 1,350 and advertising had started to fall away dramatically. In fact, Flower claimed that in the twelve-month period up to June 1803 the average number of advertisements had not exceeded sixteen weekly. To compound his problems, it had also become more difficult to collect small debts and to guard the newspaper against bad debts. Flower put all this down to the impact of Pitt's additional tax of three half pence on newspapers, introduced in 1797, which, he claimed, had affected the sale of every print in the kingdom.[47] But there were also other factors involved, one of them being Flower's imprisonment for libel in 1799. Miraculously, Flower had kept the newspaper going, even from his prison cell, but the whole incident caused him and the *Intelligencer* irreparable damage. It also made those around him a little more cautious. His wife, Eliza, for one, became increasingly anxious that he gave up the editorship of the *Intelligencer*, not least because she feared his safety might be compromised by 'a very persecuting Administration'.[48] Less easy to assess is the impact of Cobbett's *Political Register*, established in 1802. Although it initially adopted an anti-Jacobin stance, the *Register* rapidly became a leading opposition paper, filling the space left by Flower's *Intelligencer*.

Despite its untimely demise, the *Intelligencer* remains an important source for historians of British anti-slavery. Through its pages we enter an important eighteenth-century world, a world in which slavery pressed heavily on notions of guilt, just as it pressed heavily on notions of sin and retribution. As we have seen, Flower had no time for half measures and poured scorn on those who prevaricated or stressed the importance of political expediency. This is why he was so unstinting in his criticisms of figures like Pitt and Wilberforce. If his attacks sometimes appear intemperate, this is because he believed that so much was at stake. It made no sense, Flower argued, to criticise the French, or to draw attention to French enormities.[49] To his mind, Britain's crimes were much greater. In saying this, Flower consistently returned to the question of the slave trade. As he put it in his *National Sins Considered* (1796), 'it is impossible for me to use language sufficient to convey any adequate idea of the enormity of our national guilt, in resolutely persevering in such a traffic, after its atrocities have been repeatedly exposed to view'. Slavery, he insisted, was one of the nation's 'principal crimes.' It followed, therefore, that Britons needed to make amends; either that, or they risked losing everything to their enemies.[50]

Flower was hardly alone in thinking and writing about slavery in these terms. Granville Sharp, Joseph Priestley and John Newton – to name but three – all shared the same preoccupations and, for the most part, evoked the same language and imagery. Jane Bliss's research on eighteenth-century sermons has also stressed the influence of theories of providential design, of sin and retribution, on abolitionist thinking, both among Dissenting and Anglican clergy.[51] Yet, at the same time, Flower made a vital contribution to the early abolitionist movement, not least in popularising these ideas, particularly during a period of uncertainty and unrest. If we are successfully to reconstruct abolitionist discourse during the 1790s – its tensions, nuances and sharp disagreements – we need to pay more attention to figures like Flower. Self-opinionated, hard-hitting and confrontational, this tireless critic of the status quo imbued abolition of the transatlantic slave trade with an urgent moral force, reaching out to people the length and breadth of the country (with some justification, Flower could claim that his paper was read 'from the Highlands of Scotland to the lands-end of Cornwall') and helping in the process to nurture an abolitionist culture that fed indirectly into the parliamentary debates of 1804–07.[52]

Notes

1. See, for instance, Adam Hochschild, *Bury the Chains: Prophets and Rebels in the Fight to Free an Empire's Slaves* (Boston: Houghton Mifflin, 2005); J. R. Oldfield, *Popular Politics and British Anti-Slavery: The Mobilisation of Public Opinion against the Slave Trade, 1787–1807* (Manchester: Manchester University Press, 1995); Seymour Drescher, *Slavery and Anti-Capitalism: British Mobilisation in Comparative Perspective* (New York: Oxford University Press, 1987).
2. Oldfield, *Popular Politics and British Anti-Slavery*, pp. 4–5, 84, 185–6.
3. *Intelligencer*, 11 and 25 October 1794; 1 and 8 November 1794. For Coleridge's relationship with Flower, see Richard Holmes, *Coleridge: Early Visions* (London: Penguin Books, 1990), pp. 78, 112 and 116. Flower also published Coleridge's verse-drama, *The Fall of Robespierre* (1794).
4. John Feather, 'Cross-Channel Currents; historical bibliography and *l'histoire du livre*,' *The Library*, sixth series, vol. 2 (March 1980), p. 11. See also, Michael J. Murphy, *Cambridge Newspapers and Opinion, 1780–1850* (Cambridge: The Oleander Press, 1977), pp. 29–30.
5. *Oxford Dictionary of National Biography*, vol. 12, p. 274.
6. Feather, 'Cross-Channel Currents,' pp. 12–13.
7. Quoted in Murphy, *Cambridge Newspapers and Opinion*, p. 34. See also *Intelligencer*, 23 July 1793.
8. For details of this case, see Benjamin Flower, *The Proceedings of the House of Lords in the Case of Benjamin Flower, Printer of the Cambridge Intelligencer, for a supposed Libel on the Bishop of Llandaff* (Cambridge, 1800); *Journals of the House of Lords*, vol. 42 (1799–1800), pp. 177, 181–2. Flower later appealed against his sentence to the court of king's bench but all to no avail.
9. Benjamin Flower to Eliza Gould, 29 August and 2 September 1799, Benjamin Flower Papers, National Library of Wales, MS 1358F.
10. Benjamin Flower to Eliza Gould, 2, 6 September 1799, Benjamin Flower Papers; Benjamin Flower, *A Statement of Facts, relative to the Conduct of the Reverend John Clayton, Senior, the Rev. John Clayton, Junior, and the Rev. William Clayton: The Proceedings on the Trial of an Action brought by Benjamin Flower against the Rev. John Clayton, Junior, for Defamation, with Remarks* (Harlow, 1808), pp. xxi–xxiii; Timothy Whelan, 'Politics, Religion and Romance: Letters of Eliza Gould Flower, 1794–1802,' *Wordsworth Circle*, vol. 36 (Summer 2005), pp. 85–109; Murphy, *Cambridge Newspapers and Opinion*, p. 25.
11. Benjamin Flower to Eliza Gould, 6 September 1799, Benjamin Flower Papers.
12. *Intelligencer*, 16 July 1793. This was the *Intelligencer*'s motto or masthead throughout its ten-year history (1793–1803).
13. *Oxford Dictionary of National Biography*, vol. 20, p. 170; Benjamin Flower, *The French Constitution, with Remarks on Some of its Principal Articles; in which their Importance in a Political, Moral and Religious Point of View is Illustrated; and the Necessity of a Reformation in Church and State in Great Britain Enforced* (London, 1792).
14. See Flower, *The French Constitution*, pp. 500–01.
15. *Intelligencer*, 7 March 1795. For Priestley and Wakefield, see Jane Bliss, 'The Idea of Providence in Eighteenth-Century Abolitionist Discourse and its

Impact on the British Campaign to Abolish the Slave Trade,' MRes thesis, University of Southampton, 2004, pp. 83–94.

16. *Intelligencer*, 10 May 1794, 4 July 1795, 9 March, 13 April, 5 October 1799, 15 February 1800 and 18 December 1802. For Fox, see Oldfield, *Popular Politics and British Anti-Slavery*, p. 57. For Garrison, see Henry Mayer, *All On Fire: William Lloyd Garrison and the Abolition of Slavery* (New York: St. Martin's Press, 1998), esp. pp. 69–70, 103, 131, 370.

17. *Intelligencer*, 15 February 1794.

18. Ibid., 1 August 1795.

19. Ibid., 22 December 1801. See also *Intelligencer*, 15 August 1795, 19 March 1796 and 15 February 1800.

20. *Intelligencer*, 8 December 1798.

21. Ibid., 2 April 1803.

22. Ibid., 15 February 1794.

23. For Flower's preoccupation with fasting and national sins, see his *National Sins Considered, in Two Letters to the Rev. Thomas Robinson, Vicar of St. Mary's, Leicester, on His Serious Exhortation to the Inhabitants of Great Britain, with Reference to the Fact* (Cambridge, 1796), which also contains another condemnation of the transatlantic slave trade (pp. 23–7).

24. *Intelligencer*, 7 March 1795 and 19 March 1796.

25. Ibid., 1 March 1794. Charles James Fox and Samuel Whitbread, among others, made this same point in the House of Commons. Whitbread claimed that the Lords had devoted just six days to the examination of witnesses for and against the slave trade in 1793, five in 1794 and only three in 1795. See *The London Chronicle*, 6–8 February 1794 and 26–8 February 1795.

26. *Intelligencer*, 13 April 1799.

27. Ibid., 19 March 1796.

28. Ibid.

29. Ibid., 27 January 1798.

30. Ibid., 14 June 1800.

31. Ibid., 15 April 1797.

32. Ibid., 13 February 1796.

33. Wilberforce's *Practical View of the Religious System of Professed Christians Contrasted with Real Christianity*, usually referred to as *Practical Christianity*, was an immediate success and went through fourteen editions before 1817.

34. *Intelligencer*, 11 November 1797 and 12 January 1799.

35. Ibid., 25 March 1797.

36. Ibid., 7 November 1795, 3 June 1797 (Wilberforce's Christianity), 3 February 1798. Flower is here quoting Joseph Addison's *Cato*, Act 4, scene 1 ('Curse on his virtues! They've undone his country. / Such popular humanity is treason').

37. See, for example, *The Weather Cock of St Stephen's* (1795) and *The Giant-Factotum Amusing Himself* (1797), both in Mary Dorothy George, ed., *Catalogue of Political and Personal Satires Preserved in the Department of Prints and Drawings in the British Museum, vol. 7, 1793–1800* (London, 1978), pp. 168 (BM8637), 330 (BM8980). Wilberforce's changing stance on war with France was a source of particular comment, hence the reference to 'Bewilderforce.'

38. George, ed., *Catalogue of Political and Personal Satires*, p. 369 (BM9046).

39. See J. R. Oldfield, *'Chords of Freedom:' Commemoration, Ritual and British Transatlantic Slavery* (Manchester: Manchester University Press, 2007), pp. 36–49.
40. See Flower, *The French Constitution*, p. 218. For the non-consumption movement in Britain, see Clare Midgley, 'Slave Sugar Boycotts, Female Activism and the Domestic Base of Antislavery Culture,' *Slavery and Abolition*, 17 (1996), pp. 137–62; Charlotte Sussman, *Consuming Anxieties: Consumer Protest, Gender and British Slavery, 1713–1833* (Stanford: Stanford University Press, 2000).
41. *Intelligencer*, 21 April 1798.
42. Ibid., 28 September 1799. My emphasis.
43. *Intelligencer*, 21 April 1798. In his 'Lecture on the Slave Trade,' published in *The Watchman*, 25 March 1796, Coleridge also distinguishes between 'benevolence,' which 'impels to action and is accompanied by self-denial,' and 'mere sensibility.' See Kathleen Coburn, ed., *The Collected Works of Samuel Taylor Coleridge*, vol. 2, Lewis Patton, ed., *The Watchman* (London: Routledge Kegan Paul, 1970), p. 249n. This may be something more than coincidence. As Patton points out, Coleridge was certainly aware of Flower's *The French Constitution* and used it in his lecture on the slave trade. It also seems likely that he read the *Cambridge Intelligencer*, although it is just as likely that Coleridge influenced Flower, and not vice versa.
44. *Intelligencer*, 28 September 1799.
45. *Ibid*, 1 August 1801.
46. Flower left Cambridge in 1804 and later set up a printing business in Harlow. In 1807 he established another newspaper, *Flower's Political Review and Monthly Register*, which ceased publication in 1810. Soon after, Flower and his two daughters moved to Dalston in Greater London, where he died in 1829. See Murphy, *Cambridge Newspapers and Opinion*, pp. 40–1.
47. *Intelligencer*, 18 June 1803; Murphy, *Cambridge Newspapers and Opinion*, p. 29.
48. Eliza Gould Flower to Benjamin Flower, 20 November 1802, Flower Papers, National Library of Wales. Flower married Eliza Gould in January 1800. Ironically, their relationship seems to have blossomed while Flower was in prison. See Whelan, 'Politics, Religion and Romance,' pp. 85–7; *Oxford Dictionary of National Biography*, vol. 20, p. 170.
49. This was a consistent theme of Flower's editorials during the early 1790s. See, for instance, *Intelligencer*, 11 January, 3 May and 19 July 1794.
50. Flower, *National Sins Considered*, pp. 24–7.
51. Bliss, 'The Idea of Providence in Eighteenth-Century Abolitionist Discourse,' pp. 83–94. For Sharp, see *The Law of Retribution; or, a Serious Warning to Great Britain and her Colonies, Founded on Unquestionable Examples of God's Temporal Vengeance against Tyrants, Slaveholders, and Oppressors* (London, 1776).
52. *Intelligencer*, 18 June 1803.

3

'Another Ida May': Photography and the American Abolition Campaign

Jessie Morgan-Owens

Photography's potential as a persuasive visual adjunct to reform campaigns was recognised from the inception of the medium in 1839, even if before the half-tone process revolutionised printing in 1880 images had to be distributed hand-to-hand. The majority of photographs made in antebellum America were daguerreian portraits: a unique image typically the size of your palm, imprinted on a reflective mirror, encased in brocade and brass. Daguerreotypes circulated without captions; therefore, authors who utilised these early photographs to depict abolitionist ideology found a malleable and suggestive representative space. Their evidentiary power in political debate relied upon writing to instruct audiences how to 'read' these images. In this essay I will discuss images of two little girls, both in appearance white, one fictional and the other daguerreotyped, one free and the other a slave, that nevertheless illustrated the same potent message of late abolitionist rhetoric: that however impugned by the public's anxieties surrounding miscegenation, the invisibility of racial markers demonstrated a moral obstacle to defining slavery along racial lines.

In February 1855, Massachusetts Senator Charles Sumner published a letter he had written to an anti-slavery activist in Washington, DC, concerning a slave from Alexandria, Virginia, named Mary Mildred Botts. The letter was originally accompanied by a daguerreotype of Mary, who appeared white in her portrait. Sumner refers to the daguerreotype, and declaims in an impassioned postscript: 'Such is Slavery! There it is!' Earlier, he describes Mary as 'another Ida May', the title character of a popular abolitionist novel by Mary Langdon (1854), which tells the story of a five-year-old white girl who is kidnapped from her middle-class family in Pennsylvania and sold into slavery in the South. Significantly, Sumner and fellow abolitionist, Governor John A. Andrew of Massachusetts, both circulated Mary's daguerreotype as an illustration of *Ida May*. In doing so, they hinted at a confluence in American abolitionist rhetoric in the mid-1850s between the indeterminacy of race, the messaging possibilities of daguerreotypy and the iconic power of the white young heroine of sentimental fiction.

In the United States of the mid-1850s, skin colour operated as a faulty ad hoc indicator of whether a person was slave or free, or could be. Racial justification for slavery tended to disavow racially ambiguous subjects, and so as the issue of race became central to these debates in the years following the Fugitive Slave Law of 1850, photographs of enslaved persons who look white increasingly appear in anti-slavery propaganda. However, to represent a likeness accurately with photography does not necessarily reveal to which racial category the sitter belongs. The inscrutability of race in portraits of light-skinned slaves focused the rhetorical attention of the language surrounding the image, for racial ambiguity requires writing to phenotype the picture. To accomplish this, Sumner and Andrew associate the daguerreotype of Mary with a particularly powerful abolitionist tool, the sentimental novel, and by doing so, replace the facts of Mary's history with fiction.

Sumner's letter in the *Boston Telegraph* concerning Mary ran the headline 'Another Ida May', which was followed by a broadside about Mary and her family written by Andrew entitled 'The History of Ida May'.[1] Ida May is kidnapped from her white middle-class family and sold into slavery in the South. Mary, by contrast, was born a slave but rescued by fundraising. However, these headlines, written at the height of *Ida May*'s sales, overlay Ida's fictional history onto Mary's story. Mary's real experience of slavery disappears beneath the surface of their shared skin colour. The power of the female child to redeem the unregenerate was a theme of nineteenth-century popular fiction, including *Ida May* and *Uncle Tom's Cabin*.[2] The daguerreotype's association with a white sentimental heroine, Ida May, allows Mary to perform the redemptive work of the sentimental heroines who have come before her. By captioning her image with the narrative, history and race of her fictional double, Mary comes to illustrate abolitionist sentimentalism.

Viewing a daguerreotype is an uncanny, singular experience unique among visual media: due to its mirrored surface, it reflects the viewer's face behind, or in front of, the image, depending on the angle of the light. Thus, the daguerreotype did not just offer the viewer a photographic likeness of the subject, but also reflected the viewer's face in the same frame, in effect miscegenating the image of the other with an image of the self. In the case of abolitionist campaign daguerreotypes, this resemblance impedes the dissociation of another race from the self and opens channels of sympathy otherwise associated only with those who share a family resemblance. While this sensational photograph portrayed a little girl who had escaped slavery, the ubiquitous portrait conventions that governed these types of photographs domesticated even the most scandalous daguerreotypes. Recognising the self in the same frame as the slave produces a sentimental relationship that powerfully mimics the familial bonds of the parent-child relationship. Sentimental rhetoric pasted onto this photograph provoked a moral battle, with the rallying cry: protect *our* innocent.

Sumner expresses his hope that Mary's daguerreotype will circulate in the US Senate as an illustration of the quandary of racial slavery, rather than as a portrait of an exceptional child. Sumner declaims her exceptionality in an impassioned postscript: 'Such is Slavery! There it is!' He indicates that all slaves are represented by Mary's portrait.

Here in full:

> Dear Doctor – I send you by the mail the daguerreotype of a child about 7 years old, who only a few months ago was a slave in Virginia, but who is now free by means sent on from Boston, which I had the happiness of being trusted with for this purpose. She is bright and intelligent another Ida May. I think her presence among us (in Boston) will be a great deal more effective than any speech I could make.
>
> Meanwhile I send this picture, thinking that you will be glad to exhibit among the members of the Legislature, as an illustration of Slavery. Let a hard-hearted Hunker look at it and be softened.
>
> I send another copy in a different attitude to John A. Andrew. Her name is Mary.
>
> Ever yours,
> CHARLES SUMNER.
>
> P.S. Such is Slavery! There it is! Should such things be allowed to continue in the City of Washington, under the shadow of the Capitol?[3]

Sumner had purchased and manumitted Mary, along with her family, with funds raised by her father Seth Botts, a fugitive slave who had become an active member of the Boston abolitionist community. Botts, under the name Henry Williams, worked at Taft's Cornhill Coffee-house in Boston, which employed and supported fugitives. Botts took Shadrach Minkins' place after Minkins' capture on 15 February 1851.[4] In Henry David Thoreau's journal from 1 October 1851, we learn that Botts, after hearing that arrest warrants had been issued for a fugitive named Williams, fled on foot to Concord to hide with Thoreau, carrying a letter of introduction from William Lloyd Garrison. At that time, he had raised $500 of the $600 needed to buy his freedom. Thoreau mentions that Botts was 'an intelligent and very well behaved man – a mulatto'.[5] According to the broadside, 'A History of Ida May', written by Andrew, Sumner and Andrew negotiated with Botts' owner in Virginia to take $500 for the deed of emancipation, followed by the remaining $100 in two years. This accomplished, Botts turned to the emancipation of his wife, Elizabeth, their three children, of which Mary was the second, his wife's mother Pruey Bell and his wife's sister Evelina. While Botts raised most of these funds himself, Andrew forwarded the remaining $200 for Pruey and Evelina's emancipation. Three of Pruey's sons remained behind in slavery. In March of 1855, 'Crystalotype pictures', or a glass plate image that was reproduced on paper, were made of Mary to raise the $300 required to emancipate Pruey's youngest son. Andrew writes of Mary's power and popularity as a sentimental heroine: 'This sum, it is hoped, will be raised by the profits on the sale of little Ida May's picture, whose youth, beauty, and innocence, rescued from all the horrible contingencies of the bond-woman's lot, have touched many hearts and moistened many eyes.'[6]

The request made in Sumner's letter is not for funds but for accord. Sumner's published letter, as a persuasive political tool, proves first, the health of the Boston abolitionist movement, and second, a belief in the power of a photographic portrait of a little girl to change minds, soften hearts and generate votes. Sumner turns to sentimental persuasion to 'soften' the legislative deadlock that occasioned the Compromise of 1850 and characterised the political climate of the decade. He transforms the image of a slave child into an emotional appeal to the 'hard-hearted Hunkers' (contemporary slang for obdurate conservatives in Congress) by exploiting the associative conduit between sight and sympathy. Mary's portrait carries out a sympathetic performance of white girlhood for the men in Washington to sympathize with. Sumner's letter also measures the currency and potential of the five modes of persuasion he employs to disseminate the message behind Mary's image: sentimental fiction, photography, newspapers, speeches and finally, the exhibition of Mary herself to 'prominent individuals of the City' at the offices of *The New York Daily Times*, on a visit to the Massachusetts Legislature, and on stage at Sumner's lecture, 'The Anti-Slavery Enterprise; Its Necessity, Practicability And Dignity'.

The familiarity of reference to the novel *Ida May, A Story of Things Actual and Possible* in Sumner and Andrew's writing provides us with some measure of the novel's popularity; it was touted in its time as the popular successor to *Uncle Tom's Cabin*, and was at one time thought to be penned by Harriet Beecher Stowe.[7] Thomas Gossett's influential study of Stowe's novel suggests, 'political leaders rarely commented on *Uncle Tom's Cabin*, publicly or privately. It was not usual for political leaders or commentators to discuss the ideas of the time in terms of novels, and the fact that this novel had been written by a woman made it even less likely that it would be discussed by them'.[8] However, Sumner's presumption that the original addressees, abolitionist giants such as Andrew and Dr James Stone, and his ultimate audience in the Capitol, had read *Ida May* suggests how liberally abolitionists repurposed novelistic images to borrow their influence in the public sphere. Consider chapter nine of *Uncle Tom's Cabin*, 'In Which it Appears that a Senator is but a Man', which models that novel's rhetorical patterns.[9] Stowe touches upon her character Senator Bird's support of the Compromise of 1850 in a series of sympathetic strategies similar to Sumner's work on the 'hard-hearted Hunkers' in Congress. In ascending order of persuasive efficacy, first are speeches, heard and given, then pictures, followed by what Stowe calls 'the magic of the real presence of distress', or a first person encounter with the fugitive slave. Senator Bird's wife first makes appeals to his Christianity, but as her argument flags, fugitives Eliza Harris and her son Harry appear at the kitchen door:

> [Senator Bird] was as bold as a lion about [the Fugitive Slave law], and 'mightily convinced' not only himself, but everybody that heard him; – but then his idea of a fugitive was only an idea of the letters that spell the word, – or at the most, the image of a little newspaper picture of a man with a stick and bundle, with 'Ran away from the subscriber' under it. The magic of the real presence of distress, – the imploring human eye, the frail, trembling human hand, the despairing appeal of helpless agony, – these he had never tried. He had never thought that a fugitive might be a hapless mother, a defenseless child, – like that one which was now wearing his lost boy's little well-known cap; and so, as our poor senator was not stone or steel, – as he was a man, and a downright noblehearted one, too.[10]

Senator Bird's identification of Harry with his own recently deceased son occasions his decision to aid the light-skinned fugitives. The sentimental attachment of father and child or, perhaps, Senator Bird's chivalrous moral code indicated by 'bold as a lion' and 'noblehearted', trounces his allegiance to national law. Clearly, Senator Sumner hopes to engineer a 'softening' effect as instant and entire as Senator Bird's sentimental transformation on the conservatives in office, who, according to Stowe's argument, must be untried by the presence of fugitives. Further, I would argue that Stowe makes a semiotic argument which supports Marcus Wood's thesis in *Blind Memory* that standardisation of the fugitive into a typographic imprint for slave advertisements wore down the meaning, and individuality, of the iconic fugitive.[11] 'The letters that spell the word' *fugitive* had deteriorated into 'the image of a little newspaper picture of a man with a stick and bundle', when it should signify a human in an ongoing state of distress. Though Stowe repeats the word 'human' twice in her description of the fugitive icon, the adjectives she employs feminise all fugitives into a 'frail' and 'helpless' state of agony in which Senator Bird finds Eliza and Harry, and where, as Stowe's gerunds, 'imploring', 'trembling', and 'despairing', emphasise, they are condemned to remain until white men acknowledge their appeals. In Sumner's strategy, Mary's more sympathetic photographic image replaces the newspaper stick figure. Mary's daguerreotyped icon further shifts the sign 'fugitive' from signifying Eliza Harris to signifying Little Eva, the archetype of the white sentimental heroine.

As Sumner's nineteenth-century biographer Edward Lillie Pierce explains, the efficacy of Sumner's letter depends upon a bait-and-switch strategy of resemblance: 'Daguerreotypes, taken after their arrival in Boston, were distributed; and many were affected by the sight of slaves apparently white, who were unmoved at the contemplation of negroes in bondage.'[12] When Sumner exclaims in his postscript, 'Such is Slavery! There it is! Should such things be allowed to continue in the City of Washington, under the shadow of the Capitol?' he articulates what we should see when we open the daguerreotype: not an individual girl but a complete 'illustration of slavery' that specifies and enhances his audience's 'contemplation of negroes in bondage'. He superimposes her representative case onto the city of Washington, and imprints 'Such is Slavery!' on the very ground where the shadow of the Capitol falls.[13] Sumner equates the law and daguerreotypy: the Capitol building imprints its image in the form of legislative 'shadow' on the landscape, both North and South. This image powerfully recalls the masthead of William Lloyd Garrison's newspaper *The Liberator*, which depicts a slave auction in front of the Capitol. For the details of this recurrent image to change, the Capitol itself must change the image it projects across the land by legally abolishing the institution that divides it.

Charlotte Forten Grimké, a member of the Salem black abolitionist community, writes about having a portrait made the day after the Fourth of July at Broadbent's daguerreotype studio in Philadelphia. While there a friend, 'Miss J' shows her a daguerreotype of an escaped slave girl. This encounter contextualises the national mythologies that coalesced around the daguerreian campaign image. Both Grimké and the subject of the photograph are black women, but on the page Grimké's description of this encounter with the fugitive mirrors the language of Sumner's letter:

> My heart was full as I gazed at it; full of admiration for the heroic girl, who risked all for freedom; full of bitter indignation that in this boasted land of liberty such a thing could occur. Were she of any other nation her heroism would receive all due honor from these Americans, but as it is, there is not even a single spot in this broad land, where her rights can be protected, – not one. Only in the dominions of a queen is she free. How long, Oh! how long will this continue![14]

She meets the daguerreotype of the young woman with sympathy and admiration, immediately followed by indignation for 'these Americans', and she concludes by identifying this little girl as a symbol of the larger movement. Although the rhetorical formula and her use of the heart metonym are the same as Sumner's letter, her exclamation, 'How long, Oh! How long will this continue!' does not mean the same thing as 'Should such things be allowed to continue ...' Grimké models the sympathetic, daguerreian response Sumner pursues from his position of power capable of social change, but as she cannot participate in the political system as a black woman her line of resemblance leads outside that system. As Gregg Crane points out in his book on race and citizenship in this period, 'the republican and rights traditions were alloyed with and limited by a prerequisite that the members of the body politic must resemble each other in language, culture, religion, and appearance'.[15] Grimké refers to the nation as both land and political community, but she places herself, with the fugitive, outside American mythology.

The newspapers that carried the Botts story searched out the daguerreotype and Mary herself to confirm the spectacle of white slavery.
A writer who saw Mary's daguerreotype on view for some weeks at the
State House in Boston agreed with Sumner that Mary was 'a most beautiful white girl, with high forehead, straight hair, intellectual appearance,
and decidedly attractive features'.[16] The *New York Daily Times* wrote
that Mary looked 'so white as to defy the acutest judge to detect in her
features, complexion, hair, or general appearance, the slightest trace to
Negro blood'.[17] In their assessments of Mary's whiteness, the newspapers
provide us with contexts that properly establish Sumner's letter as a set
piece in a larger political movement that embraced racial ambiguity as
an opportunity for importing sentimental ideas about fatherhood into
the political arena, while disavowing how Mary's whiteness came about.
These assessors, when faced with invisible racial markers of blackness,
attribute her better qualities – her intelligence and attractiveness –
to her whiteness, a positive category constituted by the absence of
'Negro blood'. Clearly for her audience, Mary symbolised an ideal
whiteness isolated in relief to the millions of enslaved black persons
whose cause, but not race, she shares.

Mary Niall Mitchell has observed that photographs of light-skinned
slaves 'simultaneously fascinated and tormented viewers because of
the subjects' "invisible" ancestry and the sexual history that produced them'.[18] Mary's precipitous conversion from a slave child into
an illustration of slavery writes the open secret of sexual slavery into
the political discourse: whatever Mary's personal history, in this letter,
or alongside Sumner at the podium, she embodies living evidence of
miscegenation, and her skin colour foretells an anxious future of either
passing for white or sexual slavery. Karen Sánchez-Eppler writes: 'As the
child of lawless sexuality she has inherited the role of being exploited.
Her body displays not only a history of past miscegenation but also a
promise of future mixings.'[19] When these reporters and politicians look
at Mary, they see her past and future, because her skin exhibits her
mother Elizabeth, her father Seth and her grandmother Pruey's sexual-
ised light-skinned body, and Mary's future eligibility in the 'fancy girl'
trade in light-skinned slave women.

The casually reported scene of scrutinising Mary's seven-year-old
body is in fact disturbingly clinical and sexual, and thus simultaneously
performs both desire and denial. Her skin powerfully delimits a moral
obstacle to defining slavery along racial lines. Therefore, her viewers
must make an anxious attempt to harden the category of whiteness
against this aspect of slave experience, even though white offence

caused the 'problem' of Mary's race. As reported by the *New York Daily Times* on 9 March 1855:

> The child was exhibited yesterday to many prominent individuals in the City, and the general sentiment, in which we fully concur, was one of astonishment that she should ever have been held a slave. She was one of the fairest and most indisputable white children that we have ever seen.[20]

I would like to draw attention to the 'general sentiment' of 'astonishment', which suggests an overpowering of the spectator in reaction to the sudden presence of something unaccountable – a temporary disturbance in the categories of experience that rattles the understanding of the relationship between visibility, whiteness and slavery. The *Washington Sentinel* responded to this article in the *Times* by insisting that 'Ida May', or Mary, 'must be a bogus slave' because the *Times* has pronounced her white.[21] The specious astonishment of 'prominent individuals of the City' and the disbelief registered by the *Washington Sentinel* suggests either a wide scale repression of the fact of sexual slavery, or a performance of white racial classification against the appearance of racial transgressors like Mary. Mary, the article insists, was 'held' as a slave, not born a slave or identified as a slave, but instead calls Mary 'a white child'. Sumner declaims astonishment of this kind at the end of his letter, but still, even he neglects to give the history recorded in Mary's skin a name when he refers instead to 'such things' when he indicates Mary's portrait: 'Should such things be allowed to continue …'

As promised in the letter, Mary and her sister accompanied Sumner on the platform of Boston's Tremont Temple on 29 March, in a series of lectures in Boston and New York organised by the original addressee, Dr James Stone. The speech, 'The Anti-Slavery Enterprise; its Necessity, Practicability and Dignity', solidified Sumner's position as a leader in the anti-slavery movement.[22] Sumner's line of reasoning begins from a position of racial indeterminacy. He does not refer to the girls' presence on stage directly, but he makes their colour the subject of his speech when he argues that pro-slavery argument depends on an untenable distinction between the races. He opens his speech by denying the sustainability of the Mason-Dixon line drawn between black and white:

> And, first, of the alleged distinction of race … It is apparent in the obvious fact, that, unless such distinction be clearly and unmistakably established, every argument by which our own freedom is

vindicated ... must plead trumpet-tongued against the deep damnation of Slavery, whether white or black.[23]

Mary's presence on the platform next to him underlines his argument that such 'clear' and 'unmistakable' distinctions between the races are unmanageable indicators for slavery. While he leaves open the future possibility of racialism, he concludes that, to be comfortable with the institution of slavery, the American public must also be prepared to countenance white slavery. Anti-slavery rhetoric from the 1850s makes use of individuals like Mary to touch the nearest sympathies of the white reader, to engage the protective paternalism of a white male audience, even if Mary's white skin marks paternal transgression.

The racial inferiority of blacks was a mainstay of proslavery rhetoric, which Sumner rejects with a plea for our shared humanity and the instability of race. Yet, mid-way through the speech, Sumner equivocates on the issue of racial equality in a strange disclaimer that occasioned the opprobrium of Frederick Douglass as a 'falling away from ... the recognition of the entire manhood and social equality of the colored people'.[24] In both this personal letter to Sumner and in an editorial in his paper, Douglass took offence to a line in Sumner's speech that maligns racism but tolerates segregation. Sumner, speaking for the abolitionist community, said:

> While discountenancing all prejudice of color and every establishment of caste, the Anti-Slavery Enterprise at least so far as I may speak for it – does not undertake to change human nature, or to force any individual into relations of life for which he is not morally, intellectually and socially adapted.[25]

The phrase 'relations of life' disassociates the Anti-Slavery Enterprise from intermarriage between blacks and whites, as well as the right to vote or own property. As Douglass writes: 'This disclaimer assumes, or seems to assume, that the colored people of this country cannot without violence to "*human nature*", be elevated to social equality with white citizens.'[26] His editorial concludes,

> But it is possible that Mr. Sumner only means here to say that intermarriage of individuals of the two races is not contemplated by the Anti-Slavery Enterprise, for which he is authorized to speak; and if he does, it may still be doubted if such a disclaimer was necessary. By whom is the charge of amalgamation brought? Who but the people

of the South are raising the cry of amalgamation as unnatural and monstrous? And yet who but they are blotting out the distinction between white and black ... Mr. S seldom walks the broad avenues of Washington, that he does not meet the mulatto daughters of Southern members of Congress, and the best blood of old Virginia courses in the veins.[27]

Douglass's editorial repositions Mary's presence on the platform as closing the gap between qualifications used to distinguish black and white, and gives her mixed heritage the pedestrian appearance history supports.

The novel *Ida May* contends that the Fugitive Slave Law shifted the border of slavery far enough north as to threaten the freedom of all Americans, not only those with dark skin. And, as Douglass avers, the prevalence of miscegenation among slaveholders in the nation's capitol suggests that Mary's skin colour should not have occasioned such surprise. In her first narrative portrait, Langdon slips into racial ambiguity in the moments before Ida May becomes a slave:

She had taken off her hat, and her long dark curls were hanging carelessly down her cheeks, and over her neck, twined with a long spray of delicate pink flowers, with which she had ornamented herself. The mourning dress showed her clear, dark complexion to great advantage; her cheeks and lips were like blushing rose-buds, and her brilliant eyes were lighted with merriment. Seen in the softened light of her leafy resting-place, with the deep shade of the forest for a background, she formed a picture on which a painter's eye would have rested with untold delight. But other thoughts were in the mind of the dark-browed man who now approached them.[28]

This passage performs a double reading of Ida's race: first, an accurate reading by the authorial painter figure, and then a deliberate misreading by the slave trader. Curiously, Langdon creates a main character so ambiguously in the 'medium tones' that she is repeatedly misread as a slave. Other characters, time and again, ignore or mistake Ida May's race. In this exhibition scene, unlike Mary's astonishing appearance in the offices of the *Times*, Ida May is marked by blackness; her black curls, her mourning clothes, and her 'clear, dark complexion' find little contrast in the pinkness of her cheeks and the pink flowers in her hair. Are we to trust the narrator's accuracy of representation when other characters in the novel seem ready to accept the slave trader's point of view?

This injustice of visual representation was written into the Fugitive Slave Law: the concept of the fugitive hinges upon the visibility of the invisible concepts of freedom and race. The Fugitive Slave Law of 1850 reinforced the Fugitive Laws of 1793, which by this time were customarily violated, by revoking judicial process and shifting the jurisdiction over fugitives into the hands, and scrutiny, of federal commissioners. An affidavit proving ownership submitted the runaway as property. If the commissioner decided that a person was not a slave, he was paid five dollars, but if the commissioner decided that the person was a fugitive, he got ten. Clearly, this provided an incentive to rule against the runaway in doubtful cases.[29] Langdon's representational crisis over Ida May's race presents, for the abolitionist, an ideological jam: to suggest that *Ida May* is unrealistic or inaccurate denies some part of the injustices of this law that it claims to record. The title page of *Ida May* quotes John 3:11: 'We speak that we do know, and testify that we have seen.' Mary's daguerreotype provides Langdon's readers with an opportunity to see her eyewitness testimony for themselves. Sumner's reference to Mary as 'another Ida May', and Andrew's publication of the 'History of Ida May' allows Ida May's fictional history to testify in the political arena, even if the histories of these little girls are strikingly different.

In conclusion, I would like to assert that the incorporation of a novelistic character, Ida May, into Mary's daguerreian message mutually enhances the image of both girls as an accurate, compelling claim against racially defined slavery. The fictional little girl, Ida May, is white but mistaken for a slave and the other little girl, Mary, is a slave but could be mistaken as white. Because both girls are not what they seem in their portraits, the writing that attends them produces a mirror effect between fiction and reality that helps us to understand the inherent textuality of the institution of slavery. The images of Ida May and Mary could be entirely misread or exchanged with a change of caption, just as a transfer of title could legally claim either girl as property.

Notes

1. I have found three publications of Sumner's letter in my research. The first is the *Boston Telegraph*, 27 February 1855. *Frederick Douglass's Paper* reprinted the article from Boston on 9 March 1855. The letter was also published in *The New York Daily Times (1851–57)*, 1 March 1855. See also, John A. Andrew, S. P. H, 'A History of Ida May' (Boston: J. S. Potter & Co., March 3, 1855).
2. Jane Tompkins, *Sensational Designs: The Cultural Work of American Fiction, 1790–1860* (New York: Oxford University Press, 1985), p. 129. As Jane Tompkins writes of Little Eva, on her deathbed the child becomes an angel

endowed with 'salvific force' While Tompkins argues that the moment of
death precedes a salvific grief, I would contend that Mary's status as a slave
gives her the necessary tinge of mortal danger.

3. *Boston Telegraph*, 27 February 1855.
4. Shadrach Minkins was arrested at Cornhill Coffee-house. After a brief hearing before a federal commissioner, a body of men entered the courtroom and
bore Minkins away. He settled safely in Montreal. President Millard Fillmore
and Secretary of State Daniel Webster ordered that the men who aided in his
escape be prosecuted in violation of the Fugitive Slave Law. For Minkins, see
Gary Collison, *From Fugitive Slave to Citizen* (Cambridge: Harvard University
Press, 1997).
5. Thoreau, *Journal*, 1 October 1851.
6. John A. Andrew, S. P. H, 'A History of Ida May'.
7. Mary Langdon [Mary Hayden Green Pike], *Ida May, A Story of Things Actual
and Possible* (Boston, 1854). The novel has been digitised by the Antislavery
Literature Project, Arizona State University. Editorial annotations and introduction by Joe Lockard. See <http://antislavery.eserver.org/prose/idamay/
index_html>. Accessed on 21 January 2009.
8. Thomas Gossett, *Uncle Tom's Cabin and American Culture*, (Dallas, Texas:
Southern Methodist University Press, 1985), p. 183. See also, Gregg Crane,
Race, Citizenship, and Law in American Literature (New York: Cambridge
University Press, 2002), p. 78.
9. For an extended reading of this chapter see Catharine E. O'Connell '"The
Magic of the Real Presence of Distress": Sentimentality and Competing
Rhetorics of Authority' in Mason I. Lowance, Jr., Ellen E. Westbrook, and
R. C. De Prospo, eds., *The Stowe Debate: Rhetorical Strategies in Uncle Tom's
Cabin* (Amherst: University of Massachusetts Press, 1994), pp. 13–35.
10. Harriet Beecher Stowe, The Annotated *Uncle Tom's Cabin*, ed. Henry Louis
Gates, Jr. and Hollis Robbins (New York: W. W. Norton, 2007), p. 97.
11. Marcus Wood, *Blind Memory: Visual Representations of Slavery in England and
America, 1780–1865* (New York: Routledge, 2000), pp. 87–99.
12. Edward Lillie Pierce, *Memoir and Letters of Charles Sumner*, vol. 3 (Boston:
Roberts Brothers, 1893), p. 413.
13. Mary and her family had been the slaves of a John Cornwall of Georgetown.
Therefore, her case brings symbolic and geographic proximity to the legislative
body in Washington, DC.
14. Charlotte L. Forten Grimké, 'July 5, 1857', *The Journals of Charlotte Forten
Grimké*, Schomburg Library of Nineteenth-Century Black Women Writers
Series, ed. Brenda Stephenson (New York, Oxford University Press, 1988).
15. Crane, *Race, Citizenship and the Law in American* Literature, p. 26.
16. *Boston Telegraph*, 27 February 1855.
17. *New York Daily Times*, 9 March 1855.
18. Mary Niall Mitchell, '"Rosebloom and Pure White", Or So it Seemed,'
American Quarterly 54/3 (September 2002), p. 378.
19. Karen Sánchez-Eppler, *Touching Liberty: Abolition, Feminism, and the Politics of
the Body* (Berkeley: University of California Press, 1993), p. 34.
20. *New York Daily Times*, 9 March 1855. Reprinted in *Frederick Douglass's Paper*,
16 March 1855.
21. *Washington Sentinel*, as reported in the *New York Daily Times*, 16 March 1855.

22. Pierce, *Memoir and Letters of Charles Sumner*, p. 414.
23. Charles Sumner, *Recent Speeches and Addresses, 1851–1855* (Boston: Higgins and Bradley, 1856), p. 486.
24. Frederick Douglass, 'Letter from Frederick Douglass to Charles Sumner, April 24, 1855', in Philip S. Foner, ed., *Frederick Douglass: Selected Speeches and Writings* (Chicago: Lawrence Hill Books, 1999), p. 33.
25. Sumner, *Recent Speeches*, p. 493.
26. *Frederick Douglass's Paper*, 1 June 1855.
27. Ibid.
28. Langdon, *Ida May*, p. 20
29. Gossett, *Uncle Tom's Cabin and American Culture*, p. 87.

4
Exchanging Fugitive Identity: William and Ellen Craft's Transatlantic Reinvention (1850–69)

HollyGale Millette

As I write this, there is an embittered battle raging in the United States over the Democratic Party's Presidential Candidate. Senator Barack Obama, at the moment a forerunner in the race, has – at turns in his campaign – relied on, shunned, marginalised and confronted his bi-racial heritage, and his own family's legacy and living memory of the transatlantic slave trade. In a twist to the proceedings, news of an amateur genealogist's findings revealed Obama's ancestors to be slave-owners and publicised a transposition that has become common in the historiography of our modern multi-cultural societies.[1] Thus in the commemorative year of 2007, the cultural memory of slavery, fugitives and the transatlantic slave trade reaches forwards from history to involve, however unwillingly or inaccurately, the aspirations of a young American politician. Obama's ancestral past was not the only one to be publicly laundered in 2007, but his was certainly held as representative of the cultural remaking employed by generations of people who choose to live without a racialised past or with an annotated one in order to create a new future. I am very interested in those who selectively rearranged their pasts amid the immediate backdrop of abolition in the nineteenth century. I see this as an important part of the cultural memory of abolition; a performative part of that history, which is often not explored or included in the popular culture of abolition. I am struck by David Dabydeen's words in this circumstance:

> [I]n the future time each must learn to live
> Beadless in a foreign land; or perish.
> Or each must learn to make new jouti,
> Arrange them by instinct, imagination, study

> And arbitrary choice into a pattern
> Pleasing to the self and to others
> Of the scattered tribe; or perish.[2]

Dabydeen references another preoccupation in my writing: that of bi-cultural competence, either unconsciously or consciously drawn. Bi-cultural competence emerges as a necessary component in a successful assimilation of immigrants, sojourners and those seeking cultural acceptance and culture sharing. The importance of bi-cultural competence (both theoretically and in practice) is beginning to be considered as a contributory factor in successful and inclusive cultural thought, policymaking and skills development. But I have yet to find scholarship that calls for bi-cultural competence to be considered within the principles and practices of historiography, as it pertains to historical life writing and the writing of biographical material.

Gloria Gordon's recent work is a fine example of the modern discussion – in practice – of bi-cultural competence.[3] Gordon looks at the legacy left by those black Britons who unconsciously assimilated into British social systems and culture, and the subsequent problems and difficulties of engagement that followed. While her investigation encompasses mid- to late twentieth-century immigrants, it locates an important discourse in both the lived history of various players in the transatlantic slave trade and the legacy of those lived histories in our cultural memory. Beyond titillation, the buried family history of Senator Obama peaks our interest because it references the manipulation of cultural competencies necessary for his family to progress in society and figures this into his family's historical legacy of slavery. Similarly, the intrepidness of the fugitive American slave re-crossing the Atlantic to find refuge from the draconian Fugitive Slave Law of 1850 has a unique resonance. These players in the later chapters of the slave trade and the early chapters of abolition returned across the Atlantic along the third side of the trade triangle in an effort to claim back in England what had been taken from them in America. If the basic tenets of slavery are power, profit and control, and the stripping of these off the enslaved, then the reclamation of these by the formerly enslaved is a lived history worthy of note. My intention here is to develop the underdeveloped lived history of two such fugitives – William and Ellen Craft – who arrived in Britain as fugitive slaves in December of 1850. I would like to consider the nineteen years the Crafts spent in Britain and the cultural competencies they navigated and the cultural identities they assumed during their assimilation there. I propose a wider view of their narrative that draws back from the proscenium of the lecture hall and the cultures of the United States and refocuses attention on performances of cultural memory and the suasion of the host culture in the Crafts' ultimate choice of identity roles.

The Crafts were not alone in their circumstance as fugitives living abroad in Britain, nor were they the only ones whose passage and initial entry into genteel British society was sponsored by American and British Abolitionists.[4] Recent scholarship, and here I am thinking particularly of Elisa Tamarkin's work, has tended to focus on the 'sociability of antislavery'.[5] Like Tamarkin, I too am interested in the attractiveness that England presented to slavery's sojourners, but I would like to distinguish the performances of identity and negotiations the Crafts participated in from their public performances as anti-slavery agitators. In a departure from the male black abolitionist model, I choose to look at the Crafts and their sojourn as a clearer example of the identity performance and the negotiation of cultural competencies in both male and female circumstance and ones where the operation of the husband and wife unit were very evident. The Crafts' example also links these negotiations to popular culture of the period. The lived history of cultural negotiation embarked on by the Crafts extended to their progeny, and when they returned to the United States as emancipated citizens (metaphorically if not legally) they left behind two of their five children and a substantial portion of their life's history. Like Senator Obama, their reclamation lived on in the visible histories of their children who having thoroughly passed into British society live among us without a visibly racialised past, the legacy of intrepid negotiation of cultural competency.

The narrative of William and Ellen Craft began in Macon, Georgia, during the Christmas holidays of 1848. Ellen was a mulatta seamstress – the probable product of the rape of her housemaid mother by her mother's master Major James Smith – with skin so light she could pass for white. William was an artisan carpenter who was employed, though enslaved, by a local doctor. With William posing as her slave, Ellen masterminded an escape plan and disguised herself in male clothes, sling and poultice as an invalid[6] rheumatic Southern 'Gentleman' en route to Philadelphia for treatment. The sling and poultice forestalled suspicion when she abstained from either speaking too much or signing anything – neither she nor William being literate. Travelling publicly by train and steamer, they arrived into the safe arms of 'conductors' of the Underground Railroad in Philadelphia four days later. The Crafts moved to Boston, where a substantial free and fugitive black community was gaining influence in the antislavery campaign. It became clear days after the September ratification of the Fugitive Slave Act that their notoriety on the New England abolitionist circuit left them wholly vulnerable. Escorted by William Wells Brown, they left Boston for Canada and then Liverpool in November of 1850.[7] The Crafts were to become the darlings of the fugitive slave narrative circuit in Britain. Their performances at these events drew thousands, were widely reported in the British press, and helped to establish a new genre in mid-nineteenth century popular culture performance: a performance of harrowing real-life escapes to freedom customised and performed to British audiences for the benefit of the American abolitionist cause. At bottom, fugitive slave narratives were abolitionist propaganda employed for a fairly pointed goal: to alter hegemonic perception of the enslaved and further the cause of abolition.

Ellen and William insinuated themselves, via the abolitionist network, into the homes of the sympathetic social elite. Subsequently, the impact of these associations helped to determine their choice of permanent address, schooling, social circle and business interests. Their permanent or long-term address of settlement was No. 12 Cambridge Road in Hammersmith, an address that no longer exists, although an example of contemporaneous properties can be seen in the nearby Avonmore Road. Typical for this western suburb of London, this comfortable mid-Victorian family home of four to five floors offered growing space for a mid-sized middle-class or lower middle-class family with room enough for a maid/cook but, more often than not, operating without one. Both William and Ellen enroled at Ockham School near Weybridge in Surrey to improve their literacy and take vocational training in the fields of school teaching (Ellen) and agriculture (William). This was a school that advertised itself as a school for the middle classes, recommending to those interested in giving or acquiring a 'useful education'. Instruction comprised: 'Reading, Writing, Arithmetic, including Mensuration and Book-keeping, Geography, History, Grammar, with the elements of Vocal Music, Drawing, and Chemistry, and attention being paid to general information and to the moral and religious training and instruction in industrial occupations'.[8] At a time when education and scholastic pursuits, while on the rise elsewhere, were still strongly the preserve of the upper and middle classes, the Crafts' invitation and sponsorship at such an institution was a departure from the slave-turned-worker route that predominated among (mostly male) diasporic blacks in England at that time.[9] Furthermore, it placed their assimilation strategy immediately alongside domestic Victorian debates about culture, class, education and self-improvement.[10]

Various patrons with sympathetic abolitionist interests and ties arranged their introduction and sponsorship at this school following their arrival in 1850.[11] Chief among these was Harriet Martineau, who arranged for much of the Crafts' welcome, support and education in their early years in England and hosted the Crafts at her home, The Knoll, in Ambleside when the couple were lecturing in the locality in 1851.[12] Through sponsors such as Martineau and Reverend Francis Bishop (who hosted them in his home on their arrival in Liverpool) they met and were further sponsored by Unitarians, Quakers, social reformers and abolitionists throughout England and Scotland. Many of these, like Lady Annabella Noel Byron, Lord and Lady Lovelace and Dr and Mrs Lushington were of some social standing. A direct and purposeful movement through (or some might say, up) the social ladder can be noted in their first three years of sojourn, where private performances in parlours and domestic areas were enacted in tandem with their public performances in the lecture hall. Arriving on Brown's arm at these events, the 'white-looking' Ellen was often concealed in their initial introduction in these social circles only to be introduced or 'revealed' as a mulatta later in a complicit display of an abolitionist's trump card.[13]

Ellen's whiteness permitted her to pass 'up' in terms of class both in America and Britain, but in Britain this passing connected with the contemporaneous trend to embrace mulattoes as middle class. Mulattoes in emigrating or immigrating to Britain faced better opportunities and comparable privilege, and in maintaining these tropes of passing the Crafts were acknowledging and manipulating their symbolic power in the public arena.[14] In her performance of *freedom* in the United States Ellen chose to masquerade in the body of a white male; in her performance of *self* in Britain she chose to acculturate in the body of a domesticated female. Acculturation is the process of acquiring some, but not necessarily all, aspects of the host society by the individual. Immigrants, refugees, natives, ethnic groups and sojourners all have varying modes of acculturation depending on their circumstances.[15] Ellen's disguise masked her gender while foregrounding her approximate whiteness during her flight to freedom in the US. At that time, the particular white body that would have afforded her the greatest amount of purchase was the male white middle-class body. In Britain, on the other hand, the particulars of her situation benefited best from inhabiting the female white middle-class body. It was in these guises that they might best access the sharing of cultures and best prosper.

While certainly the staged management of their performances enveloped the Crafts, and other ex-slaves engaging in anti-slavery agitation, in a veil of 'male philanthropic surveillance and control' that mirrored and countered audience consensus, it is important to recall their status (or, more appropriately, their non-status) in a strange new country.[16] The power and influence these abolitionists had over the Crafts could, in their situation, be seen more as a comforting embrace rather than an unwanted manipulation. This couple, although feted guests, were – at bottom – fugitive migrants, what we would today call 'asylum seekers', and this should be foregrounded in the UK portion of their biography. Unlike other fugitive slaves visiting from America, the Crafts did not return to the US or Canada after a few months of agitation, a few years of study, or at the end of a successful tour. Unlike William Wells Brown, Alexander Crummell or Henry 'Box' Brown, they were much less temporary in their approach to settlement and displayed, not the characteristics of a visitor or tourist as these men did, but the characteristics of sojourners. A sojourner spends a medium amount of time (in parity with their life-span) in a place, with the intention of returning home. Mostly, they are awaiting a change in their nation's laws, the resolution of some national crisis, or the end of civil unrest and/or war, which will make their return possible. But, clearly, it will be some time before this will become wholly possible and thus they seek refuge and long-term settlement in a host culture. Various motives and expectations come to the surface when people sojourn or seek asylum in a foreign place. Sojourners, for example, are very focused on gaining status – and by this I mean gaining those things that mark a person as 'legitimate' in society: money, property, official papers to prove belonging – and in doing so with a considerable amount of agency. These motives and experiences help shape their reactions to, and acceptance of, their largely temporary environment. The sojourner (and especially the fugitive) suffers: degrees of alienation, feelings of powerlessness, meaninglessness, unbalance and self and social estrangement.[17] Often these feelings lie dormant in the first stages of arrival, only to reappear later causing bouts of confusion, depression or disconnectedness. Surely a powerful, instructive and perhaps prescriptive embrace by their 'abolitionist friends' would have put the Crafts at ease and enabled a more successful assimilation. Thus, it is not at all surprising that their initial decision was to tow the party line of the abolitionists while they were gaining a foothold and a locus of control in England.

Nearly all sojourners suffer from culture shock: that sudden unpleasant feeling that may violate expectations of the new culture and cause one to evaluate one's own culture negatively.[18] It is noteworthy that people who are suffering such anxieties tend to lose their inventiveness and become obsessively concerned with orderliness and boundaries.[19] This would go a long way to explaining William and Ellen's reliance on others to lead them and their attention to social boundaries and their policing. There is a relativity to the acculturation equation: 'Who am I, if not myself in relation to others?' lingers foremost in the mind of the sojourning individual and acts as a self-policing mechanism that helps to negotiate the tensions, contradictions and conflicts of identity formation and social membership. The positive side to culture shock or 'role-shock' is that as a transitional experience it can result in the adoption of new values and attitudes that ordinarily would not be considered, making a sojourner more flexible and insightful, and resulting in a wide breadth of personal growth.[20] Barbara McCaskill concurs that the Crafts 'wasted no time in procuring the physical protection, financial assistance, and emotional inspiration of militant abolitionist communities on both sides of the Atlantic.'[21] It is interesting to note that after arriving in Philadelphia they moved directly to Boston – two cities that would emerge as the centres of the black aristocracy. Likewise, in London, they would settle not in the East End, where the bulk of the black British diaspora was to be found – notably around the docks in Limehouse and Canning Town where a free black man could earn a living as a sailor – but in a respectable family home in the West of London. At all times their geographic choice and referents seem to be courting the favour of the moneyed yet conscientious classes. Culture learning differentiates between social skills and social values, between performance and compliance.[22] To learn and acculturate using the social *skills* of the host culture is *a performance*; to learn and acculturate using social *values* is *compliance*. I see William and Ellen as consciously acculturating in both senses. Their adeptness at achieving certain social skills and espousing certain sets of values negotiated the colour bar, which ordinarily may have prevented their acceptance into certain strata of society. In other words, theirs was both a quantitative and qualitative acculturation, in which their adeptness at assimilating *skills* provided them with a *point of entry into* their host culture; but their adeptness at assimilating *values* provided them with *a social position within* their host culture.

On the whole, London's dwindling black community in 1851 was distinguished by its poverty and more often than not they faced a life of begging.[23] The factors contributing to this decline were threefold: (1) the 1832 Act of Parliament that fined captains for transporting natives or fugitives from Africa or elsewhere – thus offering incentive to return them to Africa or the nearest free port; (2) the economic collapse of the West Indian sugar trade resulting in the end of many of the plantations and the formation of separate non-travelling West Indian black communities; and (3) the 4:1 male to female ratio of blacks in London, which resulted in mixed-race unions whose offspring were absorbed into existing white working class communities.[24] The astronomical increase in the white population only furthered these trends. Thus, to consider the landscape facing William and Ellen upon their arrival is to suggest that they participated in both careful planning and manipulation to secure their social advancement and survival as fugitives in Britain, or improvised judiciously and quickly on networking opportunities. Their situation was quite contrary to the lot of other blacks in Britain at that time, for whom the notoriety of a handful of prominent visiting American ex-slaves offered the means to make a penny from a ballad or an oration by borrowing the narrative style of the fugitive as pure pretence. What distinguished William and Ellen from these men and women? Predicated as it was in what Marx called 'commodity fetishism', the emerging middle-class hegemony and consciousness was deeply concerned, fascinated and fearful of objects and especially persons who symbolised or actually crossed boundaries. Ellen and William provided a popular exhibit of these fetishes and fears, and one that simultaneously, due to the philanthropy and humanitarianism embedded in the abolitionist cause, could be rationalised as both educative and virtuous. How much more acceptable and popular to see this 'respectable' sensational black couple than the single black male labourer in the streets with his broadsides? How much more palatable and reassuring to see this 'respectable' visiting black family than Britain's own second-generation of mixed race faces struggling for status amid the lower-classes?

Houston Baker refers to the fugitive slave's body as the 'negro exhibit' whose 'body, in all of its marked and visible clarity of wounding, made affective the metaphors of moral suasion propounded by white abolitionists. The silent fugitive slave's body became an erotic sign of servitude in the social, liberational discourses of white abolitionists'.[25] Their performance was a mimetic one that brought home, perhaps uncomfortably, both the otherness of the fugitive on stage and the culpability of the spectator in this process. This, specifically, refers to black males who, as a set piece of stagecraft, would silently be called forward to the podium in order to 'reveal' the remnants of their wounds as inscribed on their bodies – usually on their backs – by the dreaded whip of their ex-plantation masters. As Diamond observes, 'The body's emphatic ("live") presence is offered as a momentary habitus of what is not present – the forgotten objects and cultural detritus that constitute a piece of historical experience'.[26] In this way, cultural memory is inscribed on the fugitive body. William Wells Brown used Ellen to stir his audience into imagining her meeting the worst of these bodily fates and he used her to constitute a piece of cultural memory.[27] Before the late century's popularisation of the ethnographic exhibit, the black body as exhibit was confined to the public displays of slavery in America as written on the body: scars, wounds and other signs of torture. This kind of display and advertising produced a visual text that served both to re-inscribe and eroticise servitude and slavery back onto the fugitive's body. When editors and lecture leaders cautioned against a prurient interest and sensationalism for titillation purposes they were actually anticipating, and therefore cultivating a prurient interest in this pain fetish. William and Ellen did not, in fact they were unable to, offer any such spectacle as bodily scars, but Ellen's silent presence on the lecture platform did offer the spectator a reference point wherein they could inscribe their empathy; a reference point for the unspoken: rape, indignity, horror, courage and so on.[28] William and Ellen's bodies were participating in a dialectical narrative of social relations while simultaneously the body of the spectator was given over to enquiry and reflection; their bodies were being commodified a second time in William's physical presence at the podium and in the sale of curios – Ellen's engraved portrait, for example. It could be construed, therefore, that they were effectively 'sold' or 're-auctioned' to the fervent pro-abolitionist members of their audiences and those newly converted to the cause in the struggle to reinvent themselves and survive in a new culture.[29] But given the complexities of their contextual historiography it would do a disservice to their biographies to be so reductive. Both William and Ellen's, and certainly Ellen's, placement as products varied considerably throughout their lives and, I would argue, they exercised a fair amount of agency in choosing the avenues by which they would be commodified and reinvented.

Ellen's engraving showed no scars, but the cross-dressed Ellen fulfilled the same effect of re-inscription and eroticisation. It might be understood that Ellen *sought* the re-inscription of her body by the limitations and boundaries of a social system in order to contain and inscribe a new identity. I do not intend to suggest that she deliberately and anarchically flouted the gender conventions of her time – by all accounts, in fact, Ellen was a 'modest', 'shy' and 'sweet woman', quite the model of appropriately feminine behaviour.[30] Rather, I would posit that the emotionally vulnerable, highly-strung character Craft develops into is possibly a rhetorical figure that served as a (necessary) counterbalance to her cross-dressed identity of Mr Johnson.[31] In her marriage to William and in her member status in the 'Cult of True Womanhood' she chose a domestically inscribed meaning for herself. 'To be a "True Woman" in the nineteenth century meant being relegated to the domestic realm and embodying all that was "moral" and spiritually upright. To be engaged in matters of the body was to fall out of that realm'.[32] The domestic middle-class female, epitomised in the Steel Engraved Lady, 'divided into four cardinal virtues – piety, purity, submissiveness, and domesticity'.[33] For the bulk of middle-class, or aspiring, London housewives the image of the idle female installed, stage-like, in the proscenium of the front parlour (the public-private/private-public household performance space), was a perpetual labour of performance that involved imitating a complex and intricate 'disappearing act' on the traces and vestiges of her actual household labour (cleaning, cooking, child-rearing).[34] This was further substantiated geographically in the very architecture of the middle-class home with its kitchen in the cellar, its nursery in the attic and various hidden closets and cupboards to keep evidence of household labour well out of sight. Ellen, as McCaskill notes, is 'constantly, creatively, concealing objects'[35] throughout her fugitive escape. When considered alongside the concealment strategies employed by the domestic female engaging in the 'vanishing act' of household work, it is clear that Ellen was already so well-practiced at concealment that her sojourn in Britain represented merely *a different kind* of concealment strategy not a *new* strategy of performance. A reinvention perhaps, but given the ease of experience it was not an identity that proved hard to reach and it was one that offered social benefit.

Observing William and Ellen on stage respectably presented, and mindful of the social boundaries of dress and deportment, was testimony to their potential, willingness and achievement of acculturation. William's spoken and written text was the product of his/her/their labour by which he hoped to sustain himself and his family; gendered actions that should be read, first and foremost, as a performance of William's 'bread-winning'/'head-of-household' identity, and second as a performance of empowerment from a newly emancipated man. In taking the stage, William encountered a position of power merely by occupying the platform. For Ellen, rising to speak on the platform would have compromised that ideal of womanhood, which she had hitherto been denied and to which she deeply aspired. Such a strident transgression of bourgeois values and boundaries would also threaten her rhetorical appeal with her 'white sisters'. Choosing to curtsey demurely and fade into the curtain call of speakers imposed a certain dialogue all its own on the viewer. Rather than reinforce a conspicuous display of the wounded body, Ellen's falling in line with the domestic ideal of the middle-class female displayed her as 'slavery's silent argument'.[36] Without their performances situated in these boundaried middle-class gendered roles neither of them would have succeeded in exchanging their victimized fugitive American bodies for respectable landed meaning-filled ones, and I believe they opportunistically saw and acted on this exchange via their sojourn in Britain and in the psychology of their acculturation strategy.

The process by which individuals change their psychological characteristics, change their surrounding context, or change the amount of contact in order to achieve a better 'fit' (outcome) with other features (cultural, social, material) of the system in which they carry out their life is instructed by 'positive selector obstacles' – those culturally constructed barriers that must be passed through in order for a sojourner to acculturate.[37] These include, for instance, education, physical fitness, language ability and financial security. Male industry, female domesticity, deportment and conspicuous self-improvement were all barriers that positively selected sojourners to England: manage the obstacle and you were in, mismanage it and you were excluded into the lower classes or worse.[38] Ellen's silence, therefore, along with her 'visible embarrassment' or her demure reluctance to come forward to the edge of the stage curtain, were not so much a testimony to her subjugation as they were indicative of the performance of the domestic woman.[39]

People who migrate have, by definition, an internal locus of control and are demonstratively seeking homogeneity, and 'in order to migrate voluntarily one has to assume considerable personal responsibility and control over one's own affairs – financial, social, and familial'.[40] Whether or not William and Ellen strategically achieved this, or the degree to which it was strategically achieved, does not detract from the impact of it having happened at all. A more critical reading of both Ellen and William's participation in the abolitionist lecture circuit and their assimilation into British culture reveals a discourse of performance, agency and the brokered exchange of cultural competencies for both economic and social security. And, I hope, it offers a new and more complete historiography of their sojourn and a new translation of their cultural memory. Surely, as we mull over topics such as rendering reparation, aiding anti-slavery work, and culling exploitation based on 'evil desire',[41] a crucial underlying step of forward thinking practice is to consolidate and fully account for cultural memory and cultural history. I find it significant to add here the note made by Cherie Booth in her keynote speech at the WISE Conference in 2007. In it she chose to recount what was, to her, the most human aspect of narrating one's slavery story. In the course of her business with the International Court of Human Rights she noticed that, almost unilaterally, when victims of human rights abuses are asked – and they are always asked – what retribution they would like to see meted out on their enslavers/torturers/ aggressors, their second choice[42] is always to have their abusers hear their story; to have the ability and space to publicly tell their story, and for people to take note.[43] That the first steps towards reconstructing self and gaining status for those enslaved are to seek acknowledgement by the public of the crimes against them, firmly places catharsis in the context of self-making. The act and ability of presenting one's self-narrative, in this case, is a route through to receiving some semblance of atonement. Perhaps another encounter embedded in the cultural history and memory of the Crafts is their encounter with and the use of, the cathartic elements in their performance? Maybe they could not begin to self-make until they had witnessed, from their side of the stage, a certain sort of atonement? In presenting their life-narrative and performances, both on and off stage, they negotiated the fraught task of reinvention while purposefully 'stitching up' what had been torn apart in their lives.[44]

William and Ellen left their home in England and returned to the United States in 1869, when they were legally safe to do so. They did not take all of their family with them. Indeed, their younger son, who originally returned to Georgia with them to help them set up their school and farm, missed England so much he returned. Their eldest son never left Britain, and is listed on the 1871 Census as having a fairly middle-class job as an insurance clerk for a merchant shipping line. He lived in Battersea, with his wife and children, the eldest of whom was called Ellen.[45] It is not unlikely that the great-grandchildren of this couple still populate parts of Greater London. In more ways than one, these are the progeny of their forefathers' fugitive slave identities. In one generation (from enslaved father to gainfully employed son) the family moved from sojourner to immigrant; from acculturant to assimilant. Like Barack Obama, the vestiges of the contemporary Craft family's self-making may rest unseen, but you need only scratch the surface to find a significant memorial to cultural memory. While men and women like Obama, and perhaps even Ellen Craft's great-granddaughter, are hailed as 'self-made' men and women of our age, their making began further back and is bound up in our communal cultural history.

Notes

1. Paul Harris, 'Obama Told of Family's Slave-Owning History in Deep South', *Independent*, 27 February 2007, p. 26.
2. David Dabydeen, *Turner: New and Selected Poems* (London: Jonathan Cape, 1994), XXI. 20.
3. Gloria Gordon, *Towards Bi-Cultural Competence* (London: Trentham Books, 2007). Though Gordon's work focuses on the legacy of the 'Windrush Era' immigrants, her research and practice of competencies is useful. Gordon locates stages of assimilation beginning with the unconscious fitting in to survive, through the secondary stage of an unconscious distribution of psychological dualities (black and white identities), to the later generations' developed problems born out of this slippage.
4. Liverpool, especially, developed a geography of assimilated immigrant blacks laced with fugitive histories. See Jacqueline Nassy Brown, *Dropping Anchor, Setting Sail: Geographies of Race in Black Liverpool* (Princeton: Princeton University Press, 2005).
5. Elisa Tamarkin, 'Black Anglophilia; or, The Sociability of Antislavery', *American Literary History*, 14/3 (Autumn 2002), pp. 444–75.
6. Note the play on words of Ellen's invalid – or, in-valid – gentlemen; neither valid as a slave, nor valid as the transgressive cross-dresser.
7. Blackett provides the most exhaustive account of the Crafts' biographies. See R. J. M. Blackett, *Beating Against the Barriers: Biographical Essays in Nineteenth-Century Afro-American History* (Baton Rouge: Louisiana State University Press, 1986) pp. 86–137. See also Dorothy Sterling, *Black Foremothers: Three Lives* (Old Westbury: Feminist Press, 1998), pp. 2–59.
8. Advertisement and Papers pertaining to the Ockham School, in the Letters of Elizabeth Jesser Reid, Bedford Archives, RHC AR/GB 05005 RF 100–06.
9. While actual boarding school costs suggest that they were uniformly beyond the economic means of the bulk of the middle classes, there were less expensive schools on offer redressing the deficiency in religious education along with the more useful educations. Increasingly, however, by mid-century a major preoccupation of the middle classes and rising lower-middle classes was the education and formal training of their young – and especially their women, who where expected to manage and keep both the social diary and the financial ledger of the household. See Patricia Branca, *Silent Sisterhood: Middle Class Women in the Victorian Home* (London: Croon Helm, 1975), pp. 38–59.
10. See Audrey A. Fisch, *American Slaves in Victorian England* (Cambridge: Cambridge University Press, 2000).
11. Confirmed in the Letters of Elizabeth Jesser Reid, Bedford Archives, Royal Holloway, University of London, Egham, G 0505 RF100–06. See also D. Logan and V. Sanders, eds., *The Collected Letters of Harriet Martineua* (London: Pickering Chatto, 2007), especially 14 March 1851.
12. William Craft's narrative acknowledges Martineau as one of those responsible for their entry into England. See William Craft, *Running a Thousand Miles for Freedom or, the Escape of William and Ellen Craft from Slavery* (London: William Tweedie, 1860).
13. Brown comments in his publication on his meeting with an English 'Lady' who retired to her sewing in a 'neat room' wherein sat a 'young woman' also

sewing and reading from a spelling book. Brown pulls his cards out slowly to reveal the identity first of the 'Lady' as Lord Byron's widow and her 'companion' as Ellen; 'that poor exile' and former slave. Similar to the Walkers' meeting with members of the upper classes on their tour in 1904, the revelation that the Crafts were not only rubbing shoulders with the great and the good, but were sharing time in their parlours, validated them when the stories were reported back overseas. Brown, *The American Fugitive in Europe* (London: J. P. Jewett and Co., 1855), pp. 219–20.

14. James Walvin, *Black and White: The Negro and English Society, 1555–1945* (London: Allen Lane, 1973), pp. 194–96. Notably, the lighter-skinned children of the West Indies who often sojourned in London while receiving private school education, were treated as middle class. See Eric Williams, *History of the People of Trinidad and Tobago* (London: Andre Deutsch, 1964), especially Chapter 14.

15. John W. Berry, Uichol Kim and Pawel Boski, 'The Psychological Acculturation of Immigrants', in Margot Light and A. J. R. Groom, eds., *International Relationship: A Handbook of Current Theory* (London: Pinter, 1985), p. 62.

16. Anne McClintock, *Imperial Leather: Race, Gender and Sexuality in the Colonial Context* (London: Routledge, 1995), p. 140.

17. Adrian Furnham, 'The Adjustment of Sojourners', *Journal of International and Intercultural Communication*, 7 (1987), pp. 42–59.

18. The anthropologist, Oberg, first coined this term (1954) but it has since betrayed many facets of definition. Guthrie has used the term (1975) 'culture fatigue'; Smalley uses 'language shock' (1963); Barnes, 'role-shock'; and Ball-Rokeach interprets it as 'persuasive ambiguity'. Different researchers apply it to different isolated circumstances. See Adrian Furnham and Stephen Bochuer, *Culture Shock: Pychological Reactions to Unfamiliar Environments.* (London: Methuen, 1986), esp. Part III, pp. 159–200. In terms of the Crafts' experience, the wording 'role-shock' seems preferable.

19. Furnham, 'Adjustment of Sojourners', p. 46

20. Ibid., p. 47.

21. Barbara McCaskill, '"Yours Very Truly": Ellen Craft – the Fugitive as Text and Artefact', *African American Review*, 28/4 (1994), p. 511.

22. Furnham, 'Adjustment of Sojourners', p. 57.

23. The communities of black residents distinguished by such historians as James Walvin. See James Walvin, *Making the Black Atlantic: Britain and the African Diaspora* (London: Cassell, 2000), pp. 190–91. These communities appear as black to dark blue – designated as Poor to very Poor – on Booth's poverty maps.

24. The large majority of black men in the capital were sailors or worked on or near the docks. It is of little surprise that the residual black residents that remained were to be found closest to the docklands areas in London's East End. These areas were the very poorest. Data drawn from Walvin, *Black and White*, pp. 196–8.

25. Houston A. Baker, *Workings of the Spirit: The Poetics of Afro-American Women's Writing* (Chicago: University of Chicago Press, 1991), p. 13.

26. Elin Diamond, *Unmaking Mimesis: Essays on Feminism and Theatre* (London: Routledge, 1997), p. 150.

27. Such as in his address to the Glasgow Emancipation Society in January, 1851, 'American Fugitive Slave Bill'. See *The Glasgow Herald*, 10 January 1851. After the meeting William and Ellen were pulled forward and introduced to an enthusiastic audience of about 3,000.

28. Ellen's whiteness was key to the campaign of raising interest in American slavery among Britons. According to the Rev. R. L. Carpenter, 'when they heard that Mrs. Craft was nearly white they expressed more horror than before'. See 'American Slavery', *The Liberator*, 25 July 1851 [reprinted article].

29. Both McCaskill and Fisch offer readings of Ellen Craft and Sarah Remond, respectively, that are characterised as embarrassing wherein neither female exerted agency and was 'merchandised on the European political marketplace, with the orator's platform replacing the auction block'. See McCaskill, '"Yours Very Truly"', p. 512. Fisch, Zackodnik notes, is so 'focused on what press accounts of Remond's speeches tell us about British nationalism and anxieties about Victorian society that Remond's strategies receive scant if any critical attention'. See Audrey A. Fisch, 'Negrophilism and British Nationalism: The Spectacle of the Black American Abolitionist', *Victorian Review*, 19.2 (1993), p. 95, and Teresa Zackodnik, 'The Enslaved as Spectacle, Sarah Parker Remond, and American Slavery in England', *Nineteenth-Century Prose*, 29/1 (2002), p. 97. See also Barbara McCaskill, *William and Ellen Craft in Transatlantic Literature and Life* (Athens, GA: University of Georgia Press, 1999).

30. Sterling, *Black Foremothers*, p. 47.

31. Ellen Mary Weinauer, '"A Most Respectable Looking Gentleman": Passing, Possession, and Transgression in *Running a Thousand Miles for Freedom*', in Elaine K. Ginsberg, ed., *Passing and the Fictions of Identity* (Durham, NC: Duke University Press, 1996), p. 55.

32. Daphne Ann Brooks, *'The Show Must Go On': Race, Gender, and Nation in Nineteenth-Century Transatlantic Performance Culture* (Berkeley: University of California Press, 1997), p. 2.

33. To clarify: Piety = religiousness; Purity = abstinence from sex until marriage when conjugal duties became imperative (death was preferable to the loss of innocence); Submission = idle, inactive, passive unthinking housewife, who was – at all times – obedient; and Domestic = faithful and cheerful fulfilment of familial and social duties. This was a woman who was to bring cheer, nurse, comfort, entertain and restore all who entered her realm. See Barbara Welter, 'The Cult of True Womanhood, 1820–1860', in Edward Pessen, ed., *The Many-Faceted Jacksonian Era* (Westport: Greenwood Press, 1977), p. 48.

34. 'Woman was to work in silence, unseen "working like nature in secret" her love goes forth to the world "to regulate its pulsation and send forth from its heart, in pure and temperate flow, the life giving current". She was to work only for pure affection without the thought of money or ambition.' See Welter, 'The Cult of True Womanhood', p. 54, quoting from Maria J. McIntosh, *Woman in America: Her Work and Her Reward* (New York: Appleton, 1850), p. 25. See also McCaskill, '"Yours Very Truly"', p. 518.

35. McCaskill, '"Yours Very Truly"', pp. 518–19.

36. 'American Fugitives in England', *The Liberator*, 30 May 1851.

37. Berry, Kim and Boski, 'The Psychological Acculturation of Immigrants', pp. 63–4.

38. Furnham, 'Adjustment of Sojourners', pp. 54–7.

39. Eliza Harris, the nearly white runaway heroine of *Uncle Tom's Cabin*, who cuts her hair and dons men's clothes to runaway, is a composite of Ellen. This, in effect, gave Ellen a life and a voice centrestage in London alongside her husband's lectures and narratives. See Harriet Beecher Stowe, *Uncle Tom's Cabin* (London: Cassell, 1852); 'Anti-Slavery Meeting', *The Liberator*, 7 March 1851; *American Slavery. Report of the Great Anti-Slavery Meeting, held April 9, 1851, in the Public Room, Broadmead, Bristol, to receive the Fugitive slaves, William and Ellen Craft* (Bristol: James Ackland, 1851).
40. Furnham, 'Adjustment of Sojourners', p. 54.
41. Cherie Booth QC, Keynote Speech, WISE 2007 Conference, Hull.
42. Their first choice is almost always death to their aggressors and often at their own hands, but the Court – only an adjudicator – must disallow this (they cannot sanction killing as an option) and encourages them to think again and offer a second choice option.
43. Cherie Booth QC, Keynote Speech, WISE 2007 Conference, Hull.
44. Albert Camus, Quoted by Cherie Booth QC. Keynote Speech, WISE 2007 Conference, Hull.
45. National Office of Statistics, Census, 1871, Parish of St. Mary, Battersea.

Part II Imagining Transatlantic Slavery

5
Equiano's Paradise Lost: The Limits of Allusion in Chapter Five of *The Interesting Narrative*

Vincent Carretta

> Every part of the world in which I had hitherto been in seemed to me a paradise in comparison to the West Indies.[1]

> Disinherited as we are from [Equiano's] referential systems it is reasonable to question whether we are adequately aware of the scope of his allusions and their part in constituting the fabric of his [autobiography]. Hence, the ultimate question at issue here will be whether only the text of [Equiano's] allusion acts upon his [book] or whether it also imports its own context. If the context is indeed relevant, what are the permissible limits in our bringing that context to bear? How allusive are [Equiano's] allusions? And how functional? ... [T]he reader is not only to appreciate the allusions but is actively invited by them to exercise ... his [or her] own invention by contemplating the relevances of the entire allusive context and its received interpretation.... Such literature as this is constituted by the rich interplay between the author's text and the full contexts it allusively arouses, for these allusive resonances are not peripheral but functional to the meaning of the artistic product.[2]

Although in recent years historians and literary critics have often cited or commented on Olaudah Equiano's *The Interesting Narrative of the Life of Olaudah Equiano, or Gustavus Vassa, the African. Written by Himself* (London, 1789), they have said very little about how Equiano employs intertextual allusions in his argument against the slave trade. Few have discussed Equiano as a literary artist at the verbal level. A close look at Equiano's use of quotations and allusions, particularly in Chapter 5 of his autobiography, demonstrates that he relies on his readers' familiarity with the relevant intertextual contexts in effect to co-author or complete his arguments. He invokes other voices to render his personal experiences and observations universal. Furthermore, what Equiano does not say when he quotes from or alludes to external texts may be as significant as what he says explicitly, because such ellipses prompt his informed readers to fill in the gaps he leaves to recognise for themselves the full implications of his argument. No less than Alexander Pope in *The Rape of the Lock*, Equiano in his *Interesting Narrative* requires his readers to consider the limits of 'the rich inter-play between the author's text and the full contexts it allusively arouses' to appreciate the role his allusions play 'in constituting the fabric of his' autobiography.

Very few readers today would deny that Equiano was a skilful rheto-rician. When his *Interesting Narrative* appeared in late March 1789, millions of enslaved Africans and their descendants were given a face, a name and most importantly a voice. During the previous two years, as Gustavus Vassa, Equiano had published letters and book reviews in London newspapers attacking the transatlantic slave trade and slavery. In publishing his autobiography he revealed, either by re-claiming or inventing, an additional identity as the African-born Olaudah Equiano. A multi-generic book first published in two volumes totalling 360 quarto pages, Equiano's *Interesting Narrative* appealed to his 311 original sub-scribers and subsequent readers as a spiritual autobiography, captivity narrative, slave narrative, argument against the slave trade, adventure tale, travel book, economic treatise and *apologia*.

According to his *Interesting Narrative*, Equiano was born an Igbo in 1745, in what would become southeastern Nigeria. He tells us that he was kidnapped into slavery in 1756 at the age of 11, and even-tually taken to Barbados. After 2 weeks, he says, he was brought to Virginia, where he was bought by Michael Henry Pascal, a lieutenant on leave from the Royal Navy in command of the commercial vessel *Industrious Bee*. Pascal renamed him Gustavus Vassa, after the sixteenth-century Swedish nobleman who freed his countrymen from Danish tyranny. Equiano claims to have been first brought to England in Spring 1757, though he was there as early as December 1754 because Pascal had been recalled to military service as Britain prepared to go to war with France.[3] Equiano was baptised at St. Margaret's, Westminster, in February 1759.

Serving under Pascal, Equiano saw military action during the Seven Years' War, but as hostilities came to an end in 1762 Pascal disappointed Equiano's expectation that he would be freed. Instead, Pascal sold him into the horrors of West Indian slavery. Having acquired an education while he served in the Royal Navy, Equiano was too valuable a slave to be assigned to plantation labour when he arrived in Montserrat, and was purchased by the Quaker merchant Robert King. Consequently, Equiano's extraordinary mobility and opportunities to conduct private business enabled him to purchase his freedom in 1766.

Once free, Equiano set off from his base in London on voyages of commerce and adventure to North America, the Mediterranean, the West Indies and the North Pole. Having nearly died during the Arctic expedition, Equiano was spiritually re-born in 1774, when he embraced Methodism. In 1776 he participated in creating a slave-based plantation in Central America. Disgusted by the irreligion of his fellow workers, he returned to England the following year. He unsuccessfully applied to the Bishop of London in 1779 to be sent to Africa as missionary. The government appointed him Commissary of Provisions and Stores for the Black Poor to Sierra Leone (Africa) in 1786, but he was fired a few months later for objecting to the behaviour of fellow administrators. In the opinion columns and book reviews he published in London newspapers in 1788 Equiano opposed the transatlantic slave trade, as well as the institution of slavery. In 1792 he married an Englishwoman, Susanna Cullen, with whom he had two daughters. Equiano died on 31 March 1797, perhaps the wealthiest person of African descent in Britain. His surviving daughter, Joanna, inherited the equivalent (roughly) of £80,000 or about $160,000 in 1816.

But what rhetorical exigency or exigencies lay behind Equiano's decision to write his autobiography and publish it as and when he did in late March 1789? He tells us that he sought to issue an explanation and justification, or *apologia*, for his behaviour in the Sierra Leone affair specifically and for the conduct of his life more generally. As a spiritual autobiography, the story of Equiano's life offered his readers a conversion narrative any of them could imitate, as his frontispiece emphasises. Profit was another motive for publication, as Equiano's control of the production and distribution of *The Interesting Narrative* demonstrates. The primary motive for publication, indicated by Equiano's dedication of the book to the Members of the House of Commons and the House of Lords, was his explicit desire to contribute to the cause of abolishing the transatlantic slave trade. Equiano's related goal of abolishing the institution of slavery is less explicit in his *Interesting Narrative* than in his earlier newspaper publications. Probably intentionally rather than fortuitously, Equiano's autobiography appeared to be part of the coordinated attack from inside and outside Parliament on the transatlantic slave trade.

The care with which Equiano prepared and presented *The Interesting Narrative* is reflected in the timing of its publication. Organised and sustained opposition to the transatlantic African slave trade was a very recent development when the autobiography first appeared. Mainly through the efforts of the philanthropist Thomas Clarkson, from 1787 on the organised opposition to the African slave trade gathered, published and offered to Parliament evidence against the infamous practice. But before 1789 the evidence and arguments against the slave trade came from white voices alone. The only published black witnesses were clearly fictitious, found, for example, in the poems of Hannah More and William Cowper.[4]

Clarkson, one of Equiano's original subscribers, acknowledged the desirability of hearing the African victim's point of view. In *An Essay on the Slavery and Commerce of the Human Species* (London, 1786), Clarkson dramatised the transatlantic slave trade by placing the trade in 'the clearest, and most conspicuous point of view'. Employing the virtual reality of fiction to convey factual experience, he imagined himself interviewing a 'melancholy African'. 'We shall', he wrote, 'throw a considerable part of our information on this head into the form of a narrative: we shall suppose ourselves, in short, on the continent of Africa, and relate a scene, which, from its agreement with unquestionable facts, might not unreasonably be presumed to have been presented to our view, had we really been there'.[5]

Defenders of slavery and the transatlantic slave trade also recognised the rhetorical power a victim's voice would have. Gilbert Francklyn includes a letter dated 30 November 1788 in his *An Answer to the Reverend Mr. Clarkson's Essay* (London, 1789). He accuses Clarkson of inventing black witnesses against slavery – witnesses, Francklyn insinuates, who were actually white men speaking in blackface:

> Horrid picture of West India tyranny and brutality! And this is drawn upon the authority of people whose names Mr. Clarkson ventures not to produce ... I challenge Mr. Clarkson to produce a single man of decent character who ever gave him such an account. I do not mean a gentleman – I do not mean even a white man: I defy him to produce a Negro of character who would not *turn pale* in fabricating

such assertions. I call upon Mr. Clarkson to produce any book he ever perused ... in which he found such stories related.

(191–2).

Equiano quickly met Francklyn's challenge.

Equiano's *Interesting Narrative* was probably first published on 26 March 1789.[6] However, the subscription solicitation that Equiano sent to Josiah Wedgwood indicates that the book was ready for publication in November 1788, when illness forced William Wilberforce to delay his planned attack in the House of Commons on the slave trade, and just as King George III lapsed into the madness from which he would not recover until February 1789. Wilberforce's incapacitating illness and the King's distracting condition rendered the anticipated assault on the slave trade impracticable and impolitic before the spring of 1789. Within weeks of the appearance of Equiano's *Interesting Narrative*, Clarkson published the evidence he had gathered from white witnesses in *The Substance of the Evidence of Sundry Persons on the Slave-Trade Collected in the Course of a Tour Made in the Autumn of the Year 1788 and An Essay on the Comparative Efficiency of Regulation or Abolition as Applied to the Slave Trade*. And on 25 April 1789, less than a month after the appearance of his *Interesting Narrative*, Equiano, along with several other people of African descent, published a letter in the newspaper *The Diary; or Woodfall's Register* thanking his subscriber William Dickson for having just attacked the slave trade in his *Letters on Slavery*. Equiano and the distributor he shared with Dickson must have been delighted with Dickson's observation in *Letters* that 'no literary performance would be better received by the humane and liberal people of England, than a vindication of African capacity by the pen of an African'. On 12 May 1789 William Wilberforce commenced the delayed assault in the House of Commons on the transatlantic slave trade. In effect, and probably by intention, Equiano's autobiography was an extra-parliamentary rhetorical complement to the publications by Clarkson and others, as well as to Wilberforce's famous speech against the trade.

The attention Equiano apparently paid to the timely publication of *The Interesting Narrative* is reflected in how artfully he constructs his argument and presents his evidence against slavery, particularly in Chapter 5 of his autobiography. Equiano's literary and rhetorical art is most evident through his use of intertextuality and ventriloquism, as well as by his use of pathos, ethos and logos in the chapter that recounts one of the major turning points in his life, the point at which Pascal has sold Equiano into enslavement in the West Indies. The chapter opens, 'Thus, at the moment I expected all my toils to end, was I plunged, as I supposed, in a new slavery: in comparison of which all my services hitherto had been perfect freedom; and whose horrors, always present to my mind, now rushed on it with tenfold aggravation' (95). Consequently, 'Every part of the world in which I had hitherto been in seemed to me a paradise in comparison to the West Indies' (119).

The comparative 'paradise' Equiano had most recently lost was the state of seeming innocence he had thought he was living in with the foster-father he presumed Pascal to have been, and the familial relationship he had with his fellow shipmates. Although he knew that he had been Pascal's slave, as a minor aboard Royal Navy vessels he had been treated no differently than the servants of other naval officers, who were legally free. Like them, he had not been paid; the officers they served were given stipends for their support. Equiano had enjoyed a remarkable freedom of movement under Pascal, and he never mentions having ever experienced racial prejudice in the Navy. Given the relationship he thought he had with Pascal, he fully expected to be freed at the end of the Seven Years' War, even though Pascal had never promised to do so.

Equiano felt even more betrayed than disappointed by Pascal's decision at the end of 1762 to send him into West Indian slavery rather than manumit him. Equiano's initial response to Pascal's behaviour was despair rather than defiance. To express his suicidal feelings at the time, Equiano implicitly likens Pascal to the perfidious European trader in Thomas Day and John Bicknell's *The Dying Negro, a Poetical Epistle, from a Black, Who Shot Himself on Board a Vessel in the River Thames, to his Intended Wife*. To ensure that his readers understood the context of the lines first published in London in 1773, and reprinted with additions and changes in 1774 and 1775, Equiano included an explanatory footnote in each of the nine editions he published of *The Interesting Narrative*: '"The dying Negro", a poem originally published in 1773. Perhaps it may not be deemed impertinent here to add, that this elegant and pathetic [emotionally moving] little poem was occasioned, as appears by the advertisement prefixed to it, by the following incident: "A black who a few days before, had run away from his master, and got himself christened, with intent to marry a white woman, his fellow servant, being taken, and sent on board a ship in the Thames, took an opportunity of shooting himself through the head."'

Equiano employs pathos to appeal to his readers' emotions by representing himself as a man of feeling so overwhelmed by his afflictions that he passively anticipates death with thoughts of suicide. Appropriating, conflating and misquoting lines from *The Dying Negro*, he implores Death to deliver him to a place

> Where slaves are free, and men oppress no more,
> Fool that I was, inur'd so long to pain,
> To trust to hope, or dream of joy again.
>
> Now dragg'd once more beyond the western main,
> To groan beneath some dastard planter's chain;
> Where my poor countrymen in bondage wait
> The long enfranchisement of a ling'ring fate:
> Hard ling'ring fate! While, ere the dawn of day,
> Rous'd by the lash, they go their cheerless way;
> And as their souls with shame and anguish burn,
> Salute with groans unwelcome morn's return,
> And, chiding ev'ry hour the slow-pac'd sun,
> Pursue their toils till all his race is run.
> No eye to mark their suff'rings with a tear;
> No friend to comfort, and no hope to cheer:
> Then, like the dull unpity'd brutes, repair
> To stalls as wretched, and as coarse a fare;
> Thank heaven one day of mis'ry is o'er,
> Then sink to sleep, and wish to wake no more.
>
> (97–8)

Equiano's explanatory annotation to his quotation from *The Dying Negro* suggests that he does not assume that most readers knew the poem well enough to supplement the lines he quotes with the poem's later invocation of violent resistance in the form of an African avenger:

> For Afric triumphs! – his avenging rage
> Not tears can soften, and no blood assuage.
> He smites the trembling waves, and at the shock
> Their fleets are dash'd upon the pointed rock.
> He waves his flaming dart, and o'er their plains,
> In mournful silence, Desolation reigns –
> Fly swift, ye years! – Arise, thou glorious morn!
> Thou great avenger of thy race be born!

Equiano understandably sees Montserrat as 'this land of bondage' (98), which reminds him of John Milton's description in *Paradise Lost* of Hell:

> Regions of sorrow, doleful shades, where peace
> And rest can rarely [never] dwell. Hope never comes
> That comes to all, but torture without end
> Still urges.
>
> (*PL* 1: 65–8)

Equiano employs the pathetic fallacy – the attribution of feeling to Nature – to express the brutality he finds in the West Indies. Even the climate and shore seem hostile: 'I had been so long used to an European climate that at first I felt the scorching West-India sun very painful, while the dashing surf would toss the boat and the people in it frequently above high-water mark. Sometimes our limbs were broken with this, or even attended with instant death, and I was day by day mangled and torn' (99).

Equiano was not the first author of African descent to apply the pathetic fallacy to the West Indies. Phillis Wheatley does so in 'To a Lady on her coming to North-America with her Son, for the Recovery of her Health', in *Poems on Various Subjects, Religious and Moral* (London, 1773):

> See from *Jamaica's* fervid shore she moves
>
> ...
>
> 'Arise, ye winds, *America* explore,
> Waft me, ye gales, from this malignant shore:
> The *Northern* milder climes I long to greet,
> There hope that health will my arrival meet.'
> Soon as she spoke in my ideal view
> The winds assented, and the vessel flew.
>
> Madam, your spouse bereft of wife and son,
> In the grove's dark recesses pours his moan;
> Each branch, wide-spreading to the ambient sky,
> Forgets its verdure, and submits to die.
>
> From thence I turn, and leave the sultry plain ....[7]

Equiano moves easily from the brutality of nature to the brutality of man in the West Indian environment. About to be struck by a white man who has just cheated him, Equiano is rescued by a 'British seaman on board, whose heart had not been debauched by a West India climate' (108). He shifts from emphasising a pathetic rhetorical appeal to his readers grounded on his self-representation as a victim to an ethical appeal based on his reliability as a witness. And he shifts from using the first-person perspective to the third-person as he moves from being a man who feels almost completely for himself to one who feels for others as well. He marks these transition with another quotation adapted from Milton's *Paradise Lost*, the past tense in the original with the present:

> With shudd'ring horror pale, and eyes aghast,
> They view their lamentable lot, and find
> [View'd first thir lamentable lot, and found]
> No rest.
>
> > *(PL* 2: 616–18)

Equiano's mobility as a slave enabled him to plausibly assert the ethos and perspective of a relatively disinterested reporter and historian: 'in all the different islands in which I have been (and I have visited no less than fifteen) the treatment of the slaves was nearly the same; so nearly indeed, that the history of an island, or even a plantation, with a few ... exceptions ... might serve for a history of the whole' (111). His assumed status as an objective observer implicitly earns him the authority to editorialise about what he sees. For example, he reports that slave owners used psychological as well physical punishments to break the spirits and bodies of their slaves:

> It was very common in several of the islands, particularly in St. Kitt's, for the slaves to be branded with the initial letters of their master's name, and a load of heavy iron hooks hung about their necks. Indeed, on the most trifling occasions they were loaded with chains, and often other instruments of torture were added. The iron muzzle, thumb-screws, &c. are so well known, as not to need a description, and were sometimes applied for the slightest faults. I have seen a negro beaten till some of his bones were broken, for only letting a pot boil over. It is not uncommon, after a flogging, to make slaves go on their knees, and thank their owners, and pray, or rather say, God bless them. I have often asked many of the men slaves (who used to go several miles to their wives, and late in the night, after having been wearied with a hard day's labour) why they went so far for wives, and why they did not take them of their own master's negro

women, and particularly those who lived together as household slaves? Their answers have ever been – 'Because when the master or mistress choose to punish the women, they make the husbands flog their own wives, and that they could not bear to do'. Is it surprising that usage like this should drive the poor creatures to despair, and make them seek a refuge in death from those evils which render their lives intolerable[?]

(107)

In one of Equiano's encounters with other slaves, an old man tells him that he has often been cheated by whites: 'This artless tale moved me much, and I could not help feeling the just cause Moses had in redressing his brother against the Egyptian. I exhorted the man to look up still to the God on the top, since there was no redress below' (110–11). Equiano's elliptical allusion to Moses makes little sense to readers unless they can supply its context.[8] Equiano clearly assumes that his readers will recognise that his allusion to Moses 'redressing his brother' refers to Exodus 2:11–15: 'One day, when Moses had grown up, he went out to his people and looked on their burdens; and he saw an Egyptian beating a Hebrew, one of his people. He looked this way and that, and seeing no one he killed the Egyptian and hid him in the sand.' And if Equiano assumes that his readers will supply 'the entire allusive context and its received interpretation', he can assume that his readers will recognise the implications of his elliptical allusion: passive acceptance of oppression is not the only option available to the enslaved, and active resistance has Biblical justification. Although we cannot be sure that Equiano expects many of his readers to recall Day and Bicknell's elided invocation of 'Afric' in *The Dying Negro*, he clearly assumes that most of his readers are familiar enough with the Bible to be able to supplement his allusion to Exodus with the account of violent resistance he chooses not to mention.

Equiano's combination of personally experiencing and observing West Indian slavery allows him to make the transition to an emphasis on *logos* – reason – in his argument against the behaviour of slave owners that betrays the hypocrisy of their claim to be Christians. In less than twenty pages in the Penguin edition of his autobiography, Equiano moves from the egocentric voice, with which he opens Chapter 5, to assume a communal voice with which he addresses slave owners and their defenders. Whereas he uses the first-person *I* eighteen times in the initial paragraph of Chapter 5, in the last he uses the second-person *you* fifteen times, as he makes the transition from an opening emphasis on thoughts of self-destruction and pathos to later intimations of defiance and threat.

Equiano approaches the conclusion of Chapter 5 with an allusive passage of heightened rhetoric and controlled rage. Momentarily, Equiano reveals that his true rhetorical goal in *The Interesting Narrative* may be more radical than he claims. He does so by conflating abolition of the slave trade, amelioration of slavery and eradication of slavery in his verbal outburst. In effect, the author's rage at the evils of slavery erupts through the narrative, as his voice changes from that of autobiographer to that of preacher. The result is one of the most direct assaults on the institution of slavery found any where in Equiano's writings.

He calls on slave owners to become men of feeling like himself. He begins by identifying the causes and consequences of burying all sentiments:

> Such a tendency has the slave-trade to debauch men's minds, and harden them to every feeling of humanity! For I will not suppose that the dealers in slaves are born worse than other men – No! it is the fatality of this mistaken avarice, that it corrupts the milk of human kindness, and turns it into gall. And, had the pursuits of those men been different, they might have been as generous, as tender-hearted, and just, as they are unfeeling, rapacious, and cruel. Surely this traffic cannot be good, which spreads like a pestilence, and taints what it touches! Which violates that first natural right of mankind, equality and independency, and gives one man a dominion over his fellows which God could never intend! For it raises the owner to a state as far above man as it depresses the slave below it; and, with all the presumption of human pride, sets a distinction between them, immeasurable in extent, and endless in duration! Yet how mistaken is the avarice even of the planters. Are slaves more useful by being thus humbled to the condition of brutes, than they would be if suffered to enjoy the privileges of men? The freedom which diffuses health and prosperity throughout Britain answers you – No.
>
> (111)

Equiano turns to Milton again when his rhetoric rises to the peroration that draws Chapter 5 to its close. He employs ventriloquism, appropriating the voice of Milton's demon Beelzebub and changing it to the present tense to move from the personal to the political, from the individual vision to the communal through the use of the first person plural *we*. In effect, Beelzebub's voice provides Equiano with the avenging figure he had elided in his earlier elliptical quotation from *The Dying Negro* and allusion to Genesis 2:11–15:

> When you make men slaves, you deprive them of half their virtue, you set them, in your own conduct, an example of fraud, rapine, and cruelty, and compel them to live with you in a state of war; and yet you complain that they are not honest or faithful! You stupify them with stripes, and think it necessary to keep them in a state of ignorance; and yet you assert that they are incapable of learning; that their minds are such a barren soil or moor, that culture would be lost on them; and that they came from a climate, where nature (though prodigal of her bounties in a degree unknown to yourselves) has left man alone scant and unfinished, and incapable of enjoying the treasures she has poured out for him! An assertion at once impious and absurd.[9] Why do you use those instruments of torture? Are they fit to be applied by one rational being to another? And are ye not struck with shame and mortification, to see the partakers of your nature reduced so low? But, above all, are there no dangers attending this mode of treatment? Are you not hourly in dread of an insurrection? Nor would it be surprising; for when

> > [... for what peace will be giv'n]
> > ... No peace is given
> > To us enslav'd, but custody severe;
> > And stripes and arbitrary punishment
> > Inflicted – What peace can we return?
> > But to our power, hostility and hate;
> > Untam'd reluctance, and revenge, tho' slow,
> > Yet ever plotting how the conqueror least
> > May reap his conquest, and may least rejoice
> > In doing what we most in suff'ring feel.[10]
> >   (111–12)

Equiano's appropriation of Beelzebub's voice raises intriguing questions about the possible limits and implications of his allusions, as well as about possible influences on his decision to highlight in the debate over the abolition of the transatlantic slave trade the likelihood of revenge on the part of the enslaved, were nothing done to alleviate their oppression. Was Equiano aware that he was quoting a demon? We cannot be certain that Equiano had read *Paradise Lost*, despite his quotations from it. He may have known it only at second hand.[11] But even if Equiano had not read Milton's poem, Beelzebub is identified as the speaker of the lines Equiano quotes in Edward Bysshe, *The British Parnassus: or, a compleat common-place-book of English poetry* (London, 1714) and subsequent editions. Does Equiano knowingly quote a demon promoting violent resistance to implicitly dissociate himself from that position even as he expresses it?

The likelihood that Equiano knew that he was quoting Milton's demon raises the possibility that he is provocatively suggesting that he is more sympathetic to the cause of violent rebellion than to the status quo defended by the hypocritical Christians he has been addressing. If so, he may have influenced as well as simply preceded William Blake's far more famous claim in *The Marriage of Heaven and Hell* (engraved c.1790–1793) that 'The reason Milton wrote in fetters when he wrote of Angels & God, and at liberty when of Devils & Hell, is because he was a true Poet and of the Devils party without knowing it'. Again, we cannot prove that Blake read Equiano's *Interesting Narrative*, but Blake's employer and publisher Joseph Johnson was also Equiano's distributor and subscriber. Cleverly, though anticlimactically, Equiano ends Chapter 5 by enclosing the iron fist of threatened violence in the velvet glove of proposed amelioration: 'But, by changing your conduct, and treating your slaves as men, every cause of fear would be banished. They would be faithful, honest, intelligent and vigorous; and peace, prosperity, and happiness would attend you' (112).

Equiano knew that his prediction or threat of possible violent resistance to slavery was not unprecedented. In *Thoughts and Sentiments on the Evil and Wicked Traffic of the Slavery and Commerce of the Human Species* (London, 1787) his friend, subscriber and sometime collaborator Quobna Ottobah Cugoano had earlier taken an uncompromising position: 'Therefore, if there was no other way to deliver a man from slavery, but by enslaving his master, it would be lawful for him to do so if he was able, for this would be doing justice to himself, and be justice as the law requires, to chastise his master for enslaving of him wrongfully.'[12]

Equiano was probably also familiar with a famous and frequently re-published passage in Guillaume Thomas François Raynal's *A Philosophical and Political History of the Settlements and Trade of the Europeans in the East and West Indies. Translated from the French by J. Justamond ....* vol. 3 (Amsterdam, 1770, 4 vols.; London: Cadell, 2nd edn 1776, 4 vols.):

BUT what am I saying? Let the ineffectual calls of humanity be no longer pleaded with the people and their masters: perhaps they have never been consulted in any public transactions. If then, ye nations of Europe, interest alone can exert its influence over you, listen to me once more: Your slaves stand in no need either of your generosity or your counsels, in order to break the sacrilegious yoke of their oppression. Nature speaks a more powerful language than philosophy, or interest. Some white people, already massacred have expiated a lot of our crimes; already have two colonies of fugitive negroes been established, to whom treaties and power give a perfect security from your attempts. Poison hath at different times been the instrument of their vengeance. Several have eluded your oppression by a voluntary death. These enterprises are so many indications of the impending storm; and the negroes only want a chief, sufficiently courageous, to lead them to vengeance and slaughter.

WHERE is this great man to be found, whom nature, perhaps owes to the honour of the human species? Where is this new Spartacus, who will not find a Crassus? Then will the *black code* be no more; and the *white code* will be dreadful, if the conqueror only regards the right of reprisals.

TILL this revolution takes place, the negroes groan under the yoke of oppression, the description of which cannot but interest us more and more in their destiny. [emphasis in original]

(172–3)[13]

Equiano was less likely to have been aware of a similar passage addressing the probability of insurrection in Thomas Jefferson's *Notes on the State of Virginia*, Query 14 (written 1781, published Paris 1784, London 1787):

It will probably be asked, Why not retain and incorporate the blacks into the state, and thus save the expence of supplying, by importation of white settlers, the vacancies they will leave? Deep rooted prejudices entertained by the whites; ten thousand recollections, by the blacks, of the injuries they have sustained; new provocations; the real distinctions which nature has made; and many other circumstances, will divide us into parties, and produce convulsions which will probably never end but in the extermination of the one or the other race.[14]

Perhaps the closest rhetorical precedent for the way Equiano constructs his argument in chapter five of *The Interesting Narrative* is 'The Speech of Moses Bon Sáam', an anonymous and very likely fictional address by a former slave to his black maroon comrades-in-arms resisting white slave owners in Jamaica. Once the purported speaker had learnt to read, he discovered 'that the very Man, from whom they [slave owners] had deriv'd the *Name* they had given me, of *Moses* had been the happy *Deliverer* of a Nation! Of a Nation *chosen* and *belov'd* by *God!* the Deliverer of this chosen Nation, from such a *Slavery as ours'*.[15] More overtly than Equiano, Bon Sáam sees himself as a second Moses prepared to use violence to free his people from oppression. But like Equiano after him, Moses Bon Sáam predicts that if the slave owners ameliorate the conditions of those they have enslaved 'the proudest of your Enemies will *embrace* you, in spite of your *Colour*, when they foresee *Destruction* in your *Anger*; but *Ease* and *Security* in your *Friendship'*.[16]

Like Moses Bon Sáam, Equiano leaves open the option of violent resistance. His words may seem less passionate than the voices we hear behind them. His calm language, however, only underscores the righteous anger beneath. Equiano's enslavement in the Americas was extraordinarily unrepresentative of the lives suffered by the vast majority of people of African descent doomed to work in the fields. But it was unrepresentative in ways that enabled him to acquire a perspective on slavery in the Americas unavailable to any one individual slave. The mobility of his occupation in the Americas, his literacy and his good fortune in the masters he had, gave him access to information about the range of slave conditions throughout the British American colonies, which enabled him in 1789 to bear witness against slavery as a spokesman for the millions of his voiceless fellow slaves. He was able to transcend the limits of merely personal experiences to identify general truths about the evil institution and to convey them to his readers by appropriating the voices of others. Only someone who had borne witness to the full range of the evils of West Indian slavery in the 'land of bondage' was qualified to serve as the Moses or African avenger his 'countrymen' needed to deliver them from despair. Unfortunately, like the first Moses, Equiano was destined to direct his people to the promised land of abolition, but not to join them there: he died ten years before Britain outlawed its transatlantic slave trade in 1807.

Notes

Earlier versions of this essay were given as talks at conferences or as lectures in the United Kingdom – Chawton House, Queen Mary (University of London), University of Newcastle, University of Glasgow; Australia – University of Sydney, University of Tasmania; and the United States – Florida State University, University of Alabama, Duke University, State University of New York at Buffalo, and the 2007 annual meeting of the East-Central American Society for Eighteenth-Century Studies. I have profited greatly from the comments, questions, suggestions and encouragement from the members of my audiences, particularly Charlotte Sussman. My research is greatly indebted to the staffs and collections of the British Library, the British National Archives, the Houghton and Widener Libraries at Harvard University, the Library of Congress and McKeldin Library, University of Maryland. I am especially thankful for the support of Henry Louis Gates, Jr. I am very grateful for a Distinguished Visiting Fellowship from Queen Mary College, University of London, which enabled me to complete the research and writing of this essay.

1. Olaudah Equiano, *The Interesting Narrative and Other Writings*, ed. Vincent Carretta (New York: Penguin, 1995; revised and expanded, 2003), p. 119. All subsequent references to Equiano's writings are taken from this edition, and identified parenthetically by page number.
2. Earl R. Wasserman, 'The Limits of Allusion in *The Rape of the Lock*', *Journal of English and Germanic Philology*, 65 (1966), pp. 425–44; reprinted in Maynard Mack and James A. Winn, eds., *Pope: Recent Essays by Several Hands* (Hamden, CT: Archon Books, 1980), pp. 224–46. Quotations, pp. 224–5; 245–6; 246. In brackets, I have substituted references to Equiano and his autobiography for Wasserman's references to Alexander Pope and *The Rape of the Lock*.
3. See Vincent Carretta, *Equiano, the African: Biography of a Self-Made Man* (New York: Penguin Putnam, 2007).
4. Representative examples of fictional black voices can be found' in the volumes 4–6 in Peter J. Kitson and Debbie Lee, eds. *Slavery, Abolition and Emancipation: Writings in the British Romantic Period*, 8 vols. (London: Pickering & Chatto, 1999).
5. Thomas Clarkson, *An Essay on the Slavery and Commerce of the Human Species* (London, 1786), pp. 117–18.
6. *The World* announced on 24 March 1789 that *The Interesting Narrative* would be published on 26 March.
7. Although I have not found evidence that Equiano read Wheatley's *Poems*, he certainly was aware of her work because Clarkson quotes it in his *Essay on the Slavery and Commerce of the Human Species*.
8. See Eileen Razzari Elrod, 'Moses and the Egyptian: Religious Authority in Olaudah Equiano's *Interesting Narrative*', *African American Review*, 35 (2001), pp. 409–25; George Boulukos, *The Grateful Slave: The Emergence of Race in Eighteenth-Century British and American Culture* (Cambridge: Cambridge University Press, 2008), pp. 193–5.
9. [Equiano's footnote in editions 8 and 9.] See the Observations on a Guinea Voyage, in a series of letters to the Rev. T. Clarkson, by James Field, Stanfield, in 1788, pp. 21, 22—'The subjects of the king of Benin, at Gatoe, where I was, had their markets regular and well stocked; they teemed with luxuries unknown to the Europeans.'
10. Adapted from Beelzebub's speech in Milton, *Paradise Lost*, 2: pp. 332–40. According to Matthew 12: 24, Beelzebub is 'the prince of the devils'.
11. According to *Eighteenth-Century Collections Online*, the passage 'Regions of sorrow ... That comes to all' is included in several eighteenth-century collections of great passages of poetry, and quoted dozens of times as an epigraph or within eighteenth-century texts earlier than Equiano's *Narrative*. Samuel Johnson uses the passage 'With shudd'ring horror ... and found' in his

Dictionary (London, 1755) to illustrate *agast*, and the same passage is cited numerous times in such works as Charles Gildon, *The Complete Art of Poetry* (London, 1718) and *A Poetical Dictionary; or, the Beauties of the English Poets Alphabetically Displayed* (London, 1761). All three Milton quotations used by Equiano appear in Edward Bysshe, *The Art of English Poetry. Containing, I. Rules for making verses. II. A collection of the most natural, agreeable and sublime thoughts, ... in the best English poets. III. A dictionary of rhymes* (London, 1702; 6th edn 1718), 2 vols., which was repeatedly printed, with various titles, throughout the eighteenth century.

12. *Thoughts and Sentiments on the Evil of Slavery*, ed. Vincent Carretta (New York: Penguin, 1999), p. 59.

13. Although conventionally attributed to the Abbé Raynal, *A Philosophical and Political History* was actually a collaborative work, whose authors included Denis Diderot and Paul-Henri Thiry, Baron d'Holbach.

14. Jefferson, *Notes on the State of Virginia*, ed. Frank Shuffelton (New York: Penguin Putnam, 1999), p. 145.

15. Anonymous, 'The Speech of Moses Bon Sáam', in Thomas W. Krise, ed., *Carribbeana: Anthology of English Literature of the West Indies, 1657–1777* (Chicago: University of Chicago Press, 1999), p. 104. Emphasis in original. The periodical *The Prompter* first published 'The Speech' on 10 January 1735, and it was reprinted in the January 1735 issues of the *Gentleman's Magazine* and the *London Magazine*. Reverend Robert Robertson appended 'The Speech' to his pro-slavery *The Speech of Mr. John Talbot Campo-Bell, a Free Christian Negro, to his Countrymen in the Mountains of Jamaica* [London, 1736]. Equiano may have learnt of 'The Speech of Moses Bon Sáam' from James Tobin's *Cursory Remarks upon Mr. Ramsay Essay* (London, 1785), which mentions Robertson's work (p. 131). The Rev. James Ramsay was a close friend of Equiano and a subscriber to *The Interesting Narrative*. On 28 January 1788 Equiano published a hostile review of Tobin's *Cursory Remarks* in *The Public Advertiser*.

16. Moses Bon Sáam, p. 107. Emphasis in original.

6
Phillis Wheatley's Abolitionist Text: The 1834 Edition

Eileen Razzari Elrod

The problem presented to readers by the late eighteenth-century poet Phillis Wheatley is nearly as well known as her poetry. Alongside many readers' expressions of admiration, others have registered suspicion and disapproval, first in the eighteenth and then again in the mid- and late twentieth centuries. And nearly all of Wheatley's critics acknowledge the centrality of the poet's life in responses to her poetry. Whether the questions were framed in terms of literary authorship in the context of racist assumptions (as they were in the eighteenth century) or racial (as well as gendered) authenticity in the context of assumptions about piety and predictable conventions of neoclassical poetry (as they were in the twentieth and twenty-first centuries), Wheatley has disturbed reader's expectations in her moment and in ours. My own undergraduate students, for instance, frequently recall Alice Walker's Wheatley from their US schoolroom curriculum. Brilliant, isolated, enslaved and deeply conflicted about her race and self, Walker's Wheatley (shaped at least in part by the Black Arts Movement's hostile reception) embodies Virginia Woolf's 'contrary instincts', a fraught and unfortunately iconic representation of black women's creative expression. In the widely reprinted 1974 title essay of *In Search of Our Mothers' Gardens*, Walker presents Phillis Wheatley as a young black girl combing the golden hair of both her white mistress and the classical goddess of virtue, providing one moment among many when Wheatley served a particular rhetorical function for readers, writers and activists in the trans-Atlantic cultural milieu that first established her as a literary celebrity in 1771.[1]

But what of the intervening, nineteenth-century Wheatley who emerges from the first decade of the organised abolitionist movement in America? In 1834 George W. Light published a new edition of Wheatley's poems in Boston. Advertised in William Lloyd Garrison's *Liberator* and clearly addressed to abolitionist readers, Light's publication was dedicated 'to the Friends of the Africans'. The publication included, first, an anonymous introduction and, second, a 'Memoir', by Margaretta Matilda Odell. The publication's brief 'Introduction' makes only one specific reference to Wheatley's life or work, that is to say that the text will 'simply ... present an unvarnished record of African genius, sustained by Christian benevolence and guided by Christian faith'. The introduction further presumes that its readers support a 'great work of general emancipation', which promises 'the early dawning of that bright day', when 'the African shall be as the American, and the black man as the white'. But while the text seems to presume an abolitionist readership in an anti-slavery context, Odell's 'Memoir' undermines those assumptions in important ways.[2]

The 1834 biographical essay by Margaretta Odell warrants an attentive reading; the 'Memoirs' shaped the parameters for many readers' receptions of Wheatley's work in the nineteenth and twentieth centuries, when not only Odell's information but just as importantly her rhetorical framing of Wheatley continued to influence and inform discussions of the poet. Reprinted many times, Odell's essay served as a source of information for scores of other writers interested in Wheatley. William Robinson, in his 1981 *Bio-Bibliography*, for instance, notes repeated errors of fact and substance in publications about Wheatley, and Odell is the source for most of these, which get repeated for decades.[3] Further, Odell remains among a handful of early sources widely presumed to be reliable, in part, because she proclaims her own authority in the text of the *Memoir* on the basis of her personal connection to the Wheatley family (in her own terms as a 'collateral descendant'), and in part, surely, because of Wheatley's early death (at about age 30 in 1784), the absence of any contemporary public life-writing, and the dearth of other biographical accounts.

Wheatley left no written personal account (aside from her poems and letters), and while her letters have become increasingly important, they offer little information to readers interested in the details of Wheatley's biography. In terms of factual narrative records for Wheatley's life, then, prior to Odell there is John Wheatley's brief 1772 letter, the famous attestation note 'To the Publick' signed by eighteen of the most 'respectable characters' in Boston, and the preface to the poems, all published with the first edition of Wheatley's *Poems* in 1773. Other than brief references from the poet herself on her life and experiences in her letters and poems, then, readers have no textual descriptions of her life with the Wheatleys, her manumission, her professional/commercial ventures as a writer before or after procuring her freedom, the War for

Independence or her marriage or children. In the context of this relative silence concerning the person of Wheatley and the overwhelming fact of her life experience as a kidnapped slave and literary child prodigy, Odell's *Memoir*, though rarely actually cited, has taken on a greater authority and significance than it might have otherwise.

Odell's Wheatley shows us something of the poet's rhetorical function for abolitionists in the 1830's, revealing the 1834 edition's imagined readers' creative and sentimental construction of their own as well as Wheatley's identities. Moreover, it may well be Odell's Wheatley who becomes and remains the subject of readers' interest from the 1830s onward. She is the explicit source for some of the crucial features that consistently appear in nearly every rendering of Phillis Wheatley: the detailed portrayals and specific anecdotes of the loving, even sacrificial Wheatley family, the devoted, precocious slave, the nearly overlooked manumission, the unfortunate marriage and the apolitical and conventionally pious poet. Some of these features, of course, are clearly corroborated in Wheatley's poetry (her piety, for instance), but many are not. While there are issues in any biography where silence might accurately be read as the subject's disinterest or the event's irrelevance, it seems safe to assume that manumission from slavery would not be one of those.

Wheatley herself (intentionally or not) avoided narrative autobiographical presentations, in an era where life writing, particularly by pious Christians was extremely popular. Nonetheless, Wheatley was always embodied in her work as a racial, gendered and aged subject. Her life, her self, as an African slave girl was at least in part the point, the subject, indivisible from her literature, her artistic production. So as often as she was writing about publicly prominent others, such as her trio of tributes to famous Georges (III, Whitefield and Washington), she was, always and for every part of her audience, writing of and about herself as an ethnographic subject for Europeans, as an enslaved, then formerly enslaved, African girl. Her celebrity as a literary protégée of the Wheatleys and their famous friend the Countess of Huntingdon Selina Hastings (the enormously influential patron to whom she addressed the Whitefield elegy and later her *Poems*) depended upon her white audience's interest in her as an African slave, as a part of the extraordinarily fraught discussion of slavery, race, religion, empire and liberty in the late eighteenth century, particularly among evangelical Christians who favored Whitefield's and the Countess's equally contradictory stances on the issue. Both of these influential Methodists believed in a kind of theological egalitarianism (which suggested a dismantling of racial hierarchies), urged African Americans to take part in the work of the church and simultaneously defended the practice of slavery.[4]

Before and after her death readers found her self as interesting as her poetry. While some Bostonian white women were finding rhetorical power via anonymity, Wheatley's relative fame and power depended upon the public's interest in her identity and experience.[5] Part of the public interest in her in England and America concerned her novelty as a kind of genius who emerged despite social circumstances. Her contemporaries had demonstrated robust interest in surprising prodigies who demonstrated talent apparently inconsistent with their class and station.[6] But of course much more of the interest revolved around race. She was, as Gay Cima has pointed out, performing her own identity for readers from her first publication. Carretta suggests that if Wheatley had remained in London in 1773 (rather than returning to Boston in response to the Wheatley family summons) she might have enjoyed a more successful commercial career, trading and building on the evident celebrity and cultural capital brought by her first volume of poems and her status as a woman writer of colour.[7] Early anti-slavery activists made use of both her self and her poetry in arguments for the humanity, intellect and creative capacity of African Americans, and the corollary inhumanity of slavery: Gregory (1785), Clarkson (1786) and Stedman (1796).[8]

William Lloyd Garrison had drawn readers' attentions to Wheatley's poetry from the beginning of his publication of *The Liberator*. Between February and December of 1832 Garrison ran nearly all of Wheatley's poetry. The February issue of that year included a brief biographical sketch by Abigail Mott and an excerpt from a speech by Samuel Knapp. In the same issue, the 1834 and 1835 reprintings of Wheatley's volume of poetry were advertised. And after its 1834 publication, Light's volume with Odell's memoir was advertised among Garrison's list of available anti-slavery publications for sale.[9] The publisher would have been familiar to many American readers. George W. Light edited and published *The Boston Book* and *Young America's Magazine*, publications directed at readers interested in self-improvement, and reprinted works by well-known writers of the day (including Longfellow and Hawthorne). Joseph Kett describes Light as a machinist turned editor who began publishing somewhat coincidentally as a result of his involvement with emergent labour associations.[10] Other publications he put forward suggest a domestic and traditionally Christian focus. During this same decade he published several titles by William Alcott, notably on the duties of young wives to their husbands and children, advocating a familiar doctrine of sacrificial love and domestic efficiency (*The Young Woman's Guide, The Young Husband, The Young Wife, The Young Housekeeper, The Young Mother* and *The House I live In, or The Human Body*). Light's publications of Alcott's treatises on the young wife and the young mother were particularly good sellers. The reading audience for Odell's 'Memoir' and George Light's republication of Wheatley's poetry would have presumably shared some of the concerns represented by both publishers – Garrisonian abolitionism synthesised with moderate political reform, domestic, sentimental Christianity and conventional feminine piety.

The anonymous introduction (which preceded Odell's *Memoir*) to George Light's 1834 edition of Wheatley's poetry suggests that the pages to follow will present a sweeping argument against slavery and for racial equality, taking into account the full humanity of blacks. Noting that slavery has been 'erased' in New England, the writer of the 'Introduction' then poses a set of rhetorical questions: 'How can a free people be a slaveholding people? Surely ... where man is claimed as the property of his fellow, the cornerstone of the Temple of Liberty must be laid in the sand; and whither shall we flee when such frail foundation is unsettled? We have been told of the happiness of the Negro in his bondage ... But would the free man change places with the slave? Does he envy his condition?' The writer goes on to acknowledge the social effects, 'the poisonous operations of slavery on public sentiment', at the same time issuing a call for abolition and education. The overall tone of the 'Introduction' suggests a fairly politicised perspective, as he/she ends with a general call for emancipation and an imaginative yearning for the 'early dawning of that bright day, when, in the moral view of his fellow-men, no less than of that creator who has "made them all of one blood", the African shall be as the American, and the black man as the white'.

Despite this assertion of racial equality as well as a commitment to liberty and social and cultural enfranchisement, however, what follows is a thoroughly exceptionalist argument, an account of a unique individual, a 'genius' whose extraordinary talent, along with her extraordinary virtue, repeatedly requires the reader to understand her as not just unusual, nor even rare, but unique. Odell's essay seems, in fact, to provide a foundation for an argument *against* a more sweeping, politicised and theorised position regarding slavery and race, by distinguishing her not only from all other African American slaves, but also from all other Africans. Moreover, while Odell does not make this a part of an explicit argument (or problem for an implied argument), Phillis

Wheatley's experience in slavery is happy, even fortuitous in this narrative depicting benevolent slaveholders and dangerous freedom. The actual argument (rather than the one forecasted in the 'Introduction') that emerges from Odell's biographical narrative seems no anti-slavery argument at all, but rather an affirmation of the prevailing values held by white readers considerably less progressive than Garrison's. Christian humility and compassion are quite unsurprisingly endorsed, and the location for these virtues is not the slaveholder but rather the enslaved; conventional racial hierarchies are not only unquestioned but vigorously reinscribed.

It's worth reading these materials about Wheatley as much in terms of what seems missing as for what is actually there. Making sense of the biographical essay in light of the popular genres with which Odell's American Christian readers (to whom she specifically addresses herself) would have been familiar, several omissions seem notable, at least. For instance, she gives readers a religious biography without a conversion story. For all of the lessons of piety (and there are many) contained in the biographical sketch, Wheatley's religious experience and sensibility is assumed, rather than narrated. Her Christian virtues (particularly humility) are repeatedly extolled and presented in a conventionally religious context. But, for example, her actual conversion to Christianity (a key genre convention of nearly all Protestant spiritual autobiography and biography) is missing. And although the narrative of conversion was often particularly important to writers marginalised by race, sex or class as a crucial tool for establishing the transformation and hence authorial credentials of the writer looking to secure the interests of pious readers, Odell does not discuss Wheatley in these transformative terms.

Furthermore, conversion is only one of the transformational experiences that seems to be missing in this personal narrative. Interested readers, certainly abolitionist readers, would have been familiar with the emerging genre of the slave narrative. Though perhaps not yet seen as a distinct genre by many readers in 1834, personal narratives by slaves formed part of the rich body of religious life-writing popular with readers on both sides of the Atlantic. Many of these spiritual autobiographies featured literal, physical captivity at the heart of the narrative drama, often metaphorising it into a personal story of trial and triumph, including a story of conversion or spiritual transformation. Personal accounts featuring Africans captured and enslaved by whites, whites captured by Indians in America and Muslims in Algiers, all rendered for readers cultural and racial conflicts that personalised and spiritualised the larger story of cultural conquest, so that the individual narrative became, in many cases, not about the conflict of communities and culture, nor about the unequal power dynamics that shaped the outcome, but, instead more often, an intensely *personal* story of spiritual travail and individual triumph. The most popular personal narratives of the period featured both conversion to Christianity and liberation from spiritual and literal bondage (from slavery, and, in a related genre, from Indian captivity). The two genres were related in the readerly needs they served (for violence, horror and depictions of racial others, all packaged into a suitable didactic package with a pious narrator) and both became important ideological tools for swaying public opinion concerning race relations in the nineteenth century. The eventually more overtly polemical and politicised slave narrative genre of, say, Frederick Douglass or Harriet Jacobs, emerges from this literary, commercial and religious legacy. Equiano's 1789 *Narrative* is the best example, but there were other early examples as well, sometimes in form of a brief broadside such as Johnson Green's *Life and Confessions*, 1786.

Late eighteenth and early nineteenth-century readers were both familiar with and hungry for these ostensibly pious tales of cultural conflict, which frequently offered dramatic sensation and graphic violence. Such narratives were particularly appealing for readers squeamish about the less socially acceptable form of the novel. By way of the personal narrative, then, readers could encounter the violence and drama they craved without the social censure associated with the reading of novels (presumed by some readers to be spiritually wicked and intellectually and civically vacuous). Equiano's narrative is important in part because it crosses so many lines of genre and audience appeal. Offering readers a story of captivity, spiritual meaning (specifically Christian conversion) cultural transformation, personal triumph, commercial success and nascent political protest it captured a robust audience on both sides of the Atlantic. During the decades after Equiano, as abolition became an organised international political force, slave narrators increasingly made use of the political potentialities of the genre. And it is during the 1830s, at the time of Odell's publication and in the context of Garrisonian abolitionism, that the slave narrative shifted from a spiritual story of captivity to an antislavery polemic, as William L. Andrews describes it, from a presentation of the slavery of sin to one of the sin of slavery.[11] The slave narrative energised abolitionism (even as the Indian captivity narrative helped to lay a foundation for systematic Indian 'removal' of Andrew Jackson's presidency in the 1830s). So it is all the more notable that Odell's Wheatley is neither converted nor freed during the course of the 1834 'Memoir'.

Odell's account fails altogether to mention not only her Christian conversion, but also her manumission. The most popular personal narratives emerging from this period featured conversion to Christianity and liberation from literal bondage, but Wheatley's 1773 passage from slavery into freedom is entirely unnoted. In fact, Odell's Wheatley moves from being ostensibly within the loving Wheatley's family protection to being entirely outside of it without accompanying explanation. The shift in legal status seems to occur as a function of the deaths and removals that are noted in the biography, rather than as a result of her (or anyone else's) agency. Indeed her manumission seems to be framed as profound familial loss rather than dramatic liberation. This despite what we know of her crucial trip to a post-Somerset decision England, where she met with Granville Sharp – as Vincent Carretta notes, the most dangerous tour guide imaginable for a colonial slave visiting England.[12] Indeed, as Carretta speculates, after her return to America from her trip to England, Wheatley may well have aggressively pursued the manumission that goes entirely unmentioned in Odell's biography.

The failure to acknowledge Wheatley's manumission would have had a number of possible rhetorical effects on nineteenth-century readers. Readers might have imagined away her slavery, picturing her 12 years with the Wheatleys exclusively as a time of literary patronage and familial nurture. Or they might have assumed that she was freed immediately or early on in her time with the Wheatleys. In any case the omission of a discussion of Wheatley's transformation from slave to free puts her somehow beyond the reach of such terms. Readers are not faced with her agency, nor are they invited to see her as complicated by such questions of political or national identity. She remains relentlessly domestic, and her story is told in almost entirely personal terms, as Mrs Wheatley's servant (rather than slave), the perennial child and companion to her aging and ill mistress. She neither seeks nor secures her freedom and, like the rhetorically appealing and profoundly gendered early descriptions of the seventeenth-century Puritan poet Anne Bradstreet, her publication occurs only because others will it, not because she seeks it herself.

Odell's Wheatley, with her complete absence of agency, would have offered a reassuring antidote to an American populace riveted by Nat Turner's revolt just a little over two years earlier. Albert Stone asserts that 'no slave narrative had a swifter impact on the American public than *The Confessions of Nat Turner*'. Turner and Thomas Gray (to whom Turner dictated his memoir) tapped readers' desire for accounts of slave experience and racial violence. In the hands of court-appointed attorney Gray, Turner's *Confessions* became, to a certain extent, an anti-abolitionist tool, designed, certainly, to reassure slave-holders that Turner was a crazed aberration, neither strategic nor sensible. Gray may have designed the narrative to persuade readers of Turner's lunacy as the central point of the story. And yet, despite the rich and critically fraught history of the reception and reinterpretation of Gray's handling of Turner's *Confessions*, readers have long noted the compelling power of Nat Turner's words despite the intervening presence of Gray. Most memorable, perhaps, is the moment when Gray invites Turner to repent by asking him what was likely intended as a rhetorical question: 'Do you not find yourself mistaken now?' To which Turner responds with the rhetorically stunning 'Was not Christ crucified?' Published almost immediately after his execution, fifty thousand copies of Turner's dictated story were printed.[13]

In contrast to Turner, who embodied and articulated rage over slavery and an unconditional quest for freedom, Odell's Wheatley didn't seek freedom at all. Rather, she faced the most oppressive circumstances in her life *after* her unacknowledged manumission and the subsequent death of Susanna Wheatley. The happy years with the loving family (actually the period of Wheatley's enslavement) is bookended by two periods of dramatically depicted hardship: first, the moment before she is initially sold, and, second, after she is free and no longer with the Wheatley household. Indeed, the most dangerous periods of her adult life occur, first, as a result of the War for Independence, which Odell presents as an event that brings economic disorder rather than political liberty; and second (in that context of difficult freedom), when she acts with agency to choose to marry. Odell's intriguing reference to the war seems to cohere with her presentation of Wheatley. Political and personal liberty are dangerous; revolt, even the idealised historical revolt of the War for Independence, is unseemly. Such a view coheres with Odell's vague, entirely personal anti-slavery position, which elides any discussion of the potentially complicated and embarrassing transition from slavery to freedom.

Which brings this discussion to the genre conventions that *are* present in Odell's story. Though accounts of spiritual and political transformations are missing, the conventional signposts of a woman's life narrative are emphatically present. In fact, the biographical subject Phillis Wheatley is presented in ways quite familiar to readers of novels in the late eighteenth and early nineteenth-century. The 'Memoir' reads rather like a sentimental novel. Phillis Wheatley is, first, the pious and vulnerable orphan in need of the sacred domestic space for spiritual and material protection and survival, and, second, the virtuous, but ultimately fallen woman, tragically seduced by a bad man into fatal circumstances.

Odell's memoir emphasises the conventional female virtues marketed by the popular sentimental fictions of the day and noted decades ago by literary scholars and historians: purity, piety, submissiveness and domesticity. The sacred domestic space, important and deeply gendered in early nineteenth-century fiction, trumps political, economic and civic space (as in revolution, manumission). And domesticity seems, in the main, apolitical here, in contrast to the way writers such as Stowe employ the domestic sphere in qualified ways toward political ends. Phillis Wheatley's virtue, specifically her self-deprecation and humility, is commended to the reader from her first appearance in the narrative. Rhetorically, Odell presents Phillis's humility initially almost as a natural result of her original state, when she is first envisioned at auction as a very young child. The emphasis in the portrayal is on Wheatley's vulnerability, on her obvious need for the Wheatleys' and by extension, readers', sympathy and kind intervention. Wheatley's forcefully narrated vulnerability establishes the frame in which she will be viewed by readers for centuries. In what now seems a strange and startling rhetorical coup, the slave purchase becomes a rescue and, ultimately, an adoption, of a submissive, vulnerable orphan, perhaps even an anticipation of the orphan of mid-century novels such as the record-breakingly popular *Wide, Wide World*. The reader, perhaps, is situated to envision herself as a textual corollary to the fostering family who will for good or ill take charge of the vulnerable child. The presentation of slave as orphan then enables, perhaps even requires, readers to position the Wheatley family not as slaveholders but as a compassionate family enlarging their sacred domestic space to include a needy outsider. Odell presents a scene (repeated often in the Wheatley biographies that follow this one) featuring Phillis Wheatley as a poor, weak, child, wrapped in a dirty carpet, not so much abducted, really, as abandoned, an orphan awaiting rescue and adoption into a family. And the Wheatleys become that family – kind, even compassionate liberators, who, almost incidentally, held slaves.

The sentimental space into which the reader is invited features a highly qualified liberation. Phillis' years with the Wheatleys are presented not as bondage but, rather, as liberation from unspoken horrors that proceeded them, and as a literary apprenticeship that allowed her genius to bloom. The Wheatleys replace her lost mother (a primitive figure imagined in the vaguest of possible terms) with another (a 'benevolent' New England Christian): 'We cannot know at how early a period she was beguiled from the hut of her mother, or how long a time elapsed between her abduction from her first home and her being transferred to the abode of her benevolent mistress, where she must have felt like one awaking from a fearful dream' (11). What readers 'cannot know' is nonetheless conjured up by Odell. The Wheatleys have nothing whatever to do with the 'beguiling' that takes Phillis from her family and culture. Moreover, her abduction consists specifically not of enslavement, but instead loss of mother and loss of home. On the one hand, the powerful rhetorical effects of these losses will reverberate throughout abolitionists' antislavery arguments for the next three decades where writers will repeatedly marshal readers' feeling responses to descriptions of familial losses, sentimental passages that will underscore the inhumanity of race slavery even as it sentimentalised the grief of these losses. On the other hand, framing the immorality of Wheatley's situation in this exclusively familial context allows resolution or redemption to occur within the kind household of the Wheatley family where the fact of slavery is eclipsed, even negated, by kindness and education.

Phillis Wheatley's virtuous humility is present from the start and emphasised throughout Odell's story. She seems (essentially, even) both literary genius and humble Christian. Selected for purchase by Mrs Wheatley precisely because of her humility, Odell's Phillis exhibits virtues that, in this challenging rhetorical context, seem to humanise her, without vilifying the Wheatleys, despite the fact that they are actively engaged in the purchase of a child. While the Wheatleys' participation in the system of chattel slavery goes entirely unnoted, and in fact is hard to see in this version, their kindness, instead, along with Phillis' humility, seems to be the point of the story. Ironically, Odell emphasises Phillis Wheatley's humanity and piety as she *de*humanises Wheatley's cohort of female slaves, without a hint of self-consciousness. Even in this first instance, then, Phillis is exceptional. In contrast to other slaves, who are described as 'robust, healthy females', descriptors that reify but fail to critique their status as human chattel, Phillis's humanity is emphasised by a focus on vulnerability and virtue. She is 'slender', and 'suffering', and her 'humble and modest demeanor' attracts Mrs Wheatley's attention. Consequently Mrs Wheatley is not so much purchasing and then enslaving a child as she is coming to the aid of a vulnerable and innocent lost child. Odell's narrative invites readers rhetorically into the same compassionate stance as the one Mrs Wheatley seems to occupy in the narrative.

This rhetorical frame persists throughout the narrative, as Odell both implicitly and explicitly presents Wheatley's enslavement not as bondage but adoption. Mrs Wheatley is never slave mistress. Rather she moves from being a hospitable hostess to an indulgent adoptive mother. 'Phillis ate of her bread and drank of her cup, and was to her as a daughter; for she returned her affection with unbounded gratitude, and was so devoted to her interests as to have no will in opposition.' When she is not 'daughter', she is Mrs Wheatley's 'protegee'.[14] And Mrs Wheatley is her 'benefactress' and 'benevolent mistress'. Odell's portrayal occasionally acknowledges a more realistic description of the power relations at work here, but only as she overturns such starkness with sentiment, as in 'The chains which bound her to her master and mistress were the golden links of love, and the silken bands of gratitude. She had a child's place in their house and in their hearts'. In other passages Odell indicates dominion but only in an intensified context of love and intimacy, expressed, for example, in emphatically placed possessive pronouns as she has Mrs Wheatley repeatedly referring to 'my Phillis' in family anecdotes. Further, the unacknowledged distinctions between Phillis and all other African American slaves, explicitly made at the scene of the auction, persist. Odell describes Mrs Wheatley singling out Phillis for favour and privilege. She goes on to describe the other Wheatley slaves' bewilderment at such treatment, but offers no reflective comment, allowing the others (such as Prince) to serve as rhetorical comic relief or entertaining local colour. Phillis is special, human, known and worth a reader's attention and sympathy; her enslaved cohorts are in an entirely separate class and category.

While Odell presents the enslaved Wheatley as a rescued orphan, she portrays the free adult Wheatley as a victimised woman, perhaps even as a fallen woman from a seduction novel. Wheatley is seduced, however, not into illicit sex resulting in an illegitimate child, but, rather, into a bad marriage with a man decidedly beneath her in terms of virtue and class. The outcome remains the same: Wheatley's 'fall', specifically her marriage to John Peters, determines the same ending as for, say, Susanna Rowson's Charlotte Temple: loss of 'virtue'. Each precipitates a decline into poverty, illness, unhappy maternity and then the deaths of mother and child. Odell's Phyllis Wheatley adheres to the formulaic set of events that threatened so many other women of virtue in the fiction of the period. Like the tragically fallen heroines of the novels, she provides a negative moral lesson founded on a bedrock assumption that the central choice, the only meaningful choice, of a woman's life, concerns whom to love and marry. Sentimental language and dramatic circumstances, mirroring those featured in many late eighteenth and early nineteenth-century women's novels, dominate Odell's narrative.

Wheatley's resemblance here to stock characters (vulnerable orphans, fallen women) from sentimental novels foregrounds her gender in strikingly conventional ways, simultaneously rendering her race (specifically the way her race determines her circumstances) nearly invisible, despite her race and her enslavement constituting most readers' first concern. This, despite her experience of slavery, despite the explicitly abolitionist contexts and market for this edition. The effects of race on her narrowly circumscribed situation are entirely overlooked as the biographer presents Wheatley, first, as a vulnerable child in need of a family, and then later, post-slavery, again as a vulnerable, this time tragic, heroine, not as a newly liberated person of colour. Suddenly and sadly bereft of the love and protection of her 'family', Wheatley is prey to the designs of an apparently bad man. Her life ends as those of so many popular fictional women did – one more extraordinary woman of great promise, pious like Rowson's Charlotte Temple, brilliant like Foster's Eliza Wharton, who loves the wrong man and dies abandoned by him in a dirty garret with his unfortunate or dead child by her side.

Odell's rendering of Phillis Wheatley invites readers to imagine themselves as liberators in the benign and sentimental tradition of the Wheatleys. While the primary virtue displayed by Phillis Wheatley is her submissiveness, the primary virtue displayed by her 'family', is kindness/compassion – of a particular sort. Readers are invited to identify with the Wheatleys, who are presented as benevolent and virtuous, embodiments of Christian compassion, despite the fact that they held slaves, indeed continued to hold Phillis Wheatley as a slave, long after recognising her 'genius'. Such a message, while theoretically refuted by the arguments in the paper that advertised this volume, would nonetheless have worked effectively to reassure readers of the comfortably limited scope of the ethical demands made upon them by an anti-slavery position.

Odell's 1834 'Memoir', situated as it was at the beginning of the edition of Wheatley's poems, invited readers to see Wheatley's poetry in the context of a life story in which she becomes not so much a part of an argument for abolition, but rather contrastingly, a self-congratulatory account of the kindness and virtue of whites who, first, recognised a (rare) black genius, outstanding for her personal virtue as well as her intellect, as humble as she was brilliant, and then acted in compassion on her behalf, fostering her talent and protecting her, not because of her common humanity, nor because of their understanding of the immorality of their own actions, nor, even, because of her suffering, but, rather, because of her remarkable talent and humble Christian character. Such a story would have assured white New England readers of their moral and political safety in the face of increasingly organised and vocal blacks who made claims upon white America that were vastly different than Odell's modest and virtuous Phillis.

Notes

1. Alice Walker, *In Search of Our Mother's Gardens* (New York: Harcourt, 1983). 1771 was the year Phillis Wheatley published the funeral elegy for George Whitefield (addressed to Selina Hastings and composed in 1770) in Boston and London. She had published earlier poems, including one in 1767, and had composed poems at least two years prior to that (Vincent Carretta, ed., *Phillis Wheatley, Complete Writings* (New York: Penguin books, 2001) Introduction, p. xiv). The Whitefield elegy, however, brought her significant attention and fame on both sides of the Atlantic.
2. Margaretta Matilda Odell, *Memoir and Poems of Phillis Wheatley, a Native African and a Slave, Dedicated to the Friends of the Africans* (Boston: George Light, 1834).
3. William H. Robinson, *Phillis Wheatley: A Bio-Bibliography* (Boston, MA: G. K. Hall, 1981). Another source for biographical error and confusion regarding Phillis Wheatley is Henri Gregoire's 1808 *De La Litterature De Negres ...*, which was translated into English in 1810 by D. B. Warden. Gregoire claimed to draw his information from a letter from M. Girard who claimed to know Wheatley's husband personally, but, as Robinson points out, the Gregoire text contains numerous errors, which Warden's translation then repeats and compounds. Subsequent accounts of Wheatley's biography by John Russwurm and Abigail Mott repeat these errors.
4. David S. Lovejoy, *Religious Enthusiasm in the New World: Heresy to Revolution* (Cambridge, MA: Harvard University Press, 1985), p. 199.
5. Gay Gibson Cima offers intriguing comparative readings of Phillis Wheatley and Mercy Otis Warren as performance critics, focusing on the issues and effects of anonymity. See Cima, 'Black and Unmasked: Phillis Wheatley, Mary Otis Warren and the Limits of Anonymity', *Theatre Journal*, 52 (2000), pp. 465–95.
6. Kristin Wilcox, 'The Body into Print: Marketing Phillis Wheatley', *American Literature*, 71 (1999), p. 12.
7. Carretta, ed., *Phillis Wheatley, Complete Writings*, p. xxxv.
8. Ibid., p. xxxvi.
9. William H. Robinson, ed., *Critical Essays on Phillis Wheatley* (Boston, MA: G. K. Hall, 1982), p. 53.
10. See Joseph Kett, *The Pursuit of Knowledge under Difficulties: From Self-Improvement to Adult Education in America, 1750–1900* (Stanford: Stanford University Press, 1994).
11. William L. Andrews, *To Tell a Free Story: The First Century of Afro-American Autobiography, 1760–1865* (Urbana: University of Illinois Press, 1986).
12. Carretta, ed., *Phillis Wheatley, Complete Writings*, p. xxxvi.
13. Nat Turner, *The Confessions of Nat Turner, The Leaders of the late Insurrection in South Hampton, Virginia* (Baltimore: Thomas Gray, 1831).
14. Odell, 'Memoir', pp. 13, 18.

7
Women and Abolitionism: Hannah More's and Ann Yearsley's Poetry of Freedom

Lilla Maria Crisafulli

In 1824 the Quaker Elizabeth Heyrick published her pamphlet *Immediate not Gradual Abolition; or, an Inquiry into the shortest, safest, and most effectual means of getting rid of West Indian Slavery* (reprinted in New York in 1825 and in London in 1832). William Wilberforce, who by then had spent most of his life as a parliamentary leader of the abolitionist movement, did not appreciate this radical female stand and invited his followers not to support it. Nevertheless, Elizabeth Heyrick's pamphlet was successful and helped to bring about the liberation of slave children. It might be noted that 10 per cent of the financial support to abolitionist societies of the time came from women, and in areas such as Manchester women contributed up to half the total amount, although, while women were admitted into such societies, they were excluded from leadership positions.[1]

On 8 April of the same year, at the home of the author Lucy Townsend in Birmingham, there was a meeting of women writers, including Elizabeth Heyrick herself, Sarah Wedgwood, Sophia Sturge and Mary Lloyd, who together decided to found the Birmingham Ladies Society for the Relief of Negro Slaves (the first abolitionist women-only society). Later, similar groups were created in Nottingham (Ann Taylor Gilbert), Sheffield (Mary Ann Rawson, Mary Roberts), Leicester (Elizabeth Heyrick, Susanna Watts), Glasgow (Jane Smeal), Norwich (Amelia Anderson Opie, Anna Gurney), London (Mary Anne Schimmelpenninck, Mary Foster), Darlington (Elizabeth Pease) and Chelmsford (Anne Knight). By 1831, 73 such organisations existed, but two years later, after the 1833 abolitionist act, these societies and organisations were dismantled. In 1840, on the occasion of the first World Anti-Slavery Convention in London, an unsuccessful attempt was made to forbid women from taking part. The result of this proposed restriction caused many of the women present to become conscious that their sex was excluded even from the celebration of the newly acquired freedom granted to the slaves of the British Empire (not by chance in 1828 Elizabeth Heyrick had published *Apology for Ladies' Anti-Slavery Associations*, as if predicting the need to reassert women's role in the movement). This evident violation of women's rights as representatives and participants inspired Anne Knight to begin a campaign for the rights of equality for women, so that in many ways the movement for women's emancipation can be said to derive from that for the abolition of slavery.[2]

Let us now travel back some fifty years, to the 1780s, when women writers first began to champion the abolitionist movement. These writers, unaware of events to come, blazed the trail that would eventually lead to the historic breakthrough of 1840. This essay will argue that women's involvement in the early abolitionist campaign was not only an act of human sympathy or sentimental charity bestowed on the slaves and on their brutal condition by female hearts responding with greater *pietas* to human sufferings than their male counterparts. What I would like to suggest here is that women's participation in the anti-slavery trade movement was in part a moral and emotional duty but also a daring political act, and that it constituted a remarkable step towards that process of self-awareness that eventually led women to appeal for full social, economic and legal rights of their own.

Following Moira Ferguson's findings in *Subject to Others*,[3] I wish to underline that in many ways women's anti-slavery arguments were not only shaped by their own marginalised social status, but that their daring first-person participation in the anti-slavery campaign helped them, in turn, to pick up and articulate arguments and opinions that formed a political language, a language put to good use in shaping the rhetoric of their later plea for freedom and equality. In other words, while they saw slavery as an unjustifiable usurpation of human rights and as a distorting mirror of the larger English society in which they were living and operating, at the same time anti-slavery discourse gave them an insight into their own subalternity and social exclusion, and empowered them to speak also for themselves as the 'excluded' other.

The beginnings of women's involvement in the abolitionist movement can be traced back to 1787–9, years of fundamental importance in the history of the British movement against the slave trade. In 1787 The Society for Effecting the Abolition of the Slave Trade was founded by Granville Sharp and Thomas Clarkson, while in the same year William Wilberforce became the leader of the abolitionist movement in Parliament. In 1788 The Society for Effecting the Abolition of the Slave Trade organised its first petition campaign, presenting over 100 petitions against slavery to Parliament (the second campaign was organised in 1792 with around 519 petitions). The final upshot of such endeavours came about in 1807 when Britain passed the *Abolition of the Slave Trade Act*, which outlawed the British Atlantic slave trade.[4]

The two women writers I wish to discuss here, Hannah More and Ann Yearsley, participated in the debate of these years. Though from very different socio-economic backgrounds, both women were from Bristol, a city where, in the late eighteenth century – as in London, Liverpool and other British towns – virtually every citizen had some interest in one or more slave trade ships, and the sugar trade gave them unprecedented luxury and wealth. Inevitably, as Alan Richardson has pointed out, 'The Abolitionist campaign forced the average British citizen at least to consider connections between his or her daily life and the politics and economics of a growing colonial and mercantile empire. Such considerations would have been still more pressing in Bristol where, as a phrase common by the early nineteenth century had it, "every brick in the city had been cemented with a slave's blood". Bristol had become Britain's second largest city in the early eighteenth century through trading the "slaves and sugar"'.[5]

If, as Cora Kaplan rightly argues, the age was 'marked from the beginning by exclusion of gender, race and class', it was undoubtedly abolitionism that allowed women to develop a deeper social understanding, giving them the authority to voice their antagonism and their anger against a British economic policy whose inhumanity they denounced and challenged.[6] In the Romantic period, as Peter J. Kitson observes, abolitionism often acted 'as a coded language of opposition to the dominant culture within Britain as well as a direct campaign against the cruelties of empire'.[7] Women were at the forefront of such a campaign, making themselves heard through oral and written discourse and *becoming visible* through various social actions (such as taking part in public meetings, supporting petitions and boycotting slave trade goods), which is to say that women played a central role in the national political agenda as never before in Britain. In recent years a vigorous debate informed by post-colonial theories has surrounded abolitionist literature, seen as complicit 'with the naturalization of racial categories that characterized nineteenth-century racism'.[8] Tim Fulford and Peter J. Kitson, in their introduction to *Romanticism and Colonialism: Writing and Empire, 1780–1830*, summarise this viewpoint as follows: 'Many of the British Romantics saw themselves as being in opposition to aspects of colonialism – Coleridge and Southey actively campaigned against slavery and Blake wrote against it'. Fulford and Kitson, referring to the various contributions to their volume, go on to add: 'Discussions of their work are placed next to analyses of Evangelical women abolitionists, Hannah More and Mary Butt Sherwood – writers opposed to their politics and aesthetics. What is revealed in this contextualisation is that, on neither side of the gender and ideological divisions, was a self-consistent discourse on colonialism possible: men and women, Romantic and Evangelical opposed slavery in different ways, but both reinstated some of its informing assumption within their opposition'.[9]

If these are considerations about white abolitionist literature at large, critical readings of women's abolitionist literature are, if anything, even more severe. Deirdre Coleman, for instance, argues that 'in seeking to capitalize upon fashionable anti-slavery rhetoric for their own political objectives, women only increased the general murkiness of abolitionist rhetoric, an effect most evident in their employment of the emotive but clichéd analogy between their own disenfranchised lot and the plight of enslaved Africans'.[10] No less censorious are Alan Richardson's remarks, particularly with reference to Hannah More and Ann Yearsley. According to Richardson, 'If Romantic discourse naturalizes nation and race, however, Enlightenment discourse manifests racist tendencies of its own, and More's rhetoric also concurs with canonical Romanticism as it veers from Enlightened universalism toward British nationalism.' Besides, whereas 'More's verses also evoke Romantic rhetoric ... in their intensification of the trope of "African savagery" and their insistent connection between "darkness" or blackness and "rude", "luxuriant" African "energy", the "wild vigour of a savage root" (*Slavery, a Poem*, 87–90) ... Yearsley's text [*A Poem on the Inhumanity of the Slave-Trade*, 1788] vacillates throughout between assigning its represented slaves an African or Caribbean origin, collapsing the two exotic regions into an indifferentiated "barb'rous" (317) or "wild" (148) space of "dingy" natives vulnerable to the incursions of European slaves'.[11]

Before venturing into a closer discussion of More's and Yearsley's contributions, some further considerations, provoked by these critical perspectives, may be useful. First, it is by no means evident that women's open dissent and firm opposition to the trade of human beings, which had made Britain the wealthiest and the most powerful country in the world, were without public risks or private consequences. The idea of the slave-as-commodity, and that of the necessity of the slave trade to the prosperity of the country, were widely shared, and the personal lives of those who openly opposed them – especially if members of the female sex – were in various ways exposed to the arbitrary power of the traders and their political supporters: that is, to the people who in practice ruled British society. As Eric Williams long ago observed, transatlantic slavery was inextricably linked to Britain's economic and political hegemony. More recently, Franca Dellarosa has underlined the intensity of the involvement of city life in the slave trade in cities such as Liverpool: 'As a contemporary historian remarked, the "real annual return of wealth" deriving from the slave trade "may be said to pervade the whole town, increasing the fortunes of the principal adventurers, and contributing to the support of the majority of the inhabitants; almost every man in Liverpool is a merchant [...] almost every order of people is interested in a Guinea cargo" [Wallace 1797, p. 229]'.[12] Such a glory of 'the town and the city' is sadly documented by the abolitionist Thomas Clarkson, who describes with bitterness and astonishment the failure of the English to be touched by the atrocities of the African trade, the material signs of which were exhibited in shop windows, where 'iron shackles, handcuffs, and thumb-screws were sold'.[13]

Abolitionism inevitably became a contemporary issue in which women writers considered themselves relevant participants, able to exploit artistic skills and creative imagination in order to articulate a convincing argument. As women intellectuals, they were privileged and marginalised at the same time: privileged because they succeeded in making their voices heard, marginalised because they were unrepresented beings, deprived of civil and economic rights, thereby anticipating Mary Wollstonecraft's polemical affirmation that 'Men will endeavour to enslave woman: and who can tell, how many generations may be necessary to give vigour to the virtue and talents of the freed posterity of abject slaves'.[14]

What is strikingly modern in women's abolitionist poems, however, is their opposition to the economic transaction at the basis of colonialism. If as women they felt almost physically the separation between mothers and children, protesting vigorously at the disruption of parental relationships in slave families, as intellectuals they began to pose disquieting questions that go well beyond the sentimental sympathy for the sufferers in question. They started looking at the slave trade in terms of a huge and ferocious deception that a ruthless and wealthy ruling class imposed on the defenceless and the unrepresented.

Women poets signal a radical transformation in the conception of consumable goods and related commercial transactions. For these authors, superfluous or luxurious goods had been turned into everyday necessity, altering, as a result, the scale of social and moral values: there was no questioning of how and why these goods were produced; all that counted was to increase their perceived necessity. From this awareness, which in many ways anticipates Marxist analysis, derives the understanding that slavery was not only an unjust, and morally and emotionally condemnable, human economic transaction, but also a constructed need that created a constructed world. Such a transaction was based on false values that had not only betrayed the traditional principles of British dignity and freedom, but, worse, had also abandoned the inherent sphere of human morality in order to give priority to the material sphere of economic interest and monetary gain.

Women writers adumbrated a demystification of the money nexus, disguised as necessity, in calling – albeit sentimentally – for a readjustment of the scale of values. A radical demystification would have involved the creation of the concepts of labour and of production, both concepts alien to women who had been so far employed as a workforce in home industry and in agriculture, but who, with the introduction of the capitalist division of labour, were to be dramatically discriminated against and exploited in terms of working hours and salary. More generally, the passage to a capitalistic society had as a consequence the transformation of the British Protestant work ethic into a profit ethic that gradually drew lines of irreconcilable separation between the different spheres of social identity and belonging: class, gender and age. It is precisely this ethic of profit and the ruthless separation of social groups into conflicting spheres that women authors challenged. From this perspective the role and commitment of Quaker and Evangelical women writers, of dissenting women authors and of women spokespersons for the working class, can be said to have been irreplaceable. Their liberating action was useful not only in the gradual escalation and in the final success of the abolitionist movement, but even more so for their capacity to throw light on the contemporary materialistic and consumerist processes that were progressively destroying all social cohesion and community ties, leaving the weak and the defenceless exposed to collective exploitation and individual abuse.

Reading across these women poets' texts, it is possible to see a progression in their determination to trace the parabola of cause and effect underlining the slave trade and thereby remove any possible alibi. But this awareness opened the way to an understanding of their own situation, and, unavoidably, the critique of the slave trade by women implicated the ideology of nationalism, and especially male-centred nationalism. Although Britannia was female-gendered, the designation

'Britons' seemed to be reserved for men; on the other hand, many British women were not ready to identify themselves with every single connotation that this label implied, as is shown by three of the most popular anti-slavery poems written, namely those by the Evangelical Hannah More (1745–1833) –'Slavery, a Poem' and 'The Sorrows of Yamba; or, The Negro Woman's Lamentation. To the Tune of Hosier's Ghost'[15] – and the working-class writer Ann Yearsley (1756–1806) – 'A Poem on the Inhumanity of the Slave Trade'.

Although coming from different social classes and antithetical ideological positions, the two poets deal with the slave trade as a fundamentally British male domain. In 'The Sorrows of Yamba' (1795) More – while advocating religion and, in particular, organised religion as a possible form of relief for the enduring suffering of the poor slave Yamba – does not hesitate to denounce the brutality of the British traders and sailors who, away from home, betray what at home they seem to cherish as inviolable and sacred, namely, domestic life and familial affections:

> Whity man he came from far,
> Sailing o'er the briny flood;
> Who, with help of British tar,
> Buys up human flesh and blood.
>
> With the Baby at my breast;
> (Other two were sleeping by)
> In my hut I sat at rest,
> With no thought of danger nigh.[16]

Towards the end of the poem, More daringly launches a frontal attack on the traders responsible for Yamba's fate. Through the poetics of allegory (for example, in the phrase 'British Sons of Murder'), as well as an emphatic syntactic rhetoric (a series of vocatives and imperatives such as 'Mock no further' or the anaphorically reiterated 'Cease' and 'bid'), More places her female poetic voice in a powerful and permanent antagonism with the British history of national values and patriotic pride:

> Cease, ye British sons of murder!
> Cease from forging Afric's Chain;
> Mock your Saviour's name no further,
> Cease your savage lust of gain.

Ye that boast *'ye rule the waves'*,
Bid no Slave-ship soil the sea;
Ye that *'never will be slaves'*
Bid poor Afric's land be free.[17]

It might be noted that in line 136 ('Cease your savage lust of gain') More cleverly reverses – very much as Thomas Clarkson does in his *An Essay on the Slavery and Commerce of the Human Species* (1785), with the term 'barbarian' – the contemporary use and meaning of the word 'savage' as a label for the British slave traders rather than their human goods. She also quotes ironically two of the lines of the popular patriotic song 'Rule, Britannia' ('Ye that boast *"ye rule the waves"*, / Bid no Slave-ship soil the sea; / Ye that *"never will be slaves"* / Bid poor Afric's land be free')[18] in order to mock the putative love for freedom traditionally attributed to the British people, but that from More's viewpoint is not equally bestowed by them on other peoples, races or nations.

It should also be pointed out that 'The Sorrows of Yamba' was published during the years of the French Terror, when the British establishment had launched a severe crusade against radicals and dissenters in general: a period of war and social instability that obliged even the most committed abolitionists to withdraw from the public scene. Hannah More was not a radical but she was not at all new to firm opposition to the slave trade, having published in 1788 – at the outbreak of the movement and on the eve of the mass petitions presented to Parliament by Wilberforce – another abolitionist text, 'Slavery, A Poem'. The latter is not a popular ballad easy to sing or to remember, like 'The Sorrows of Yamba', but is framed in the polite form of narrative verse and offers to the reader an interesting interplay between notes and text, prose and poetry, the notes contextualising through quotation and personal explanation what the poetical text theorises.[19] If occasionally More appears to negotiate with some of the stereotypes of the time, more frequently she overturns British contemporary assumptions and confronts white supine connivance: no one can pretend not to see or not to know any longer; every British citizen has to answer for his/her own share of responsibility in the obscene trade.[20]

From this point of view, it might be argued that Hannah More, rather than merely inaugurating, as Ferguson suggests, 'a normalizing discourse', casting 'slaves into a mode of radical alterity', is in fact accusing an entire community – that is, contemporary society at large – of complicity. It is also difficult to accept that we are simply facing a 'racist and colonialist' discourse, as Richardson states, since More seems genuinely

committed to expressing an irreducible antagonism to the present
and past history of her country, deconstructing much of the supposed
glory and appeal of the current Imperial discourse.[21] More's anti-slavery
poem, while electing literature as a powerful means of spreading liberal
ideas and arousing sympathy and support, dismisses its fictional and
subjective aspects, calling instead for facts and actions:

> O, plaintive Southerne! Whose impassion'd strain
> So oft has wak'd my languid Muse in vain!
> Now, when congenial themes her cares engage,
> She burns to emulate thy glowing page....
> Tho' not to me, sweet Bard, thy powers belong,
> Fair Truth, a hallow'd guide! Inspires my song.
> Here Art wou'd weave her gayest flowe'rs in vain,
> For Truth the bright invention wou'd disdain.
> For no fictitious ills these numbers flow,
> But living anguish, and substantial woe;
> No individual griefs my bosom melt,
> For millions feel what Oronoko felt:
> Fir'd by no single wrongs, the countless host
> I mourn, by rapine dragg'd from Afric's coast.[22]

As is well known, British culture of the period, compared with that of
other European countries, was characterised by a high degree of literacy
and a widespread readership, of which a good percentage were women.
Knowing that they had many potential readers provided women with a
new power that many late eighteenth-century female writers made use
of by making their voice audible and their needs and desires known.
As Ferguson notes, 'As for the white British women themselves, their
participation inevitably challenged tradition. On the one hand, they
enhanced their prescribed role as sentimentalists, yet on the other they
asserted a right to power, however limited, by claiming forceful identities as public polemicists voicing themselves into the body politics'.[23]

Hannah More was fully conscious of the power of the press and of the
appeal exercised by poetry and, more extensively, by literature. In late
December 1787 she hurriedly wrote 'Slavery, a Poem' to coincide with
the Parliamentary debate (that was eventually postponed), explaining:
'if it does not come out at the particular moment when the discussion
comes on in parliament, it will not be worth a straw'.[24] Verse by verse,
More demolishes all alleged reasons that the Parliamentary pro-slavery
lobby had produced over the decades, constructing an uncompromising

counter-discourse that is not only, and powerfully, humanitarian but also stringently political. Her humanitarian rhetoric can be discerned in the description of the spiritual and bodily sufferings of the slave, and his being sung as a creature of God. This divine origin is heavily underlined by More in her reversal of the stereotyped racial and social ladder of the time, whereby she dubs the pro-slavery exponents themselves 'murderers', 'barbarians' and 'white savages', including in such accusatory definitions all the British who claim not to know about 'Th'opprobrious commerce', and turning the slaves, instead, into the 'living' image of the divine: 'Respect *his* sacred image which they bear'.[25]

More's political force is as unwavering as her humanitarian commitment, albeit somewhat more difficult to decipher. This can be seen, for example, in the comparison that she draws in the poem between the Africans and the ancient Romans. The simile yoking the African slaves and the ancient Romans – even if the former are 'scourged' and the latter 'deify'd' – has an important common semantic and moral ground that More underlines, namely their shared pride and fearlessness:

> A sense of worth, a conscience of desert,
> A high, unbroken, haughtiness of heart;
> That self-same stuff which erst proud empires sway'd,
> Of which the conquerors of the world were made;
> Capricious fate of men! That very pride
> In Afric scourg'd, in Rome was deify'd.[26]

The comparison between Africans and ancient Romans – whose rise and fall in civilisation and power had been largely analysed and debated during the eighteenth century and used as a warning for other peoples and countries – seems to have here a hidden implication, beside the more rhetorical gesture of prizing the Africans for their 'indigenous' nobleness. In other words, if Rome's freedom and greatness were poisoned by the thirst for power of the Empire that corrupted the Republican and stoic character of the Romans, leading finally to the Barbarian invasions and destruction of Rome, Africans' power and freedom – from an antithetical perspective – had been put to an end by the greed of the British Empire that, acting like modern Barbarian tribes, trampled down African civilisations:

> Hold, murderers, hold! Nor aggravate distress;
> Respect the passion you yourself possess, ...
> Barbarians, hold! Th'opprobrious commerce spare,

> Respect *his* sacred image which they bear....
> And thou, WHITE SAVAGE! Whether lust of gold,
> Or lust of conquest, rule thee uncrontrol'd!
> Hero, or robber! – by whatever name
> Thou plead thou impious claim to wealth or fame.[27]

From this viewpoint, the suicide of Qua-shi, which the poem narrates immediately after the parallelism between the Africans and the ancient Romans, has much to do with the Stoic philosophy of self-sacrifice. Qua-shi, as a long footnote in the poem explains, kills himself rather than hit his cruel master, but does so to protest against human perfidy and disloyalty and to teach his master more noble and manly behaviour. It has very little to do, therefore, with the passive response of a tamed being.

On the other hand, suicide – or, alternatively, the act of letting oneself die as a sign of protest (as Yamba does in More's poem) – is a topos not only of abolitionist poetry but also, on closer consideration, of late eighteenth and early nineteenth-century women's literature at large, especially when dealing with female characters' destiny within a patriarchal society. Examples may be found in the heroine of Mary Wollstonecraft's novel *Mary, a Fiction* (1788) (but also, in some ways, in *Maria or the Wrongs of Woman, 1796–1798*); or, again, in Mary Shelley's *Mathilda* (1819) as well as in *Valperga* (1823) (I am thinking here, in particular, of the death of Beatrice, the prophetess).

Hannah More's subversion of British nationalistic values, and her estrangement from patriotic discourse and social practice, are extended in Ann Yearsley's 'A Poem on the Inhumanity of the Slave Trade' (1788):

> I know the crafty merchant will oppose
> The plea of nature to my strain, and urge
> His toils are for his children: the soft plea
> Dissolves my soul – *but when I sell a son,*
> *Thou God of nature, let it be my own!*
>
> ...
>
> Away, thou seller of mankind! Bring on
> Thy daughter to this market! Bring thy wife!
> Thine aged mother, though of little worth,
> With all thy ruddy boys! Sell them, thou wretch,
> And swell the price of! Why that start?[28]

The paradoxical but unequivocal rhetoric of these lines is in some ways reminiscent of Swift's *A Modest Proposal* (with less irony). The poetic

voice defies the slave trader and destroys any moral justification that
he may allege, or indeed any material need that he may aver, in favour
of his wicked trade. Yearsley's accusatory poem ends by challenging a
society built on the name of the father, and by defining as decadent
and unjust a national institution traditionally considered a guarantee
of British freedom, that is, Parliament, seen here as a male-oriented
centre of power whose aims have to do only with merchandising goods
and further enriching the already rich. Parliament, suggests Yearsley,
rather than being a haven of human rights and of Christian charity,
has become a sanctuary of private property and of individual egotism.
And it is to underline the neglected duties of the nation towards the
weak and the powerless – as well as the infringement of the sanctity of
institutions such as the House of Commons by those who preside over
them – that the final lines present a series of challenges and charges in
an apocalyptic tone:

> Is this an English law, whose guidance fails
> When crimes are swell'd to magnitude so vast,
> That *Justice* dare not scan them? Or does *Law*
> Bid *Justice* an eternal distance keep
> From England's great tribunal, when the slave
> Calls load on *Justice only*? Speak, ye few
> Who fill Britannia's senate, and are deem'd
> The fathers of your country! Boast your laws,
> Defend the *honour* of a land so fall'n
> That Fame from ev'ry battlment is flown,
> And Heathens start e'en at a Christian's name.[29]

More's and Yearsley's writings, together with the work and actions of
many other women of the time, not only belied the iconic image of a
subdued and frozen woman, but ventured out directly into the political arena in order to deconstruct the gendered language of nationhood.
More and Yearsley also re-traced a mechanism of causality within British
national and political history, re-enacting the individual stories of the
slaves Yamba, Qua-shi and Luco. Theirs is a gendered appeal regarding the
breaking of familial ties through the separation of mother and child, wife
and husband and more generally the uprooting of all the bonds that link
the individual to everything that defines his/her identity, such as 'motherland', house (or hut) and home and parental affections. In projecting
their anxiety for their own social status onto the deprived human
creatures that Yamba, Qua-shi and Luco represent, they also achieve a

mode of sympathetic or empathetic identification that goes beyond the
mere rhetoric of sensibility of the time, becoming a formidable political
weapon able to shake consciences and mould public opinion.

Fully aware that contemporary British society was constructing a
national model of woman that corresponded to the idea of the nation as
family, where women were the pivotal centre of the extended domestic
sphere as perpetuators of the British race, More and Yearsley anticipate
this 're-feminisation' of Britannia. Britain is seen ideally as a mother-
centred Christian community, and the women poets skilfully deploy
this model centred on their sex, in applying it to the slaves who are
thereby identified as individuals unreligiously torn from the familial
bonds and domestic affections on which the national model is based,
and, indeed, uprooted from their native motherland itself.

Notes

1. See Clare Midgley, *Women Against Slavery: The British Campaigns, 1780–1870*
   (London: Routledge, 1992), pp. 17–23.
2. Ibid., pp. 43–51, 158–62. See also the 'Women's Anti-Slavery Association', http://
   www.spartacus.schoolnet.co.uk/REslaveryW.htm (Accessed 21 July 2009).
3. Moira Ferguson, *Subject to Others: British Women Writers and the Colonial
   Slavery, 1670–1834*, (London: Routledge, 1992).
4. See J. R. Oldfield, *Popular Politics and British Anti-Slavery: The Mobilisation of
   Public Opinion against the Slave Trade, 1787–1807* (Manchester: Manchester
   University Press, 1996), pp. 41–69.
5. Alan Richardson, 'Darkness Visible? Race and Representation in Bristol
   Abolitionist Poetry, 1770–1810', in Tim Fulford and Peter J. Kitson, eds.,
   Romanticism and Colonialism: Writing and Empire, 1780–1830 (Cambridge:
   Cambridge University Press, 1998), p. 131. Richardson is reporting a quota-
   tion from Peter Fryer's *Staying Power: The History of Black People in Britain
   Since 1504* (London: Pluto Press, 1984), p. 33, but, according to Eric Williams
   ('The Golden Age of the Slaves System in Britain', in *The Journal of the Negro
   History*, 30/1 (January 1940), pp. 60–106), the quotation refers to an actor in
   Liverpool who, 'hissed by the audience for appearing, for the first time, in
   a drunken condition, steadied himself and declared with offended majesty:
   "I have not come here to be insulted by a set of wretches, every brick in
   whose infernal town is cemented with an African's blood"', p. 69.
6. Cora Kaplan, 'Pandora's Box: Subjectivity, Class and Sexuality in Socialist
   Feminist "Criticism"', in G. 'Greene' and C. Kahn, eds., *Making a Difference:
   Feminist Literary Criticism* (London and New York: Routledge, 1985), pp. 146–
   76 (p. 150).
7. Peter J. Kitson, 'Romanticism and Colonialism: Races, Places, Peoples,
   1785–1800', in Fulford and Kitson, eds, *Romanticism and Colonialism*, pp. 13–34
   (p. 25).
8. Ibid., p. 33.

9. Tim Fulford and Peter J. Kitson, 'Romanticism and Colonialism: Texts, Contexts, Issues', in Fulford and Kitson, eds., *Romanticism and Colonialism*, p. 11.

10. 'Conspicuous Consumption: White Abolitionism and English Women's Protest Writing in the 1790', *English Literary History (ELH)*, 61 (1994), pp. 341–62 (p. 341), quoted in Kitson, 'Romanticism and Colonialism: Races, Places, Peoples, 1785–1800', p. 34.

11. Alan Richardson, 'Darkness Visible', pp. 129–47.

12. See Williams, 'The Golden Age of the Slave System in Britain', pp. 65–78; Franca Dellarosa, 'Questioning "the Enterprising Spirit of the People": Abolitionist Poetry in Liverpool, 1784–1788', *La Questione Romantica*, 18–19, (Spring/Autumn 2005), p. 18. Dellarosa is here referring to J. Wallace and the text quoted is *A General and Descriptive History of the Ancient and Present State of the Town of Liverpool [...] together with a Circumstantial Account of the True Causes of Its Extensive African Trade* (Liverpool, 1795, 2nd edn).

13. I am referring to Thomas Clarkson's *The History of the Rise, Progress, and Accomplishment of the Abolition of the African Slave Trade by the British Parliament*, vol. 1 (London, 1808), pp. 375–78.

14. Mary Wollstonecraft, *A Vindication of the Rights of Woman*, ed. Carol H. Poston (New York, 1988, 2nd edn), p. 77.

15. In his introduction to the poem, Alan Richardson suggests that it may have been originally written by a 'rather obscure poet', Eaglesfield Smith, and then extended and revised by More who included the poem in her *Cheap Repository Tract* in 1795. Smith's first publication of his version of the poem, however, came out two years after More's *Cheap Repository Tract*, leaving the case open to further question. In any case, what matters here, I believe, is More's decision to publish the poem, thereby accepting and sharing its outspoken contents. See Alan Richardson ed., *Slavery, Abolition and Emancipation: Writings in the British Romantic Period*, vol. 4, Verse (London: Pickering and Chatto, 1999), p. 224. In 2002 Alan Richardson dedicated an entire article to 'The Sorrows of Yamba', pointing out the different ideologies expressed in the two separate versions of the poem, Eaglesfield Smith's and Hannah More's: Alan Richardson, '"The Sorrows of Yamba"', by Eaglesfield Smith and Hannah More: Authorship, Ideology, and the Fractures of Antislavery Discourse', in Michael Eberle-Sinatra, ed., *Romanticism on the Net*, 28 (November 2002), pp. 1–17.

16. Hannah More, 'The Sorrows of Yamba; or, The Negro Woman's Lamentation. To the Tune of Hosier's Ghost' (from *Cheap Repository Tracts*) in Richardson, ed., *Slavery, Abolition and Emancipation*, vol. 4, pp. 225–6.

17. Ibid., pp. 231.

18. The patriotic song 'Rule, Britannia' was written in 1748 by John Thomson to the music of Thomas Arne.

19. Ann Yearsley used the same instrumental interplay between footnotes and text in her abolitionist poem.

20. Ferguson, *Subject to Others*, p. 163: 'By stereotyping Africans and emphasizing their own cultural command while recognizing the denial of full constitutional rights to all and their own historical exclusion from parliamentary debate, white female polemicists centerstaged themselves as classic doubled subjects. They were involved in "a form of power which subjugates and makes subject to"; they were split between acting as agents and identifying with victims'.

21. See Ferguson, *Subject to Others*, pp. 150, 153; and Alan Richardson, 'Women Poets and Colonial Discourse: Teaching More and Yearsley on the Slave Trade', in Steven C. Behrendt and Harriet Kramer Linkin, eds., *Approaches to Teaching Women Poets of the Romantic Period* (New York: MLA, 1997), p. 78. Ferguson herself, however, does not entirely dismiss More's genuine commitment, and she frequently underlines More's contradictions in her social and political statements. On the other hand, Debbie Lee acutely underlines the ambiguities and the problems that British antislavery literature in the Romantic period have caused for contemporary critical discourse (*Slavery and the Romantic Imagination* (Philadelphia, University of Pennsylvania Press, 2002), pp. 4 and 224 – note 10). In this regard Lee quotes Malcolm Kelsall ('"Once did she hold the gorgeous East in fee ...": Byron's Venice and Oriental Empire', in Fulford and Kitson, eds., *Romanticism and Colonialism*, pp. 243–60) and Stephen C. Behrendt (Behrendt, ed., *Romanticism, Radicalism, and the Press* (Detroit, Wayne State University Press, 1997), pp. 13–29), where Kelsall argues that such a literary production is inevitably put in the shade of contemporary postcolonial reading: 'But that history is read retrospectively from the instantaneous present [...] discussion of the empire in the East has become involved with the guilt of the post-colonial West [...] The "culture of complaint" places the liberal in a position of apologetic retreat', p. 245. Behrendt warns us that we must be aware of 'actual, historical and cultural differences that separates us from our forebears', p. 13. I believe that this critical prudence should also be exercised towards Hannah More's antislavery commitment.

22. Hannah More, 'Slavery, a Poem', in Richardson, ed., *Slavery, Abolition and Emancipation*, vol. 4, ll. 37–40, 49–59, pp. 108–9.

23. Moira Ferguson, *Subject to Others*, p. 162.

24. Ibid., p. 150.

25. Hannah More, 'Slavery, a Poem', pp. 135–36.

26. Ibid., vol. 4, ll. 77–82, p. 111.

27. Hannah More, 'Slavery, a Poem', ll. 111–2, p. 113, ll. 135–6, p. 115, ll. 211–14, p. 120.

28. Ann Yearsley, 'A Poem on the Inhumanity of the Slave Trade', in Richardson, ed., *Slavery, Abolition and Emancipation*, vol. 4, pp. 133–4.

29. Yearsley, 'A Poem on the Inhumanity of the Slave Trade', pp. 154–5.

Part III Remembering and Forgetting

8
Representing Slavery in British Museums: The Challenges of 2007

Douglas Hamilton

The bicentenary of the parliamentary abolition of the slave trade in 2007 was marked by an extraordinary array of commemorations across the United Kingdom. Exhibitions sprang up from Scotland to south-west England, and in often in places not traditionally associated with the slave trade. For university academics, the slave trade, slavery and their abolition have, of course, been at the heart of decades of detailed and groundbreaking research. Until comparatively recently, however, these issues had not been regarded as central to the work of museums and galleries. A corollary of museums' increasing engagement with these issues was a growing interest by slavery scholars in the work of museums, both as advisers to exhibitions and as commentators in the increasingly fertile field of public history.[1] 2007, then, was not just about commemorating the bicentenary, but fostering a much closer dialogue between academics, museums and their audiences. This dialogue, however, should not imply that there was consensus; indeed, it is clear that representing slavery was about finding acceptable compromises between competing voices and interests.

Slavery or, more accurately, abolition, has been displayed in Britain since 1906, when Wilberforce House in Hull opened as a museum. Despite this century-long tradition, however, a widespread museum engagement with issues of slavery and abolition took a great deal longer to develop. Wilberforce House opened two new galleries – 'The slave trade' and 'Wilberforce and abolition' – in 1983, but it was not until the 1990s that the sector as a whole began seriously to take an interest.[2] Major new exhibitions, firstly 'Against Human Dignity' at Merseyside Maritime Museum in 1994 and then, in 1999, 'A Respectable Trade?' initially at Bristol City Museum and Art Gallery, then the Bristol Industrial Museum, showed the potential for this subject to provide a way for museums to engage more actively with a broad public audience.³ Crucially, it also encouraged museums that had not previously displayed a great interest in slavery and abolition. In so doing, though, many (if not all) found that representing slavery posed many challenges that were more profound than they had hitherto confronted. This essay explores some of these challenges, many of which are common to all museums. It takes the National Maritime Museum in Greenwich as a case study in order to offer a particular insight into the way that museums could respond.

Set in the UNESCO Maritime Greenwich World Heritage Site, a particularly leafy part of southeast London, the National Maritime Museum (NMM) stakes a reasonable claim to be the biggest and most important maritime museum in the world. It opened its doors in 1937 and now houses an extraordinarily large and varied collection of material that represents and illustrates 'the importance of the sea, ships, time and the stars and their relationship with people'.⁴ In 1999 the NMM was re-launched, with new galleries surrounding the central glass-roofed Neptune Court. One of those new galleries was 'Trade and Empire' within which, and among a series of other imperial themes, was a section on the slave trade, slavery and abolition. That such a display was included in the Museum's newly imagined vision of itself was striking. As the then Deputy Director noted, '[t]raditionalists may be uncomfortable'. He went on to defend the absence of 'reassuring, massed displays reflecting notions of British supremacy', arguing 'that if they were ever there, those values were never a reality for a large part of the population, and will never be accepted by the citizens of the next century'.⁵ This sentiment finds echoes in Lonnie Bunch's insistence that museums 'find a past that is useful and meaningful to living generations', but it also implied that museums (and in this case the NMM) should address themselves to a wider public; that their target audience should not only be 'traditionalists'.⁶

The problem for museums in the late 1990s (and which to an extent remains the case) was the danger of alienating the traditional audience. The launch of the NMM's Trade and Empire Gallery in 1999 unleashed a number of vitriolic responses, notably in the pages in some of Britain's more right-wing newspapers. A series of commentaries and outraged letters in the *Daily Mail*, the *Daily Telegraph*, and the *Mail on Sunday* attacked the 'political correctness' of an exhibition that *Telegraph* readers in particular described as disgraceful, shoddy and crass.⁷ While such responses were not unexpected, the NMM was also confronted by more liberal commentators, who, while less strident in tone, were nonetheless critical of some elements of the display. One argued that the NMM had 'more than a little catching up to do with those [exhibitions] in Bristol and Liverpool'.[8]

What is striking is the way the NMM responded to the critiques. To its right-wing critics it offered a robust and public response: the then Director wrote that it was 'no surprise to have provoked critics who would have us play *Rule Britannia* for the umpteenth time, so its adherents can pretend that the past 50 years of maritime *post-imperial* history have not really happened'.[9] In setting itself against the *Rule Britannia* brigade the NMM did two things: it challenged those people who most needed to be challenged, and it recognised what they did not – that Britain had become a diverse and multi-ethnic society. Lawrence James was perhaps right to argue that the sea 'has made us what we are today', but he signally failed to acknowledge that for museums across the country, 'us' and 'we' needed to be defined much more broadly than white men with a penchant for dead admirals.[10] The NMM did, on the other hand, respond positively to the more measured responses and amended or removed elements of the exhibition.

Although the reception of this gallery was traumatic for the museum, it is clear that subjects like empire and slavery had become firmly positioned as part of the NMM's understanding of its role. There are probably two key reasons why this was so. The first influence was an emerging conception of maritime history as being rather more than the history of the Royal Navy, its battles and its heroes. The 'new' museum was now interested in the sea as a social and cultural space, as well as an arena for naval battles.[11] The second element was the combination of the growing influence of Black History Month (that had been founded in 1987); the launch in 1994 of the Heritage Lottery Fund (HLF); and the introduction of free entry to national museums in 2001 – with its requirement to help meet the strategic aims of the Department for Culture, Media and Sport – all of which demanded that the museum sector actively engage a wider public.

These factors ensured that, far from returning to the safe harbour of admirals and battles, the NMM maintained its course. Indeed, it sought actively to extend its commitment, partly by the acquisition, with HLF assistance, of a new collection of slavery-related material. The 450-strong Michael Graham-Stewart Collection transformed the scope and depth of the NMM's holdings, and provided the basis for a series of new initiatives.[12] Not the least of these was the Understanding Slavery Initiative, which aimed to connect museums, teachers and young people and to engage them in developing resources to support the teaching of issues related to slavery, the slave trade and abolition.[13]

By 2004, the amended Trade and Empire Gallery covered a series of imperial themes: slavery, the slave trade and abolition (strengthened by the addition of some pieces from the new collection); the East India Company and trade with Asia; the exploration of Australasia; and the impact of empire in Britain. The narratives in the gallery were fairly traditional. They explored the history of the slave trade from the Elizabethan 'buccaneer' John Hawkins to William Wilberforce and John Clarkson. Another section tracked the transformation of the tropical islands of the Caribbean into the economic powerhouses of the British empire, and surveyed the role of the Royal Navy as their protector. There was material on the abolition campaigns and on the Navy's anti-slavery patrols. The vibrancy of African societies was evident, albeit in an ahistorical way.[14] The overall narrative tended to move towards abolition as if it were the natural conclusion to slavery. It had become clear that this was insufficient to meet the demands of 2007. The acquisition of the new collection also demanded a wholesale reinterpretation of the existing display, which was already five years old and, in the normal course of things, was likely to require a revamp within the next three to five years. Moreover, the success of public engagement programmes made it clear that the physical spaces and layout of the gallery were no longer able to accommodate the size of groups visiting. Equally significantly, the NMM (along with museums across the country) now also understood far better the state of academic research in slavery studies and the demands of its publics. As a result, the narratives in Trade and Empire had begun, even in the space of five years, to look out-dated. It is at this point that the real challenges began: it is relatively easy to critique a five-year-old gallery and to decide that it needs to be changed. It is (as all who worked on displays for 2007 will attest) very much more difficult to determine what should replace it, and at which audiences it ought to be directed.

Audiences

The NMM's Greenwich site (which includes the Royal Observatory and the Queen's House as well as the Maritime Museum) attracts over 1.6 million visitors every year, many of whom come from overseas.[15] Much of its audience tends to be white and middle class. Indeed, only a tiny minority are drawn from black and minority ethnic groups: one survey from early 2007 suggested that 85 per cent of visitors described their ethnic background as 'white'. The same survey showed that only 9 percent of visitors were 'working class' from social groups 5–8.[16]

This is not a situation unique to the NMM – it is probably true across much of the museum sector – but there is evidence that the 'brand image' of the NMM presents particular challenges. For some potential visitors the impression that the NMM is only about the sea and ships is off-putting; others, though, expect and want only to see those things. Still more are intimidated by the grand and imposing architecture of the museum, which makes them think that 'it's not for them'. This immediately created two quite distinct challenges: firstly, how to persuade under-represented groups that museums have something for them; that, to use the example of the NMM, it's not just about dead white admirals and sea battles? Secondly, and simultaneously, to continue trying to convince more 'traditional' visitors, who like displays about dead admirals and sea battles, that the history of the enslavement of Africans has any place in a British national museum.

The 'public', of course, is even more complex than these very broad social and ethnic groupings: within all of them there are wide divergences of opinion about the slave trade and its commemoration. And while these issues were common to all museums, at the NMM they seemed to have a particular edge. Here was a museum still scarred by the assault on its first attempts to display slavery, yet situated in a diverse and multi-ethnic part of London some of whose residents were unaware even of the museum's existence. The challenge, then, was to put together a display that would engage (if not necessarily please) peoples of different ages, genders, social classes, ethnic groups and education levels.

The challenges

Like other institutions, the NMM explored a range of solutions. Among the many considerations was the length of the exhibition: should it be a short-term exhibition or a permanent gallery? What should be in it? How should it be structured? Options that were discussed ranged from a relatively straightforward chronology of slavery and abolition to an issues-based display focusing on racism and human rights. Like many museums, the NMM found that the solution needed to draw on a series of principles and accept areas of compromise between competing voices.

In the first place, and perhaps most fundamentally, museums needed to develop a narrative that accurately reflected the current state of scholarly understanding of the slave trade, slavery and abolition. Secondly, in order to develop this narrative, museums committed themselves to consultation. Although some museums now have in-house expertise, the advice of external academic advisors was still sought to help ensure balance in the narrative. At the same time, comments and responses were sought from various public community and cultural commentators. Drawing on a series of advisers and generating a narrative in committee has its pitfalls, as Katherine Prior has noted.[17] Nonetheless, it is incumbent on museums to listen to their audiences. While the insistence among some quarters that the gallery should tell 'the truth' was problematic, knowing which 'truths' people wanted to hear helped to generate a sense of balance in the narrative and, at the very least, allowed museums to be prepared for any future criticisms.

An emphasis on the centrality of Africans as people rather than statistics was the third key element. It was very clear that the complexity and sophistication of African societies needed to be shown, so that Africa would not simply be equated with slavery, or, even more basically, that Africa itself not be regarded as a country rather than a continent. Equally important was the need to show the various forms of African resistance, agency and survival throughout the process of enslavement. The requirement to show African agency also made it essential to indicate the levels and forms of African involvement in the slave trade as suppliers and merchants, alongside the positive messages and role models.

Fourthly, museums tried to ensure that their displays did far more than simply celebrate, or even commemorate, the abolition of the slave trade. While it is clearly a matter of pride for many white Britons, the emphasis on abolition (and on the role of Wilberforce, Clarkson et al. in particular) at the expense of the horrors of slavery itself, is regarded as a whitewashing of the past by some black community groups, who describe the 2007 commemorations as either 'Wilberfest' or 'Wilberfarce'.[18] In truth, this separation between slavery and abolition in the British imagination is longstanding. Joseph Collyer's version of Henry Moses' painting *Abolition of the Slave Trade*, which depicts Britannia bathed in sunlight while the chains of slavery lie broken at her feet, was distributed as an official commemoration in 1808 (See Figure 8.1).[19] This image of Britain as the enlightened abolitionist is central to a widespread public memory of the slave trade. There was a tension here for museums. Without the focal point of the bicentenary it is difficult to imagine so many institutions discovering an interest in the slave trade and slavery. Yet museums were also wary of placing too great an emphasis on the abolition itself, partly for fear of being accused of celebrating Wilberforce and ignoring slavery. As a result, the majority of

Figure 8.1 Joseph Collyer after Henry Moses, *Plate to Commemorate the Abolition of the Slave Trade*, 1808. Reproduced by kind permission of the National Maritime Museum, Greenwich, London.

museums in Britain came to regard 2007 as a year to commemorate the abolition of the slave trade, certainly, but also to place heavy emphasis on the evils of the trade and on the fact that slavery (and indeed slave trades themselves) were not eradicated in 1807. In the fifth place, there was a need for exhibitions to show that the slave trade and slavery, as well as abolition, are part of a British past, and not simply something that happened to other people 4,500 miles away.

Finally, and critically, how could all this physically be displayed: did the collections exist? For some aspects, collections are particularly strong. Some of the brutal 'hardware' of slavery (chains, manacles, and whips) has survived, as has a great deal of material (of all media) generated by the abolition campaigns. Where collections in Britain are weakest is in relation to the lives and cultures of the enslaved.[20] Museums, then, if they planned to develop collections-based exhibitions, were obliged to rethink their interpretations of existing material that has, in the past, sometimes been used in ahistorical or uncritical ways.

Ultimately, museums had to come to terms with developing narratives that are defensible. It is almost inevitable that representing slavery in a museum will annoy someone. The key is to find a way to do it so that the target audiences are engaged and that the exhibition can be justified to the outraged. But how could museums do this in the contexts of competing public voices, limitations of collections and, occasionally, institutional doubts about the wisdom of it all?

A new gallery

The bicentenary was marked in all sorts of ways across the country in March 2007. Rather than latch on to that date, however, as early as 2005 the NMM took a conscious decision to uncouple its display from the bicentenary moment itself. It decided to use 2007 as a way into a wider subject that is central to the Museum's strategy, rather than as an occasion to be celebrated in the way it had done with anniversaries such as, for example, the bicentenary of the battle of Trafalgar in 2005. A short-term exhibition would not provide a long-term resource for visitors to the museum, nor would it provide the basis for the planned range of associated programmes. The particular strengths of the NMM's collection, some of which had not been seen in public for many years, if ever, enabled the museum to think on a grander scale. As a result, two major new permanent galleries, one on the Atlantic Worlds from autumn 2007 and one on the Asian Worlds, were envisaged. Both are sustained by the NMM's collections' strengths, are thematically connected and both feature slavery. In other words, slavery was not just to be for 2007, but was to be situated in permanent galleries in different parts of the museum.

The Atlantic World, which opened first, was the major focus for the slave trade, slavery and abolition in 2007.[21] It is housed in one of the NMM's largest and most central exhibition spaces, itself a clear statement of how importantly issues of this kind are regarded in the museum. It covers 390 square metres and contains over 200 objects and images, only two of which are on loan at the time of writing.[22] By focusing on the ocean, the gallery aimed to concentrate, not on Britain, or, for that matter, on Africa or the Americas, but on the elements that connect them. It set out, therefore, to explore a variety of themes including European emigration, encounters with Native Americans, trade and exchange, wars and conflict, as well as the slave trade, slavery and abolition. The idea of the Atlantic World provides the overall framework within which to understand the slave trade, slavery and abolition, and their importance to eighteenth-century British history. Within this conceptual framework, however, which narratives of slavery ought to be represented?

Clearly, representing slavery for 2007 could not simply be a matter of transferring the old narratives from 'Trade and Empire' into a new gallery. For the slave trade itself, there needed to be a more sophisticated understanding of the Middle Passage. The gallery needed to generate a sense that the Middle Passage was not just the 6–10 weeks spent crossing the Atlantic, however unimaginably awful even that was. For many, perhaps most, of those Africans enslaved, the experiences of the Middle Passage – of captivity, of brutality, of indignity – began long before ships left the African coast, as is suggested in François-Auguste Biard's famous painting, *The Slave Trade* of 1835.[23] Those people depicted by Biard being sold on the coast might have waited weeks enduring terrible conditions on board a ship, in a floating factory, or at somewhere like Cape Coast Castle or Anomabu before the voyage proper began. But perhaps the true horror of the trade apparent in the painting is the perception of it as a mundane, everyday transaction. The sheer ordinariness of a ledger, like that of the slave ship *Molly*, which sailed to Bonny in the Bight of Biafra in 1759, that shows people being commodified as objects – literally in black and white – is perhaps more revealing to the public than a discussion of the volume of the trade.[24]

One of the problems of talking about numbers is that it tends to obscure the people involved and so the display needed to be much better at depicting slave life. On the one hand, it had to suggest the awfulness of the slave trade and the hardships endured by plantation slaves and of the stripping of slaves' identities, which can be represented by displaying neck chains, manacles, whips and identification bands. But it also needed to show agency and a sense that the enslaved were sentient humans who did react and resist. This requirement behoved deeper interpretation of some material, like an identification band worn by a slave (See Figure 8.2).[25] This band bears the name of the planter and the plantation and appears to be yet another example of the stripping of the identities of the enslaved. However, it is likely that the band was locked on to the slave's wrist to allow him to leave the plantation for some purpose, perhaps to carry a message or deliver goods or livestock. This kind of 'legitimate' mobility allowed the slave to convey other information between plantations: this was a potential means by which news of friends, family or revolts might spread between enslaved communities on different plantations. In other words, then, this is an object that at first appears only to be about oppression, but with closer interpretation can be used to represent an important aspect of enslaved life.

The agency of the enslaved and their capacity to resist and survive enslavement is a key theme in the gallery. It needed to show the acts of resistance that were common on the slave ships – from individual protests to shipboard insurrections – and demonstrate that they continued on the plantations. These acts of opposition took many forms, of course, and not all can be shown through collections. Some can, however, and newspaper advertisements for missing slaves give an indication of running away as a form of resistance, while images of markets in Caribbean help give a sense of the slaves' ability to form lives of their own (See Figure 8.3).[26]

Figure 8.2   Identification Band, 1746. Reproduced by kind permission of the National Maritime Museum, Greenwich, London.

Figure 8.3 Cordon after W. E. Beastall, *Negroes Sunday-Market at Antigua*, 1806. Reproduced by kind permission of the National Maritime Museum, Greenwich, London.

The sense of black agency, and of black resistance in particular, also affected the way the abolition itself is represented. Wilberforce and Clarkson are still present, as is an emphasis on the contribution of the public campaigns. These aspects are both easy to represent: many museums have strong collections of objects and images from the campaigns. What is noticeable, though, is the extent to which museums have sought to integrate black abolitionists. Here men like Sancho and Equiano figure prominently, but so too do much more radical voices. Active resistance by the enslaved themselves is often presented by museums as being central to the ending of the slave trade, as well as slavery. This perhaps goes further than some of the scholarly literature might suggest, but the bigger problem arises in its representation. Eighteenth-century slave revolts in the British islands were important features of Caribbean life, but none was ultimately successful in overthrowing colonial authority. As a result, many museums have turned to the Haitian Revolution, which began in French Saint Domingue in 1791, to stand surrogate for risings in British islands, as well as for its role in the abolition debates. The revolution in Haiti, followed by its independence in 1804, has an important place in black political consciousness. In responding to these specific audiences, museums have enabled compromises between what the historical record suggests and the limitations of their collections.

There was also emphasis on longer-term impacts. 1807, important date though it is, did not mark the end of slavery. It is equally plain that even 1838 did not imply equality in the post-emancipation world. At the NMM, there was a desire to show the role of the Royal Navy in its capacity as suppressor of the slave trade after 1807 (See Figure 8.4). The Navy's role was complex. Until 1807 it was the protector of what had, until then, been a legitimate branch of British commerce, and the implications of its sudden transformation to suppressor of the trade after

Figure 8.4 John Moore, *The Capture of the Slaver Boladora, 6 June 1829.* Reproduced by kind permission of the National Maritime Museum, Greenwich, London.

1807 is not yet fully understood. Nonetheless, existence of the patrols tells us that slave trades (some illicit, some still legal) remained a problem. The anti-slavery patrols also allowed another key point to be made. As museums and others commemorate 1807, their focus ought to be wider than the Atlantic. Preventing slaves from east Africa reaching the Atlantic and, especially later, from being trafficked around the Indian Ocean, was central to the Navy's work into the twentieth century as photographic images in the NMM's collection demonstrate.[27] These are likely to feature in the next major gallery on Asian Worlds.

Looming over all representations of slavery in twenty-first-century Britain is the issue of racism. It was important for museums to recognise this connection, even if space did not permit a detailed examination of the relationship between slavery and the evolution of racist ideas. The NMM has a large collection of nineteenth-century caricatures that portray non-Europeans, and particularly Africans, in racist and prejudicial terms.[28] A number of them are well known to scholars and some, like George Cruikshank's *New Union Club* (1819), have been analysed by them.[29] They allowed museums to acknowledge what we now understand as racism in British society and, indeed, to note the prevalence of this kind of material in precisely the period often associated with abolitionist sentiment.

'More than a gallery'

In recent years the idea of museums as spaces within which dialogue and exchange between visitors, museum staff and academics can occur has taken hold, albeit still incompletely.[30] But a gallery on its own is insufficient to deal with complicated issues and provide a forum for such discussion, for two reasons. In the first place, some subjects are highly complex and controversial and require additional explication that is impossible on a museum text panel of, at most, 200 words or an object label of 50 words. In the second place, merely opening a new gallery is no guarantee that the new audiences at which it is directed will come and visit. As a result, the two new NMM displays, which were in part developed following a range of public consultations, were conceived, like many across the country, as 'more than a gallery'. That is to say that although the galleries are of critical importance, they are also part of a wider process of engagement. This takes many forms, ranging from individual lectures or short courses in museums, through to major community events, like those held annually on International Slavery Remembrance Day on 23 August, or as part of national Black History

Month every October. These latter events are often marked by a high degree of community participation, rather than just attendance.

The Internet has been central to the wider process of public engagement. Many exhibitions now have an online component: the Atlantic Worlds' website displays all the objects in the gallery. The objects in turn provide the basis for a series of poems by the NMM's writer-in-residence, John Agard, which offer an alternative interpretation to those of the curatorial team. The web has also been an important medium for the Understanding Slavery Initiative (USI).[31] First piloted in 2003, the USI is a consortium of museums in London, Liverpool, Bristol and (latterly) Hull, and is funded by the Department for Education and Skills and the DCMS. It was designed to bring together museum staff, teachers and pupils to develop teaching and learning resources and programmes for slavery and abolition. In all the museums, it drew on particular collection strengths and produced a series of outcomes, including teaching packs and DVDs. In developing these resources, the partner institutions aimed to increase engagement with the subject, particularly among young people aged between about twelve and fourteen. This engagement brought young people into museums, many of whom visited for the first time, and into contact with museum staff. For many participants, on both sides, it was a learning experience and one that informed the development of exhibitions. In most modern museums, object label cards are written in ways that an educated eleven or twelve year old might understand. Sometimes, however, this is regarded patronisingly as 'dumbing down'. Perhaps the most important thing these sessions taught museums was that the public, and the young public in particular, are perfectly capable of understanding complex issues, and many want to be challenged. This awareness, however impressionistically acquired, allowed curators to be bolder in representing complex issues.

The primary objective of the USI was to contribute to and advance school education. Although there were a number of places in the National Curriculum in England and Wales where issues relating to the slave trade and slavery might be taught, there was still a widespread perception that these subjects were not taught in schools. The announcement, in late autumn 2007, of their inclusion as compulsory elements in the National Curriculum should address some of those concerns. The growing awareness of issues of slavery (both historical and contemporary) demands an even greater programme of public engagement and museum exhibitions that can support them. Indeed, the USI has applications far beyond the school curriculum, with its website providing resources both for the general public, and for teaching at more senior secondary and tertiary education levels.

Museum programmes also targeted academics, in part to encourage greater research into their collections, but also to promote partnerships that allow museums to become key fora for the public dissemination of scholarly research. This can take many forms, from the publication of exhibition and collections catalogues, participation by academics in public museum events, to the promotion of new research.[32] Over the last decade there has been a growing tendency by many museums to regard themselves as active research institutions, rather than as the repositories of research material. Many prefer to conduct this research in collaboration with academic partners: at present, for example, the Arts and Humanities Research Council funds a project on Anti-Slavery and the Navy run by the NMM and the Wilberforce Institute for the study of Slavery and Emancipation at the University of Hull. This three-year project uses the Navy's anti-slavery patrols as a way of explaining and interpreting changing attitudes to race, empire and identity in nineteenth-century Britain and its empire. Its findings are likely to inform the two main galleries at the NMM as they evolve over the years to come.

Conclusion

For all these forms of engagement, and despite (or perhaps because of) the extensive coverage of the bicentenary in March 1807, it is clear that those who disliked the old Trade and Empire Gallery in the NMM still exist. When English Heritage announced a project to research links between historic buildings and slavery, a Conservative MP railed against 'politically correct hand-wringing'. *Daily Mail* readers' responses to the news went further: 'Get out your whips ... it's time to flagellate Britain again! Is there no end to this PC garbage?', or 'It's a pity that English Heritage haven't got better things to do. I really worry about the state of the UK'.[33] But museums and heritage organisations are not in the business of trying to make people feel ashamed or to encourage them to engage in an 'orgy of breast-beating', not least because they need the return visitors.[34] Instead, these displays were meant to address Britain's collective amnesia about aspects of its past. They were not trying to be 'PC' (whatever that is) but were instead showing a willingness at least to recognise Britain's role in what many black groups prefer to call the *ma'afa* (great disaster) and thereby to begin a process of repairing some of the damage caused.[35] If Britain's part in abolishing and suppressing the slave trade after 1807 is genuinely something of which to be proud, then it must also come with an acknowledgement that Britain helped to create an institution so marked by suffering, brutality and injustice that it had to be abolished.

Notes

The author was Curator of Eighteenth-century Maritime and Imperial History at the National Maritime Museum between 2004 and 2006. This essay draws on his experiences of the slavery programmes and planning a new gallery there. He is grateful to Dr Robert Blyth, Dr John McAleer and Dr Nigel Rigby for their comments and suggestions. The views expressed here are his own, and do not necessarily reflect those of the National Maritime Museum.

1. See, for example, Marcus Wood, *Blind Memory: Visual Representations of Slavery in England and America, 1780–1865* (Manchester: Manchester University Press, 2000); Elizabeth Kowaleski Wallace, *The British Slave Trade and Public Memory* (New York, 2006); J. R. Oldfield, *'Chords of Freedom': Commemoration, Ritual and British Transatlantic Slavery* (Manchester: Manchester University Press, 2007); Katherine Prior, 'Commemorating Slavery 2007: A Personal View from Inside the Museums', *History Workshop Journal*, 64/1 (2007), pp. 200–11.
2. See Oldfield, *'Chords of Freedom'*, pp. 117–20.
3. For a discussion of the Liverpool display, see T. Tibbles, 'Interpreting Transatlantic Slavery: The Role of Museums', in T. Tibbles, ed., *Transatlantic Slavery: Against Human Dignity* (Liverpool: Liverpool University Press, 2005), pp. 132–3. The Liverpool and Bristol displays are critiqued in Kowaleski Wallace, *The British Slave Trade and Public Memory*, pp. 25–64.
4. This is from the NMM's mission statement. See http://www.nmm.ac.uk/server/show/nav.3180 (accessed 28 January 2008).
5. Roger Knight, 'Making waves', *History Today*, 4 (April 1999), p. 4.
6. Lonnie Bunch, 'The Challenge of Remembering Slavery', in Tibbles, ed., *Transatlantic Slavery*, p. 126.
7. Lawrence James, 'Heroes No More', *Daily Mail*, 3 April 1999; Tom Pocock, 'Was Britain's Empire so Evil?', *The Mail on Sunday*, 29 August 1999; 'Empire Gallery is a Disgrace', Letters to the Editor, *Daily Telegraph*, 18 August 1999. I am grateful to Dr Nigel Rigby for these references.
8. Ratan Vaswani, 'A Respectable Trade?', *Museums Journal*, vol. 100 (May 2000), pp. 16–18.
9. Richard Ormond, 'Aims of the National Maritime Museum', Letters to the Editor, *Daily Telegraph*, 20 August 1999.
10. James, 'Heroes No More'.
11. Knight, 'Making Waves', p. 4; M. Lincoln and N. Rigby, 'Reinventing Maritime History', *History Today*, 7 (July 2001), pp. 2–3; A. Day and K. Lunn, 'British Maritime Heritage: Carried Along by the Currents?', *International Journal of Heritage Studies*, 9/4 (2003), pp. 289–305.
12. The NMM's collection can be seen in D. Hamilton and R. J. Blyth, eds., *Representing Slavery: Art, Artefacts and Archives from the Collections of the National Maritime Museum* (Aldershot: Lund Humphries, 2007), pp. 156–314.

13. For the current incarnation of the USI, see http://www.understandingslavery.com. Accessed on 21 February 2009.

14. Using objects from late nineteenth-century Africa to show sophistication in pre-slavery African societies is a problem common to a number of museums. See Kowaleski Wallace, *The British Slave Trade and Public Memory*, pp. 37–8.

15. *National Maritime Museum Annual Report and Accounts, 2006–2007* (London, 2007), p. 8, see http://www.official-documents.gov.uk/document/hc0607/hc06/0633/0633.pdf (accessed 28 January 2008).

16. NMM visitor research, April–June 2007. For a definition of these social groups, see http://www.statistics.gov.uk/methods_quality/ns_sec/default.asp. Accessed on 18 October 2008.

17. Prior, 'Commemorating Slavery 2007', pp. 200–02.

18. See, for example, views expressed on the website of Ligali, a pan-African human rights organisation. See http://www.ligali.org/article.php?id=637 (accessed 1 February 08).

19. National Maritime Museum, PAF 7367, Collyer after Moses, *Plate to Commemorate the Abolition of the Slave Trade* (1808). The image, along with a commentary, can be found in Marcus Wood, 'Popular Graphic Images of Slavery and Emancipation in Nineteenth-century England', in Hamilton and Blyth, eds., *Representing Slavery*, pp. 139–41, fig. 48.

20. For this gap in collections, see Prior, 'Commemorating Slavery 2007', pp. 208–09.

21. The NMM launched its new 'Atlantic Worlds' gallery in November 2007. An online version, which includes all the objects and images in the exhibition, can be viewed at http://www.nmm.ac.uk/server/show/ConWebDoc.22091.

22. Dr John McAleer, NMM, private correspondence.

23. For prints based on Biard, see Hamilton and Blyth, eds., *Representing Slavery*, fig. 2, pp. 20, 237.

24. NMM, MS/76/027.0 Account book of the snow *Molly*, a slave ship, 1759, in Hamilton and Blyth, eds., *Representing Slavery*, p. 182.

25. NMM, ZBA2474, Identification Band (1746), in Hamilton and Blyth, eds., *Representing Slavery*, fig. 17, pp. 20, 237.

26. See, for example, NMM, MGS/43-5 *The Jamaica Mercury and Kingston Weekly Advertiser*, 1779; ZBA2594 Cordon after Beastall, 'Negroes' Sunday-market at Antigua, 1806', in Hamilton and Blyth, eds., *Representing Slavery*, fig. 16, pp. 58, 208; fig. 15, pp. 57, 257.

27. Hamilton and Blyth, eds., *Representing Slavery*, pp. 224–33.

28. Ibid., pp. 284–96.

29. Wood, *Blind Memory*, pp. 165–71.

30. Prior, 'Commemorating Slavery 2007', pp. 202–07.

31. http://www.understandingslavery.com. For an early evaluation of the USI, see Eilean Hooper-Greenhill et al., *Inspiration, Identity, Learning: The Evaluation of the Impact of DCMS/DfES Strategic Commissioning 2003–04: National/Regional Museum-education Partnerships* (Leicester, 2004), http://hdl.handle.net/2381/20 (accessed 16 January 2008).

32. Among many publications relating to 2007 have been catalogues linked to displays at the new International Slavery Museum in Liverpool, the National Maritime Museum and Parliament, respectively: Tibbles, ed., *Transatlantic Slavery*; Hamilton and Blyth, eds., *Representing Slavery*; S. Farrell, M. Unwin

and J. Walvin, eds., *The British Slave Trade: Abolition, Parliament and People* (Edinburgh: Edinburgh University Press, 2007).

33. See   http://www.dailymail.co.uk/pages/live/articles/news/news.html?in_article_id=412575&in_page_id=1770&in_page_id=1770&expand=true#Start Comments (accessed 24 January 2008).

34. Melanie Phillips, 'The Enslavement of History, *Daily Mail*, 26 March 2007.

35. For positive signs of what might be achieved by such an approach, see the conciliatory response from *The New Nation* to then Prime Minister Tony Blair's expression of 'deep sorrow', in *The New Nation*, 27 February 2006, pp. 1–3.

9
Coram Boy: Slavery, Theatricality and Sentimentality on the British Stage

Elizabeth Kowaleski Wallace

Despite its spectacular success on the British stage, in the spring of 2007, *Coram Boy* bombed in New York. According to the *New York Times*, it lost $6 million capitalisation and was 'one of the most expensive failures in the history of plays on Broadway'.[1] Some of its astounding loss was due, perhaps, to its expensive production costs: with 40 cast members and a chorus of 20, the play was a pricey import. Still, the producers cannot be faulted for their optimistic investment. In a city that embraced *The History Boys* and that tendered an unprecedented 15 Tonys to *The Coast of Utopia* (itself not that warmly received in London), why not *Coram Boy*, with its promise of historical spectacle, fantastic staging and music by Handel, played by a live seven-piece orchestra?

New York critics faulted the play for its sentimentality, as well as its one-dimensionality. Writing for the *New York Post*, Clive Barnes opined that 'rarely has so much stuff – some of it grisly, even ghostly and all of it dour – produced so little', while in the *New York Times* Charles Isherwood criticised the play for being 'big and broad' but 'anything but deep'.[2] Yet neither sentimentality nor superficiality accounts for the play's dismal failure in New York. Rather, in this essay I argue that the producers did not fully understand how *Coram Boy* addressed a particularly British set of historical concerns: in the UK, the lavish and appealing production worked especially well to express a series of cultural themes that have been circulating in the British popular and mainstream press since the end of the last millennium. Those themes have to do with Britain's attempts to become a hybrid, multicultural society in the wake of its colonial past.

Like other western European democracies since the Second World War, the UK has found itself struggling to accommodate waves of post-war immigration, the former inhabitants of its empire. By the turn of the last century, it had become imperative to revise public history and to explain, contextualise and reflect upon the brutal sequence of the eighteenth-century events that had first brought disparate populations together.[3] As a production on a national stage, *Coram Boy* directly addressed this cultural mission. It spoke as well to a special, British understanding of race relations, an understanding quite different in mood, manner and style from an American take on race. Without arguing for the superiority of either national discussion, my purpose here is to expose what the producers overlooked in bringing *Coram Boy* to New York – namely, the extent to which its cultural work was peculiar to the British time, place and theatrical tradition that generated it.

In this essay, then, I will survey the background of the play, paying special attention to the publicity materials that accompanied the play and announced its social purpose. The second part of the essay highlights the theme of slavery – a theme apparently overlooked altogether by the New York critics – to argue that British stage tradition has long linked theatricality and slavery in its own problematic fashion and that this play is haunted by the spectre of that tradition. The play references a history of racially based violence with which it does not quite fully engage.[4] In short, in the UK political context, the problem lies with the way that the emotions are deployed to deflect attention away from an unfolding contemporary cultural history. In its advocacy of interracial adoption, in particular, *Coram Boy* turns away from the very history it purports to expose, and it short-circuits it own important cultural work. Thus my message about *Coram Boy* has two concurrent arguments. Firstly, the play itself could indeed be faulted for what it failed to accomplish. But, secondly, its failure in New York says less about its virtues as a deeply sentimental spectacle and more about its powerful – and distinctly British – political vision, a vision that was easily missed by an American audience.

Part one: The cultural work of *Coram Boy*

The play *Coram Boy* was adapted from a prize-winning juvenile fiction written by an author whose biography itself belongs to the story of Britain's new multi-ethnicity. Born in Mussoorie, India, in the foothills of the Himalayas, Jamila Gavin is the child of an English mother and an Indian father. She moved to the UK at age 11 (where for a time her home was, according to her webpage, a flat in a bombed out street in Shepherd's Bush) and she now lives in Gloucestershire.[5] Her fiction is a long novel in two parts, and in many respects it possesses the grim realism that has, within recent decades, come to typify the genre of young adult literature. Gavin only sensationalises slightly when she mentions in her preface that 'Children in the eighteenth century were routinely brutalised, whether it was at home or at Eton College, whether it was in the parish orphanages, which were no more than dying houses, or in the cathedral choir schools'.[6] Her novel is accurate as well in placing a black foundling at the Coram Hospital, a charity hospital near Brunswick Square, London, which was established by Thomas Coram in 1739 to receive abandoned children. Apparently records indicate the presence of one child named Thomas Africa and another with the last name Othello, indicating his African descent.[7]

At the National Theatre, Helen Edmundson's adaptation was largely faithful to Gavin's novel.[8] On stage, a cast of twenty actors, plus a choir of sixteen, played children, adults, animals, trees, angels and even gargoyles. The action was set in a Gloucester cathedral, an elegant country house, a London orphanage and a slave ship on the Thames. For reasons that appear to have entailed the logistics of casting, the parts of the young boys were played exclusively by young women.

Edmundson's adaptation is divided into two parts, each one telling the story of a generation. In part one, the musically gifted Alexander Ashbrook runs away from his home and inheritance when his father threatens to bar him from the musical world of the Gloucester cathedral school. Before leaving, he falls in love with the beautiful Melissa Melicote, whom he leaves behind, unaware that she is carrying their child, Aaron. Melissa is told that her child was born dead, but in fact he is rescued from his fate. Taken by the mentally disabled and sorely mistreated Meshak to the Coram Hospital – and not buried alive as Meshak's sinister father had insisted – Aaron, in Act II, grows up in the close camaraderie of Toby, another Coram boy, the son of an enslaved African who is said to have been passing through England on a slave ship. The same young actor plays the part of Alexander Ashbrook in Act One and then Aaron in Act Two, demonstrating that the son inherits the father's musical talent, but also proving how deep is the family bond. The action of the play resolves when Aaron and Toby – having miraculously escaped death by drowning – reveal themselves to Alexander and Melissa, at the very moment that Handel prepares to debut his 'Hallelujah Chorus' at the Coram Hospital.

When I saw the play on a Tuesday afternoon in early January 2007, the house was packed with a demographic cross-section of old age pensioners, a handful of American tourists, a large concentration of visually-impaired spectators, who enjoyed the show with the aid of headphones, and an inordinate number of high-spirited – though well-behaved – adolescent school groups. Unlike the rest of the audience – almost entirely white – the school groups were varied in race and ethnicity. Mostly in school uniform, many also sported dreadlocks, Sikh turbans and headscarves. The play seems to have held their attention well, and indeed the production aimed for a nearly over-the-top theat-ricality designed to enthral those more used to video games than live theatre: from the grand guignol effect of gory little baby skeletons to the spectacular illusion of an underwater scene, from a levitating angel to the full choir rendition of the 'Hallelujah Chorus', this was a production designed to exploit the full potential of the theatre.

Like other stages in the early twenty-first century, the National Theatre seems all too aware that its future depends on capturing the attention of a generation – and a demographic – not naturally inclined to after-noons at the theatre. Toby's story, in particular, seemed to have served as a 'hook' – as a sign that live theatre can tell a story of immediate relevance to young people of all ethnic and racial backgrounds – and it can do so as other forms of entertainment cannot. Indeed, the produc-tion was accompanied by extensive web pages, designed for classroom use, with links to curricular materials. On one link, actor Akiya Henry was singled out for her role as Toby – 'the only black character'. As the webpage explained, Henry 'thinks that people should be aware of where they came from and of how hard people have worked to have the luxu-ries we have today. Akiya says that she tries hard to learn as much as she can about her roots and where she comes from'. In her own words, in a live-stream video, Henry elucidated, saying she hoped her role as Toby helped children to understand 'what their ancestors went through [so that] they can have clothes on their backs' or so that 'they can walk down the street and not be called Nigger': so that 'they can walk into a shop or sit in a restaurant with a white man at the same table and it's all OK'.[9]

Though such comments seem to be a long way away from the eighteenth-century world depicted in the play, arguably a compelling logic links them. To tell the story of modern race relations in Britain, one would have to turn back to the history of transatlantic slavery, and in particular to the slave trade that first brought Henry's ancestors into contact with the white world. In its second part, *Coram Boy* alludes to this history and reminds its audience of this first interracial contact, even as it soft-pedals its full import by eventually suggesting that Toby can be happily taken into the Ashbrook family. Production materials made it clear that *Coram Boy*, introduced in the proper context, could be used to introduce a series of 'teachable moments' concerning race relations in the UK.

Thus, *Coram Boy* did double cultural work: it was designed to create the next generation of theatre goers while it extended the project of adjusting public history to accommodate all of Britain's citizens. *Coram Boy* was a small part of a major cultural shift to reinterpret Britain's colonial history in a darker, yet also more inclusive, way. It belongs to a list of other, similar cultural events. Such events include the opening in the 1990s of museum exhibits featuring the history of transatlantic slavery in Bristol, Liverpool and London; movies such as Patricia Rozema's 1999 controversial adaptation of *Mansfield Park* or *Amazing Grace*, the story of abolitionist William Wilberforce, directed by Michael Apted in 2007; or the publication of several novels by white and black UK authors, including Barry Unsworth, Phillipa Gregory, Caryl Phillips and David Dabydeen.[10] In many ways, this cultural shift was especially apparent in 2007 – the bicentennial anniversary of the abolition of the slave trade – as church groups, local communities and government agencies geared up to participate in a national conversation about the historical slave trade and its legacy.[11]

Yet what is especially notable here is the idea that Toby's character is a *necessary part* of the play's theatricality: in tapping the performative potential of Toby's story, *Coram Boy* participates in a much larger representational tradition in which slavery has been, by its very nature, understood *to be theatrical*: first, since the early days of the abolition movement, the British stage has, in its own way exploited the theatrical potential of enslaved bodies – even when those enslaved bodies were those of white actors in blackface. Although an American theatrical tradition also has a problematic tradition of rendering blackness, at this moment in the UK, as Britain approaches the question of what it means to be a 'multi-cultural' western European democracy, the question of how to represent blackness on stage has special relevance to a UK audience. In addition, the facts of transatlantic slavery – especially the Middle Passage but also the physical conditions of the enslaved themselves – have been historically cast, on both sides of the Atlantic, in overtly dramatic, even spectacular terms. To see the cultural work of *Coram Boy*, then, it is useful to turn to the theatrical tradition that generated it.

Part two: Theatricality and slavery in Britain

Though the history of race on the British stage does not begin with
Othello, many scholars would turn there first for the representational
issues concerning race that persist on the twenty-first century stage.
Indeed, since the earlier days of the theatre, English actors have imper-
sonated individuals of African descent, sometimes by blacking up their
faces but also by using fine lawn fabric, wigs, masks and stockings to
impersonate race. Engravings from the seventeenth century provide
further evidence of characteristic costuming and blocking used in early
productions of *Othello.*[12] However, the full portrayal of characters with a
notably 'African' or 'black' identity awaited the end of the seventeenth
century, when Thomas Southerne's adaptation of Aphra Behn's fiction
Oroonoko first appeared on the boards. Behn's novel had taken up the
story of an African prince from Coramantien (or the Gold Coast) who
is tricked into slavery and taken to Suriname. After an unsuccessful
attempt at a rebellion, he is executed in an especially gruesome way,
his hacked off genitals thrown into the fire while he calmly smokes
his pipe.[13] Departing from Behn – a playwright herself who, curiously,
never adapted her own popular tale – Southerne did not dismember
Oroonoko's body on stage, but he exploited nonetheless the full dramatic potential of the suffering 'Royal Captive'.

After its debut in 1695, *Oroonoko* became a popular staple of the
English stage, appearing in its several adaptations at least once every
season in London until 1801. A full discussion of the many adaptations,
their productions, actors and audiences would take us far from the
main thread of our discussion. Still, what is remarkable is the enduring status of this play taking up the topic of African suffering. Many
prominent actors – including Jack Verbruggen, David Garrick and, later,
American actor Ira Aldridge – played the part of Oroonoko.[14] The adaptations, done by John Hawkesworth and David Garrick in 1759, Francis
Gentleman in 1760 and John Ferriar in 1788, differed somewhat in their
emphasis and political message, yet all retained the idea of Oroonoko
himself as an apologist and martyr for the slave trade. The text calls for
him to rationalise that if he and the other enslaved Africans are 'slaves,
the planters did not make us slaves'. 'They bought us in an honest way
of trade', says Oroonoko, 'as many have done before them, bought and
sold many a wretch and never thought it wrong'. 'They paid our price',
he reasons, 'and now we are their property'.[15]

Thus, whatever nobility the eighteenth-century stage afforded
Oroonoko, whatever agency he was briefly allowed in his attempt to

lead a slave rebellion, in the end, theatrical tradition reduced him to a heart rending spectacle – an African prince tragically unable to provide a future for himself, his family, or his people. Not until the late twentieth century was the attempt made to restore Oroonoko to his West African contexts and to flesh out an African perspective within the story. Nigerian-born playwright 'Biyi Bandele was the first to take seriously the possibility that a diasporic story might underlie Behn's efforts, as, for the first time on the stage of the RSC in 1999, *Oroonoko* became an 'African' story.[16]

It is, no doubt, a long journey from eighteenth-century *Oroonoko* to twenty-first century *Coram Boy*, but I would argue that the shadow of that theatrical tradition loomed over the contemporary production. On some level, consciously or not, this production had the burden of 'correcting' the representational mistakes of the past: it could not overlook the question of the black experience on stage and it had to appear responsive to recent political shifts in emphasis – as the comments of Henry pointedly suggested. But the play was equally shadowed by the idea that *transatlantic slavery itself* is theatrical in nature. With the notorious Middle Passage at the heart of its narrative, the story of the eighteenth-century slave trade has always involved spectacular, if distressing, visual representations of human suffering, representations that have often been staged dramatically to elicit an especially visceral response.

It is incontrovertible that the enslaved lived horrific lives: from the notorious conditions of the transatlantic journey, to the forced labour of plantation slavery, to the even more brutal circumstances of Caribbean labour, the facts are well documented. What has arisen as a key interpretative issue in the UK, however, is *how best to convey* such facts to a broad popular audience that, until very recently, would have known little to nothing about its country's involvement in the sinister trade. Within the last few decades, artists, writers and cultural critics have been holding a rich and productive debate over a range of questions, including: what kinds of museum exhibits, monuments, or events best promise to convey the necessary historical background? How can such commemorative events avoid polarising their audience on the one hand and downplaying crucial questions of guilt and complicity on the other? Moreover, what should be the role of physicality in such representation? What representation can hope to capture the debilitating spiritual effects of enslavement? What happens when transatlantic slavery is represented first and foremost as shocking, spectacular and dramatic bodily suffering?[17]

Among the voices engaged in this debate are those of Marcus Wood and Saidya Hartmann. Theirs is a complex body of work that is not easily summarised. Among his other arguments, Marcus Wood warns against the scopophilic – and indeed the often pornographic – impulse behind many representations of slavery. Wood convincingly argues that it is a mistake to encourage the notion that an audience can take on or experience the suffering of the enslaved. To suggest as much, he states, is inevitably to downplay the full scope of human suffering.[18] Yet a widespread, misdirected inclination toward 'living history' suggests not only that the audience can fully assume the suffering of the enslaved, but that, unless they imaginatively take on the burden of this suffering, no connection to the issue can occur.[19] And so museum exhibits in the UK continue to simulate the Middle Passage, using a combination of visual and audio technologies to draw the audience into an 'experience' of the grisly scene.[20] But, following Wood, we might ask here 'what is being experienced in such a moment? How do shock and horror lead to moral insight? How do fascination and revulsion transmute into a higher understanding of the moral issues brought on by the fact of such spectacular suffering?'

American writer Saidya Hartman takes the discussion one step further: she argues for the necessity of turning away from the more dramatic, oftentimes gruesome representation of slavery to the more mundane experiences because *only the latter offers a full rendering of human subjectivity under severe trauma.* As she points out, the deepest human suffering lies in the debilitating routines of everyday life.[21] Whips and chains get attention like nothing else, but how do you get an audience to focus its attention on *the lived experience* of the enslaved? How do they arrive at a reflection on the extraordinary fact of a humanity that persisted, despite extraordinarily repetitive and demeaning labour? It is in response to this set of questions that museums in both the UK and the US currently borrow effectively from performance theory, turning away from the morally dubious idea that extreme trauma can (or should) be recreated and seeking instead to teach embodied lessons about the lived experience of slavery.[22]

To summarise the argument thus far, the representation of transatlantic slavery has been embedded within a problematic tradition where spectacular suffering – an especially dramatic rendering in which physical suffering is framed in an overtly theatrical way – has often occurred at the expense of an alternative kind of representation. This alternative representation, less spectacular, less obviously dramatic, might seek to understand the endurance of the enslaved, as well as the capacity to transcend debilitating physical conditions. It might, too, be content to focus on interiority, on the complex internal processes that characterised the lives of the enslaved. In short, what has been eclipsed when slavery is understood on the British stage and elsewhere first and foremost as a 'dramatic' spectacle is a full rendering of human subjectivity.

As a cultural text, *Coram Boy* becomes especially relevant when it is understood as a response to the ongoing British debate about how best to teach the historical lessons of transatlantic slavery. As the only black character, Toby stands in for 'the lived experience' of an eighteenth-century enslaved African, yet he does not appear until Act II, or the second half of the play. To be fair, the production avoids several of the representational traps under discussion here: Toby is never beaten or otherwise physically abused (though he does appear with blood marks on his shirt later in the play). Instead, slavery as spectacle in this play is confined to one rather uncomfortable scene. Having finished up his time at the Coram Hospital, Toby is sent to the house of the sinister Mr. Goddarn to be a liveried servant.

Scene Seven finds Toby attired in 'the costume of an exotic African prince, with satin pantaloons and a richly embroidered jacket. On his feet he wears gorgeous, jewelled slippers which turn up at the end, and on his head is placed a silk turban with a huge shining ruby in the centre of it'.[23] In his upturned hand he holds a silver tray. In other words, the scene visually references an entire tradition of small black boys as pets, a tradition recognised from Plate II of Hogarth's *Harlot's Progress*, among many other places. In her commentary, Henry describes how eight-year old Toby slowly realises the full meaning of his costume when he is told to smile – and then to smile wider still. But the full meaning of the costume does not dawn on him until Mr. Goddarn threatens to cut out his tongue should the boy ever tells a soul about anything he sees in the house. The actor playing Mr. Goddarn leans in close enough to suggest that the 'anything' Toby might be asked to perform is a veiled threat of sexual abuse.

However, the scene is potentially explosive for the actor playing it: there is a very uncomfortable line between demonstrating Toby's exploitation and becoming complicit in that exploitation. When the costumed boy first appeared in the matinee I attended, the audience laughed – but in a way that suggested they were delighted with the scene: the costume seems to have elicited a visual pleasure. The director tried to 'correct' their possible misconceptions concerning the innocence of the costume, as the script quickly establishes the spiritual and possibly physical abuse that the costume signifies. But the audience's attention to Toby's enslavement is then quickly diverted by another subplot that has Mr. Gaddarn involved in the trafficking of *white* slaves as well. Young girls, 'sponsored' by Goddarn and released under his auspices from Coram House, are being sent, by means of a subterranean passage in his house, directly onto slave ships bound for the Barbary Coast. While this thickens the plot, it seems also an extraneous development: is the point to make the issue of slavery more relevant to a white audience who might otherwise think slavery has nothing to do with them? Why not trust the audience to understand the issue without the reference to 'white slavery'? Why not allow Toby to represent the experience of enslaved Africans without universalising the issue? Moreover, why not linger over the issues of Toby's experience, offering the audience a rare opportunity to explore the psychological burden of enslavement?

In the penultimate scene, Toby finds himself forced on board a slave ship. He leaps into the sea in a suicidal attempt to avoid his fate. Aaron and Meshak (Aaaron's surrogate father) soon follow. What ensues is a spectacular 'underwater ballet', a powerful illusion created by having the actors hang from imperceptible ropes, while a gigantic plastic sheet hanging in front of them distorts their movements, giving them the thrilling appearance of fighting for their lives under water. Yet here this scene both remembers and does not remember the actual historical circumstances it references: the deck of the slave ship is arguably the most important icon in the history of enslaved Africans, the Middle Passage being the single most important real and imagined event.[24] The production seems simultaneously aware of the powerful semiotic potential of what it references – and disinclined to give it its due. The image of the drowning slave, thrown overboard, evokes the memory of the 1781 *Zong* incident, in which Captain Luke Collingwood had 133 sick slaves thrown overboard to their death, in order to claim the insurance money on their heads. Or it suggests the innumerable suicides of enslaved Africans, individuals who chose death over slavery. Yet here the stunning spectacle eschews actual historical reference in favour of a cinematic thrill. In the end it is Meshak, and not an enslaved African, who dies this particular death. In this and other ways, then, *Coram Boy* retains a cultural memory that it exploits without offering its audience the chance to fully engage with its meaning.

Part III: Slavery and the family

When New York critics complained about the sentimentality of *Coram Boy*, they might well have had in mind the extremely emotional final scene: as Alexander rehearses Handel's 'Unto Us a Child is Given' at the Coram Hospital with an on-stage choir, Aaron and Toby, having escaped death, unexpectedly appear. The parents reveal themselves at long last to their son, who is astonished to discover he is not the orphan he thought. Melissa then turns to Toby, and after hesitating only so slightly, suggests to him 'and I could be your mother too – if you'd like'. (At this point the sobs in the audience were audible.) But here again *Coram Boy* was shadowed by a theatrical tradition that has privileged the family as a sentimental spectacle. In this tradition, domestic affection trumps all evil, as a basic denial of *human* rights is relayed instead as an infraction to be corrected within the nuclear family. To make this point is no doubt to walk a very fine line, and I must be clear here: this is not an argument that in the real world white families should never adopt black children. (Indeed, I reject the essentialist line that asserts that black children are necessarily denied some aspect of their heritage when raised by white parents.) Rather, here the questions worth asking are: what is the nature of this deeply sentimental gesture in the context of this particular play? Why *this* fantasy that offers Toby not the return of his biological mother, but a surrogate mother in Melissa instead?

To answer these questions, it is necessary to see how *Coram Boy* deploys a trope once familiar to eighteenth- and nineteenth-century abolitionists: in abolitionist literature, it was not uncommon for the abuses of slavery to be depicted, first and foremost, as the estrangement of husband from wife and parents from children. These abuses could then be corrected by means of recuperating lost family members. The logic of this move is obvious: abolitionists believed that they could engage and mobilise broad public support for their cause by appealing to British citizens in terms that they could themselves understand, that is, in terms of 'shared' human experience of affiliation.[25] Innumerable instances from abolitionist literature support this point. To take just one example, writing in 1792, seventeen-year-old Quaker Mary Birkett wrote a poem entitled 'A Poem on the African Slave Trade: Addressed to her Own Sex' to urge women to boycott sugar, the product of enslaved Africans in the Caribbean. Her African is a young 'family' man: surrounded by a network of kin, both his parents and his future spouse:

> Then when his soul youth's joyous feeling knew,
> And manhood, ripening manhood, rose to view,
> He to his parents eye perhaps appears,
> The only staff of their declining years;
> And he with ceaseless love and anxious care,

Does oft for them the hunted food prepare:
Perchance soft passion does his bosom move,
And his fond nymph return his constant love;
Perhaps his offspring hail their honour'd sire,
And each to again the envy'd kiss aspire:
On him a pleasing weight of care attend,
As father, husband, brother, son or friend.[26]

Obviously, what Birkett does here is what so many others had already done and would continue to well into the nineteenth century both: in order to fix the attention of her (almost exclusively) female audience (for they are the ones who would most effectively boycott the sugared tea), she gives them a subject with whom to identify. In making his story into a story of lost family connections, she touches a deeply sentimental nerve. But in rendering him as the lost son/husband/father, she also feminises and domesticates her subject, and in the process, deprives him of the agency that might exist in a more militant, more proactive African subject: we don't have to travel very far to arrive at the famous kneeling, suppliant 'slave' of the famous Wedgwood medallion.[27] Of course, in *Coram Boy* Toby is not suppliant slave, but he is, as a deeply sentimental object, a motherless son appealing to maternal sensibilities.

No doubt there has always been something powerful about the sentimental idea that individuals should mobilise themselves to keep the family together, or that one should do whatever necessary to put fractured families back together once slavery has torn them apart. Yet ironically the family was also deployed by anti-abolitionists, who sometimes argued that slavery made for better families. Such is the case, for example, in Maria Edgeworth's short fiction *The Grateful Negro* (1804), where the 'benevolent' master assumes the role of a patriarchal figure characterised by his selfless interest in all those below him. As Lynn Festa persuasively argues in her incisive study of sentimentality, 'abolitionists did not possess a monopoly on sentimental feelings'.[28] Moreover, 'sentimentality does not authorise feeling for all, but rather claims it for a happy few'.[29] Festa analyses the more troubling aspects of the sentimental tradition, pointing out, for example, that 'the slave about whom one has feeling does not possess feelings or consciousness of his own: he must wait until those feelings are "imparted" to him. The attribution of lyric subjectivity does not translate into the attainment of political subjectivity'.[30]

In the case of *Coram Boy*, if Toby stands in for innumerable enslaved Africans, then sentimental feelings for his status as orphan eclipse the question of his rights. As he joins the Ashbrook family, his story closes around an image of home, but the broader discussion of social justice for others who have been enslaved is short-circuited. Moreover, what Festa writes about sentimental readers of abolitionist literature is relevant for the viewers most likely to be affected by this scene: they do not identify with the sentimental object – in this case, Toby. Instead 'they bond with each other through the medium of the sentimental object. The precipitation of the self into the role of the other is thus not a reciprocal and balanced exchange that produces a community of like equals, of men and brothers'.[31] In other words, though *Coram Boy* announces itself as important cultural intervention, its sentimentality keeps it from fulfilling its purported commitment to social justice.

The final scene of the play taps a powerful fantasy that the best way to engage in social justice, or to redress grievous social wrong, is to knit the wronged party back into the family unit: the play heals the Ashcroft family as it symbolically heals the British nation by reflecting to the audience an image of inclusiveness and wholeness. Toby's mother is most likely dead, and no doubt she has been a victim of the slave trade, but *the audience* will find a place for her son in their hearts and all will be made well, not only in their families, but in their nation as well. However, this fantasy raises the important question of *what is not being said* in this moment of apparent catharsis.

With its sentimental image of the family, the final tableau evokes the mythic 'family of man', an ideology that was most powerfully critiqued by Roland Barthes fifty years ago. Barthes was writing, of course, about the once-famous photography exhibit, but his point is nonetheless relevant here. In his essay, Barthes asked what has been repressed in the moment when the human family is represented as sharing the same transhistorical moments – birth, work, love and death.

> Everything here, the content and appeal of the pictures, the discourses which justify them, aims to suppress the determining weight of History: we are held back at the surface of an identity, prevented precisely by sentimentality, from penetrating into this ulterior zone of human behavior where historical alienation introduces some 'differences' which we shall here quite simply call 'injustices'.[32]

In other words, the default to understanding humanity as one large family eclipses *history itself*. By focusing on family connections, the audience for *Coram Boy* looks away from the injustices that have divided and continue to divide it into separate racial communities. In *Coram*

Boy – as elsewhere – sentimentality about the family urges its audience to think that significant differences in cultural or socio-economic circumstances do not really matter. Sentimentality also tolerates a wilful forgetting. It prematurely assures its audience that it can go 'beyond history' before they have fully reckoned with the burdens and responsibilities of history.

In conclusion, *Coram Boy* failed to engage an American audience because it referenced a complicated, unfolding history of race that would not have been audible to American ears. Having positioned itself in a specifically British conversation about the history of transatlantic slavery, it addressed a set of concerns distinct in tone from those that circulate in American popular culture. However, for all its gestures at historical recovery, *Coram Boy* did not see the history of transatlantic slavery as well as it purported to do. It was embedded in theatrical traditions that it referenced without advancing their purpose. As an immensely popular public spectacle, it offered its British audience a vision of social wholeness and cohesiveness before it encouraged the kind of introspection that makes true social integration possible. Its use of the family suggested that the history of transatlantic slavery could be incorporated into existing narratives about British national identity. But it failed to ask fundamental questions about what it means *to be* a family – and it never required that the audience consider its own complicity in the historical injustice that first sundered the families of enslaved Africans.

Imagine, then, an alternative ending for the play: with the music of Handel swelling in the background, Toby's mother returns, reclaiming not only her son, but also the opportunity to engage the audience in a meaningful dialogue about how he came to be there and what might be his future as a result.

Notes

1. Charles Isherwood, 'Imported Doesn't Always Mean Important', *New York Times*, 3 June 2007.
2. Clive Barnes, 'Do Not Handel', *New York Post*, 3 May 2007; and Charles Isherwood, 'Orphans of the Storm, Assailed by Lurid Evildoers', *New York Times*, 3 May 2007.
3. For an account of some efforts toward this end, see my book *The British Slave Trade and Public Memory* (New York: Columbia University Press, 2006).
4. By focusing on these themes in particular, by no means do I intend to deny that the US has had it own, long, and complicated history representing race and slavery on stage. To be sure, even before the publication of *Uncle Tom's*

Cabin in 1852, US theatre also has struggled to represent blackness on stage. In a separate but parallel history, one could trace a long line from the earliest melodramatic and sentimental renderings of blackness in early nineteenth century America to Bill T. Jones' spectacular choreography of *Last Supper at Uncle Tom's Cabin* in 1990 – and now, in the twenty-first century, to additional representations. Moreover, by focusing on the theme of sentimentality in *Coram Boy*, I do not mean to say that a sentimental tradition of representing race belongs to the British stage alone, but rather that, on the stage of the National Theatre in the early decades of the new millennium, sentimentality reappears in a new and particularly troubling form.

5. See http://www.jamilagavin.co.uk/biography.html (accessed 4 June 2009).
6. Jamila Gavin, *Coram Boy* (New York: Farrar, Strauss, and Giroux, 2000), p. v.
7. Email correspondence with Alison Duke, administrator at the Foundling Museum, which still continues the work begun by Thomas Coram.
8. *Coram Boy*, adapted by Helen Edmundson and based on the novel by Jamila Gavin (London: Nick Hern Books, 2005).
9. 'The productions: *Coram Boy*, Research, "Playing the Only Black Character"', see http://www.stagework.org (accessed 14 June 2007).
10. For a fuller account of these events, see *The British Slave Trade and Public Memory*.
11. Many of these events were described in a pamphlet, published by the British Home Office, under the auspices of the department of Culture, Media and Sport, entitled *Reflections on the Past and Looking to the Future: The 2007 Bicentenary of the Abolition of the Slave Trade in the British Empire*.
12. See Virginia Mason Vaughan, *Othello: A Contextual History* (Cambridge: Cambridge University Press, 1994); Anthony Barthelemy, *Black Face: Maligned Race: The Representation of Blacks in English Drama from Shakespeare to Southerne* (Baton Rouge: Louisiana State University Press, 1987); and Ruth Cowhig, 'Blacks in English Renaissance Drama and the Role of Shakespeare's Othello', in David Dabydeen, ed., *The Black Presence in English Literature*, (Manchester: Manchester University Press, 1985), pp. 1–25. See also Felicity Nussbaum, *The Limits of the Human: Fictions of Anomaly, Race, and Gender in the Long Eighteenth Century* (Cambridge: Cambridge University Press, 2003), Chapter 6.
13. Aphra Behn's *Oroonoko* appears in many contemporary editions, including two of note: *Oroonoko: A Norton Critical Edition*, ed. Joanna Lipking (New York: W. W. Norton, 1997) and *'Oroonoko' A Bedford Cultural Edition*, ed. Catherine Gallagher (Boston, MA: Bedford St. Martin's, 2000).
14. For a full history of the play, see Chapter 4 of *The British Slave Trade and Public History*. See also the excellent collection *Troping Oroonoko from Behn to Bandele*, ed. Susan Iwanisziw (New York: Ashgate, 2004). Though he made his theatrical debut in a production of the play, Garrick was not successful in his role as Oroonoko. See Thomas Davies, as cited by Arthur Richard Nichols in 'A History of the Staging of Thomas Southerne's *The Fatal Marriage* and *Oroonoko* on the London Stage from 1694 to 1851', PhD dissertation, University of Washington, 1971, pp. 187–8. Ira Aldridge, on the other hand, was a hit in the role. See Herbert Marshall Mildred Stock, *Ira Aldridge: The Negro Tragedian* (Carbondale: Southern Illinois University Press, 1968), pp. 54–5.

15. *Oroonoko: A Tragedy as it is now acted at the Theatre Royal in Drury Lane. By Thomas Southerne. With alterations by John Hawkesworth.* (London: 1775), p. 34. The other major issue throughout the eighteenth century was Imoinda's race: Behn's heroine was not only black, but spectacularly tattooed. Southerne altered her patrimony, making her white and thereby allowing English actresses to play the role without blacking up. 'Biyi Bandele, as mentioned below, gave back to Imoinda her African roots and identity.

16. 'Biyi Bandele, *Aphra Behn's Oroonoko in a New Adaptation by 'Biyi Bandele* (London: Amber Lane Press, 1999).

17. For a comprehensive discussion of these two questions, see two books by Marcus Wood, *Blind Memory: Visual Representations of Slavery in England and America 1780–1865* (Manchester: Manchester University Press, 2000) and *Slavery, Empathy, and Pornography* (New York: Oxford University Press, 2002). For an account of the debate over the forms of appropriate commemoration in Bristol and Liverpool in the 1990s, see Chapter 1 of *The British Slave Trade and Public Memory*.

18. See, for example, Wood's assertion in regard to the display of instruments of torture, once used upon the bodies of the enslaved: 'The artifacts which were applied and attached to the bodies of slaves, and were then preserved either in museums or in printed representations in books, are not a gateway to knowledge of the events that produced them, or a substitute for the experience of anyone, white or black, involved in the process of their use' (pp. 219–20).

19. First circulated by Cambridge historian Raphael Samuel in the 1990s, the term 'living history' has become something of a cliché in museums, where it is now applied to events as disparate as soap making and simulated experiences of the Blitz in wartime London.

20. For example, in an otherwise commendable exhibit in Bristol entitled 'Breaking the Chains: An Exhibit to Commemorate the British Parliamentary Abolition of the Transatlantic Slave Trade in 1807', curators undermined their own purposes of evoking full agency and dignity of its Afro-Caribbean citizens by asking visitors, within the small space of a dark gallery, to focus on a contemporary rendering of the infamous Brookes slave ship, with its closely packed enslaved Africans. During one visit, several school children remained fixated on the idea that dead were left to lie close to the living (like Zombies?) while the same students remained uninterested in the more salutary lessons about the ability of enslaved Africans to make communities or to profit from economic opportunities.

21. Saidya Hartman, *Scenes of Subjection: Terror, Slavery, and Self-Making in Nineteenth-Century America* (New York: Oxford University Press, 1997).

22. For example, in the recent New York Historical Society exhibit entitled 'Slavery in New York', a weighted bucket, designed to help simulate the labor of an enslaved child, taught the lesson of back-breaking labor. On one visit, I observed a father supervising his small son's efforts to lift the bucket, with the lessons of drudgery and exhaustion easily accessible.

23. *Coram Boy*, p. 74.

24. See *The Black Imagination and the Middle Passage* edited by Maria Diedrich, Henry Louis Gates, and Carl Pedersen (New York: Oxford University Press, 1999).

25. For a comprehensive analysis of the role of sentimentality in late eighteenth-century literature and political discourse, see Brycchan Carey, *British Abolitionism and the Rhetoric of Sensibility: Writing, Sentiment, and Slavery, 1760–1807* (Basingstoke: Palgrave Macmillan, 2005).

26. Mary Birkett, 'A Poem on the African Slave Trade', reprinted in Alan Richardson, ed., *Slavery, Abolition, and Emancipation*, vol. 4 (London: Pickering and Chatto, 1999), pp. 199–217.

27. For a critique of the Wedgwood medallion, see Lynn Festa, *Sentimental Figures of Empire in Eighteenth-Century Britain and France* (Baltimore: Johns Hopkins University Press, 2006), pp. 164–6.

28. Ibid., p. 178.

29. Ibid., p. 187.

30. Ibid., p. 203.

31. Ibid., p. 171.

32. Roland Barthes, *Mythologies*, translated by Annette Lavers (New York: Hill and Wang, 1995), p. 101.

10
Significant Silence: Where was Slave Agency in the Popular Imagery of 2007?

Marcus Wood

One of the high points in the media coverage of 1807/2007 was Lola Young's long article entitled 'The Truth in Chains', published in the *Guardian* on 15 March, on the brink of the Bicentennial carnival week.[1] This constituted a brilliantly compressed, but not reduced, account of the different forces swirling within the culture wars, and inheritance debates, thrown up by the anniversary. Young clearly outlined how interest groups with axes to grind, and chips on their shoulders, could only see the opportunity of hijacking the event. She clearly saw through, with a weary wisdom, the manoeuvrings of New Labour. Here we had an insider explaining, while naming no names, why the jaw-breakingly dull, and safely impotent, hypocrisies of Blair and his official anniversary front man, John Prescott, MP for Hull, were so inevitable. There is no space to summarise her excellent general take on things here, but I do want to excise two of the central truths she enunciated, because they jus-tify the following discussion. Firstly, she said: 'Africa is still a blank space in most European people's consciousnesses', adding that 'One downside of the commemorations is that the emphasis on enslavement reinforces the belief that there was no African history before European domina-tion'. This fact, and it is a fact, has terribly destructive effects on how slavery is perceived throughout the Atlantic Diaspora. Secondly, she con-cludes simply that, 'In popular public consciousness Wilberforce ended slavery'. Sad, but true, and she continued: 'A damaging side effect of the focus on white people's role in abolition is that Africans are represented as being passive in the face of oppression.'

I think that the heroic intervention of Toyin Agbetu when he so boldly and sanely transformed the Westminster Abbey Memorial service commemorating the 200th anniversary of the abolition of the Slave Trade was very much an attempt to confront this problem.[2] When all was said and done the big memorial service, complete with ancestors of Wilberforce carrying abolition fetish objects up the isle, had been arranged to keep the blacks on their respectful seats. Agbetu was having none of it. He did not, as the press would have it, mount a protest, but his lengthy intervention did achieve a transmogrification of the event; suddenly it meant something different and rather moving. He has explained his actions subsequently with some eloquence:

> The 'Wilberfest' abolition commemoration had eradicated any mention of resistance, rebellion and revolution instigated by millions of African people ... I stood up with my arms raised in a gesture of non-violence and said 'Not in our name' to Dr. Rowan Williams who was attempting to lead the congregation, which included a number of African people, to their knees to beg God's forgiveness for the slave trade ... I went to the Queen and told her that in the history of the Maafa the English are the Nazis, I then turned to Tony Blair and told him he ought to be ashamed for his behaviour, he quickly averted his gaze. The rest of what I said was directed to members of our community, I don't believe it was right for us to have remained in a venue in which the British Monarchy, Government and church, all leading institutions of African enslavement during the Maafa, collectively refused to atone for their sins. Then a gang of men attempted to drag me out through the back door on my knees. I strongly asserted that I would be walking out of the front door, on my feet, as an African.'[3]

And I for one would have welcomed a much bigger emphasis on black resistance to slavery in all its forms during 2007, and the more extreme the better. Which brings me to the central question addressed in this discussion: why was the black body represented according to such outmoded stereotypes of passivity in 2007?

This paper contends that Britain's participation in and domination of the Atlantic slave trade have been registered with the visual culture of 2007 in predominantly revisionist and unchallenging ways. My sense of increasing tedium, and I suppose my feeling that we have been largely cheated, in 2007, now the dust is settling a bit, result from the fact that in so many ways nothing has changed much in two hundred years. All in all, Britain's societal response to 2007 hid behind a date, and used 1807 as a monolith, (or is it a shibboleth?), to avoid thinking of the wider implications of the outfall of the slave trade now. This avoidance had two major manifestations, both remarkably conservative in their processes. The first lay in an undue emphasis upon a celebratory approach to a supposed magical and chimerical moment of transformation. The following discussion is not, however, devoted to an analysis of that side of the memorial equation dealing with the celebration of the 'heroes of abolition', but to its equal and opposite element, namely the anonymous and passive representation of the slave body. Surveying all areas of popular display, within the media and within museum culture, the slave body appeared trapped within a series of visual motifs that prioritised slave inactivity, slave suffering and slave anonymity. In drawing upon a body of visual material developed by the abolitionists in the late eighteenth and early nineteenth centuries, British popular visual culture in 2007 perpetuated a series of controlling stereotypes for the configuration of Atlantic slavery.

It was inevitable when the 2007 bicentennial arrived that the key elements within the visual archive of slavery would be drawn upon, reproduced, re-circulated, re-invented, recombined, reappraised, reactivated and for the most part reduced. There is a sort of visual shorthand now used in popular treatments of slavery and the slave trade, to essentialise its memory. Although they are so familiar the key elements of this shorthand are worth briefly rehearsing one more time because they communicate en masse the message of passivity and impotent suffering isolated in their different ways by Young and Agbetu. These short cuts, these instant access ways into the archival savings account of slave trauma, are as follows: the abolition seal, in its male form asking the question 'Am I not a man and a brother?' and in its female 'Am I not a woman and a sister?'; the male and female runaway slave motifs; the horrific image generated during the American Civil War, of the slave Gordon's whipped back, corrugated with keloid scarring. Beyond these individual icons there is the collective body of imagery consisting of the tools used by the slave power to terrify and abuse its property consisting of yokes, whips, paddles, brands, collars, chains, shackles, the *speculum oris* and the thumb screws.[4] And finally above and beyond all of these popular images, in terms of its ubiquitous dismemberment and endless recycling, is the 'Plan' or 'Description' of the slave ship *Brookes* (see Figure. 10.1).

Surveying the representational archive thrown up in 2007 it is evident that all of these icons were shuffled, re-dealt, played out and played to death. The processes of appropriating and parodying this historical legacy reached a low point of surreal performativity in the so-called 'March of Shame'. Restraints were donned by a group of mainly white evangelicals belonging to the group 'Lifeline'.[5] They also wore blue sweatshirts with a 'So Sorry' logo. The march's participants produced a

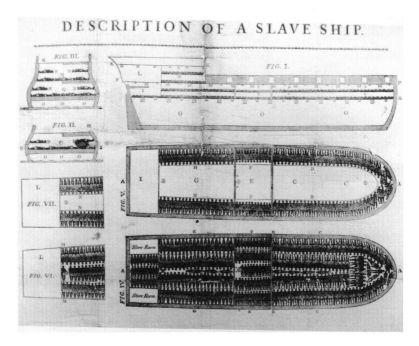

Figure 10.1 Society for the Abolition of the Slave Trade, London Committee, *Description of a Slave Ship*, April 1789. Reproduced by kind permission of Hull Museums.

grotesque parody of a slave coffle. On 25 March the core activists arrived at the Houses of Parliament in London, after a 24-day trudge down from Hull, chained and yoked together. It was supposed to be a symbolic act of atonement for the British sin of the slave trade. But what concerns me about this sorry performance is not the misplaced motivation but the bondage aspect. What did this discomfort mean, what space did their pantomime slave coffle function in? Did they feel that they were, through briefly submitting themselves to a little pain and mimicking the physical conditions in which Africans were forced to march to the slave forts, somehow atoning for the suffering of the slaves, or even worse for white guilt? The pretend slave coffle was objectionable because it seemed to see the suffering of slaves as so easily approached, and the impossible trauma of slaves so easily appropriated. We had the bizarre phenomenon of black enslavement and torture being mimicked by white slave wannabes, who re-enforced with an obscene ignorance the notion that slaves had always been silent victims.

But to return to the central theme, I have fairly continuously talked about these key sites of representation at great length, in different places, in different ways, over the last twenty years. 2007 made me wonder if I had anything more to say about them, if they still have any cultural value, or if they have been worn into smooth meaninglessness through the unending processes of re-circulation. Owing to their enormous quantity it is not possible to survey, let alone to analyse in detail, even the core materials, which recycled, quoted or parodied the key images of the earlier visual archive. The following discussion is consequently restricted to the analysis of the reconfigurations of a single image, the notorious broadside wood engraving of the *Brookes*.

Cutting and pasting the *Brookes* in 2007, the limits of cultural re-circulation

The 'Description' was reworked in 2007 in a remarkable number of ways, some of them intensely creative, some of them conservative, some of them effective and some of them dangerously close to irre-sponsible. In thinking about what happened to this image and why it happened, a great deal can be uncovered in relation to the dominant cultural agendas, which conditioned the visual archive that 2007 generated. There are different semiotic sub divisions covering how the 'Description' was re-circulated and marketed, which require clarifica-tion at the outset. In the first place, there were a plethora of straight-forward reproductions of the image, in which it was used as shorthand for what a slave ship looked like and was packed like. These can be categorised as uninflected, or relatively uninflected quotation. There are thousands of examples, but I will just give three, which give some idea of the range of processes involved. Firstly, there are the media quotations, in which any article or television documentary dealing with the subjects of abolition or the slave trade flashes the image of the *Brookes* as a sort of instant contextual filler. A typical example is the following, where the Plymouth Committee version of the plan is stuck in, without any comment whatsoever, as a visual backdrop to a Jackie Kay article demanding that Scotland acknowledge its part in Atlantic slavery.[6]

Secondly, there is the *Brookes* as trauma fashion accessory. I saw the image on this young man's T-shirt in the forecourt of Cape Coast castle, Ghana in August of 2007 (see Figure 10.2). He ran a tourist stall outside the slave dungeons, and when I photographed him he was in the process of trying to persuade a group of American academics

Figure 10.2 'The African Holocaust Never Again', 10 August 2007. Author's own collection.

attending the bicentennial slavery conference 'The Bloody Writing is Forever Torn' to buy his slave trade kitsch. He would not, however, sell me this shirt, because he had been sent it from a friend in New York, but he said he was a designer and could get me some made. I was impressed by his typically Ghanaian entrepreneurial flair, and ordered ten. This textile again simply reprints, three times over, the key section of the middle deck of the *Brookes*, this time as an instant shorthand for the 'slavery holocaust'. Thirdly, there are the uses of the image as historical background in popular educational contexts, in travelling exhibitions and museum displays. The exhibition mounted on behalf of the British Government in the Palace of Westminster to commemorate the bicentennial furnishes a rich example. This time the 'Description' of the *Brookes* was logically related to its place in parliamentary history. A case displayed the original engraving as a backdrop to a reproduction of the miniature scale model of the *Brookes*, which William Wilberforce had ordered to be constructed (**see** Figure 10.3). The bodies from the engraving were pasted down on the decks of the model, and the 'Description' was consequently developed from two to

Figure 10.3 Model of the slave ship *Brookes*, 1790. Reproduced by kind permission of Hull Museums.

three dimensions. Wilberforce then used this model as a visual aid and had it passed around the chamber during slavery debates.

In the Commons exhibition the 'Description' and the scale model of the boat were exhibited beside a bulky African slave-yoke, about seven feet long, borrowed from Anti-Slavery International. This assemblage was carefully planned months in advance by the design team responsible for hanging the show. Their little architectural plans show the yoke, the slave ship and the original plan, reduced to a series of side views and elevations. The graphic conventions used to render the slave ship *Brookes* diagrammatically in space have now been re-applied and take the 'Description' into a new abstract space where its original content is lost (see Figure 10.4). Viewed from above the 'Description' becomes a simple line, while the yoke and the ship keep their outlines as objects. Occupying real space in a way that a sheet of paper does not, are they therefore more real than the 'Description'? This display, and its diagrammatic configuration, dramatically force us to confront the artificiality, the decided unreality, of the 'Description'.[7]

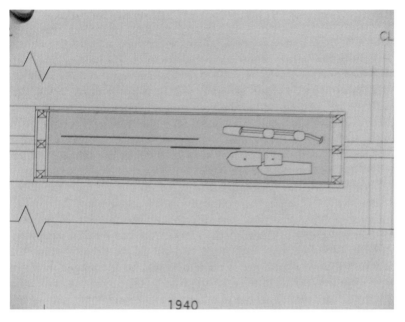

Figure 10.4 Design for the *Brookes* display, 'The British Slave Trade: Abolition, Parliament and People', Palace of Westminster, 17 May 2007. Author's own collection.

These adaptations and visual quotations of the *Brookes*, whether in the form of the T-shirt, the model boat or the diagram of the display case, underline the extent to which the *Brookes* has now entered that fluid semiotic terrain reserved for a very few images which enjoy, or must endure, global currency. It lies, in all senses of the word, along-side Munch's 'The Scream', or the photograph of the bearded Che Guevara in his beret with a single star on it, as an ever-open parodic resource. The ubiquity, the promiscuity, of the image forces us to ask whether it still has any power to shock, or if it does retain mean-ing, what this meaning is. The very familiarity of the image appears to have given it a reassuring rather than a horrific affect. Cultures throughout the Atlantic Diaspora are now, it seems, only too happy to accept this idealised vision of a slave deck as the standard version of events. Although the *Brookes* image was made to look so palpably unrealistic it paradoxically seems to represent the truth, or at least a truth.

Burnt out cases? High-art appropriations of the *Brookes*

Which leads me to my second adaptive territory, namely the radical
re-workings by artists who do not merely quote the image, intact, in
slightly altered contexts, but who dive in and attempt to shake it about,
re-invent it, parody it and generally wrestle it to the death. I will start
with the most trumpeted of the high profile adaptations. The Beninese
artist Romuald Hazoumé had worked for eight years, and completed in
2005, *La Bouche du Roi*. Named after an ancient slave port on the coast
of Benin the work was exhibited in and bought by the British Museum
in 2007. The British Museum is not renowned for the importation of
sub-Saharan African installation artists, or for buying their work, but
under Neil MacGregor, the politically canny and economically wired
museum politico who took over directorship of the museum in 2002,
all that was going to change.[8] The whole work combined a video running on a loop with an installation laid out on the floor in which the
sawn-off tops of plastic petrol containers had been arranged, more or
less, to mimic the aerial view of the middle section of the slave ship
Brookes as represented in the now universally recognisable plan of the
slave ship drawn up by a naval officer and a board of abolitionists in
the late 1780s. Some of the petrol container tops were personalised by
the attachment of small symbolic and fetish objects to each – beads
associated with African deities, dolls symbolising death and so on – the
idea being that each mask would then have a personalised identity, and
some relation to the African culture so starkly absent from the original
plan (see Figure 10.5).[9] Other elements were included that related to
the transatlantic slave trade: Cowrie shells, tobacco, glass bottles standing in for the masts, mirrors, a gun. The work was acquired by the
British Museum. Then with the backing of the National Lottery, the
Arts Council of England and the Board of the Trustees of the British
Museum, *La Bouche du Roi* was immediately sent out on a two-year
national tour, a process that continued into 2009.[10]

When a piece of work gets this sort of exposure and official rubber
stamping, then it is legitimate to ask exactly why this has happened
and what it means. Why was *La Bouche du Roi* made the way it was
made, why did the great and the wise of the British Museum see it as so
desirable, and is it is all it is cracked up to be? There was a sea of publicity in which this particular take on the 'Description' of the *Brookes*
was launched and now floats (see Figure 10.6). I do not have time to
go into much of the advertising campaign generated around this work,
but I will briefly consider the British Museum's flagship poster. This does

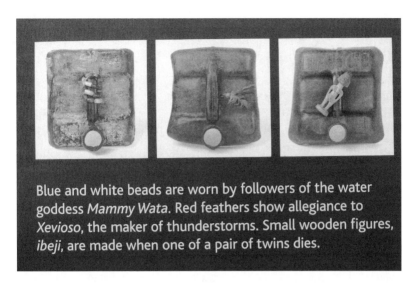

Blue and white beads are worn by followers of the water goddess *Mammy Wata*. Red feathers show allegiance to *Xevioso*, the maker of thunderstorms. Small wooden figures, *ibeji*, are made when one of a pair of twins dies.

Figure 10.5 Romuald Hazoumé, *La Bouche du Roi*, detail, 2007. Reproduced by kind permission of Romuald Hazoumé/ADAGP, Paris, and DACS, London, 2009.

very strange things to the original 'Description'. The middle section of the 1789 London broadside version of the print is excised and it is then printed over black in what might be described as an extreme off-white, or a light grey. In other words, the slave deck has been turned black, and the slave bodies off-white. They float barely visible, like fungus spores, or an intricate pattern of cigarette ash, above an aerial photograph of Hazoumé's installation. The two images have been scaled to match. Why have the black bodies from the original print been albinified while Hazoumé's petrol can lids exist against a dark yellow hardwood floor background in a range of deep browns and greys, apart of course from the black and white heads at the stern? Is this supposed to be a comment on how the slave bodies were imagined by a white abolition committee and engraved by a white artist and are therefore not really white but black, while Hazoumé's appropriation of the slaves is really black in comparison?

Coming at the *Brookes* as an image that has been manipulated and reinvented without cessation from the moment of its production over two centuries ago, it is hard to see in *La Bouche du Roi* anything but yet another predictable variation in a long line of relatively straightforward adaptive moves by installation artists and performers. The plan of the

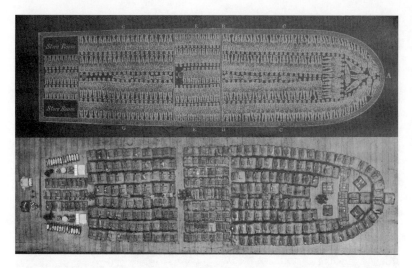

Figure 10.6   La Bouche du Roi, poster, 2007. Reproduced by kind permission of Romuald Hazoumé/ADAGP, Paris, and DACS, London, 2009, and the Trustees of the British Museum. Photo: Benedict Johnson.

slave ship has been more adapted and played with than any other image generated by Atlantic slavery, and my feeling is that it may be all played out, that it may be on the point of cultural exhaustion. What sort of icon can hold up after such unremitting processes of recirculation? There must come a point when the semiotic well runs dry, when the stuffing is knocked out of it and we cannot see the wood for the trees, or the slaves for the banana boxes, bottles of blood, tar fetishes, animal skulls, excrement or gasoline cans. There must come a time when it is pointless to rock that particular boat any more. For me that point came when I stood in the theatrical gloom, something like the light of the ghost train tunnel at a fairground, bathed in the exotic odours created by Hazoumé as an olfactory cocktail to accompany his installation. As I breathed in the fumes and looked at the pile of rubbish on the floor a terrible feeling of pointlessness and ennui came over me. Was I witness to the moment when that strange and oddly perfect eighteenth-century print of an imagined slave ship was simply incapable of bearing the weight of yet another set of borrowed robes?

Kevin Bales, the modern antislavery campaigner and author of the hugely significant book on modern forms of slavery *Disposable People: New Slavery in the Global Economy*, gave a lecture at the South Bank Centre in March 2007 in which he talked about the relation of the

2007 Bicentennial and the activities of the first abolitionists in relation to the bourgeoning forms of slavery that exist in the world today.[11] It was an uneasy talk because he was attempting to set up certain parallels between contemporary antislavery activism and the organisation, ideals and activities of the original Society for Effecting the Abolition of the Slave Trade. At a certain point, he threw a slide of the *Brookes* up on the wall, and his commentary was all about how we have now lost the power to be shocked the way an eighteenth-century audience would have been shocked by this image. At the end of the talk Mark Sealey, the inspirational force behind Rivington Place and Autograph ABP, and a black photographer and intellectual who refused to have anything to do with straightforward 'celebrations' of 2007, asked Bales a question. Why did he think contemporary antislavery activists were unable to come up with an image that could generate an equivalently powerful message to that of the plan of the *Brookes*? Why, with all our new technologies, arts sponsorship, human rights organisations and NGOs had we not produced any single image that instantly conveyed the idea of slavery and the certainty that slavery was evil the way the 'Description' of the *Brookes* seemed to? Bales' response was telling, in that rather than counter the assertion, he completely agreed that no visual work had been produced since the *Brookes* that came anywhere near its power.[12]

Over the last decade, I have seen banana boxes set out as a full scale plan of the *Brookes* in Bristol, bottles filled with blood as the *Brookes* in Hamburg, Kangaroo skulls as the *Brookes* in Australia, tarred and feathered objects on a bed of feathers as the slave bodies in London. I saw three Brazilian artists draw a full-scale parody of the *Brookes*, in which they substituted the slave bodies for crudely drawn sexual imagery, on the sands on Copacabana. Then the sea, that same Atlantic in which so many millions of slave bodies still lie dissolved, came and washed the image away. Should these parodic interventions be graded? Are some of them better than others, do some work and some fail, do they all operate in the same gestural ballpark? For over ten years now a black British artist called Paul Hope has been patiently working his way through a response to the *Brookes* (see Figure 10.7).[13] The piece is entitled 'Jam Packed Berth Place', a title that for a start suggests that Hope has located himself rather differently from the other satiric variants out there. The work consists of re-imposing, or ghosting in, one set of imagined black bodies upon another, and at that level is not a million miles from Hazoumé. Yet the type of imposition involved is I think more interesting and more intellectually lean. Hope's comical golliwogs float

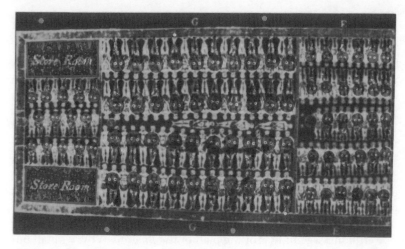

Figure 10.7   Paul Hope, 'Jam Packed Berth Place', 2007. Reproduced by kind permission of Paul Hope.

in and out of the tragic black manikins of the original, which are left as in a palimpsest; there is no attempt to obliterate his source.

Within the adaptive history of race stereotypes evolved in Britain, and across the Diaspora, in order to simultaneously bind down and ridicule the image of Black masculinity, the golliwog holds a central and notorious position.[14] But why the Robertson's golliwog? Robertson's is of course a famous jam manufacturing company, and its strawberry jam was a staple most English people over forty grew up with. Jam is a wonderfully rich metaphoric substance to throw into the mix of the slave ship. Jam could not be made without sugar, and sugar is of course the precious export that drove the Atlantic slave trade. Jam is sweet and luxurious, but it also suggests human blood and guts. Motorway police and ambulance drivers talk about 'scraping the jam off the tarmac'. And I do not know if it is appropriate to mention here that Hope, before he made 'Jam Packed Berth Place', had had hands-on experience in his job seeing the very worst things that high speed car crashes can do to human bodies.[15] But whether the artist's biography inspired the visual pun or not, the holds of slave ships were responsible for the production of vast amounts of such horrendous human jam. If we go back to the original plan, it was printed as a broadside, and at least half of the space was given over to a closely printed descriptive text. This gives appalling eyewitness accounts of the degeneration of the black slave body into human jam. Thomas

Clarkson quotes from Alexander Falconbridge's *Account of the Slave Trade* when talking of conditions on the slave decks; he begins by approaching the impossibility of description – 'When attacked with fluxes their situation is scarcely to be described' – and then continues:

> Some wet and blowing weather having occasioned the port holes to be shut and the grating to be covered fluxes and fevers among the negroes ensued. While they were in this situation, my profession requiring it, I frequently went down among them till at length their apartments became so extremely hot, as to be only sufferable for a very short time. But the excessive heat was not the only thing that rendered their situation intolerable. The deck, that is, the floor of their rooms was so covered with the blood and mucus which had proceeded from them in consequence of the flux, that it resembled a slaughter house. It is not in the power of human imagination to picture to itself a situation more dreadful and disgusting.[16]

Here we have human bodies boiled down through disease into an obscene jammy effluvia. And, of course, this filth and suffering are unrecoverable and indescribable in literal terms, which is exactly why the hands-off and clinical descriptive method of the 'Description' is so effective. The 'Description' finds no room for this slaughterhouse vision, it will not go in that direction, will not take on the challenge that 'it is not in the power of human imagination' to show something so dreadful. What Hope does, in throwing his golliwog badges into the mix, is to raise this spectre and, crucially, at the same time not to descend into any attempt at descriptive realism. Hope, in isolating the Robertson's golliwog, lighted upon an image brilliantly suited to set up a dialogue with the original design. It is the outrageous whimsicality of Hope's gesture of substitution that is so effective. His solution is a very dark humour that links the literal jam of the Robertson's golliwog with the quite inconceivable fact that the slave bodies decomposed into a very different sort of condiment.

I stress that it is the ability to avoid the incorporation of any realistic attempts at historic memory that makes Hope's work artistically success-ful, and that maintains the spirit of the original, which in its clarity and cleanness is so completely unreal. When it came to approaching the reality of the filth and the decay of the slave decks, Hazoumé's solution was to mix up a literal cocktail, which combined slave-trade products and human waste products. We were told that he flavoured his exhibit by mixing up human faeces and urine with tobacco, spices and alcohol to produce a heady brew that conjoined the suffering of the slaves with the products to which their suffering was being sacrificed.[17] Yet what finally is the status of this smell, what does it do or mean? Why use real human waste products and whose products are they anyway? Did Hazoumé use his own excretion, or another black person's, or a white person's, or a male's or a female's, or a child's? We are never told. If he used his own, then was he claiming for himself the agonised body of the slave, or was he placing himself alongside all those Western artists who have played so lovingly and profitably with their own excretion? Surely we have the right to ask, finally, what on earth is the relation of the excrement Hazoumé used to the real filth on the slave decks? Ironically, the only people who really suffered as a result of this installation were the poor, and mainly black, museum guards, forced to sit there breathing in the shit for hours on end. I asked the victims what they thought about their predicament. Several laughed and said they just got used to it after a while.

The last thing I want to do is to try to take the moral high ground here. To be honest, when it comes to Britain's involvement in Atlantic slavery there is not a lot of moral high ground going around. But I do think there are right ways and wrong ways of coming at the memory of the Middle Passage, and that we need to be clear about how much abuse the 'Description' of the *Brookes* can take. And so I should make a confession at this point. *Maxima mea culpa* I contributed to the horrible flotsam and jetsam, which the *Brookes* now tows along with it. Six years ago, in 2001, I built a parodic installation of the *Brookes* under the title 'High Tar Babies' and exhibited it in London in the Henry Moore galleries of the Royal College of Art. I laid out a genuine eighteenth-century ship's hawser in the shape of the *Brookes*. I filled the pool of space within the rope, the symbolic slave deck, with white duck down, and then put my substituted version of the slaves' bodies upon this soft bed. They were a motley crew of tar babies, fetish objects created by a series of artist collaborators, and then dipped in tar. And then I hung a giant eight-foot slug, stuffed with feathers and painted with tar, above my version of the slave deck of the *Brookes*, a new kind of deity overlooking their destiny.[18] What do I think about it now? Well, as with Hazoumé's work, it is easy enough to construct a knowing defence of it, to talk about how I questioned gender roles, animal and human rights, the nature of testimony, or broke up, while being in dialogue with the rigour of the original. But now I realise as with Hazoumé's work there was too much going on, it was too big and too noisy and too confused, and it was certainly as big a failure as *La Bouche du Roi*, if not as widely-publicised a failure.

I am not questioning the good intentions behind *La Bouche du Roi* or its undoubted seriousness, any more than I question my own seriousness in 2001.What I do question is the ability of either installation to develop the information encoded in the original 'Description' in any new or powerful direction, or in other words the effectiveness of either work as art or propaganda.

Youthful discretion, the *Brookes*, revivification and the humility of the photocopy

As I walked down the staircase of the great court in the British Museum, and away from *La Bouche du Roi* on that anniversary day in March, I came across a stall run by the Youth Concern Global Network exhibiting a series or works produced by young people in Southwark as part of the Youth Bicentenary Project, titled, 'Following the Trail 2007 and Beyond'. Among these visual experiments, lying in piles on a trestle table were modest sheets of A4 photocopies, and many of these played around with the *Brookes* image. All were satiric but humorous. There was a map of Britain with the slave bodies cut and pasted on to it, another of Southwark, the borough where this organisation is based.[19] The graphic gesture of substitution is ambiguous. Do these images say that this is how white people in Southwark still see black people today, that their slave origins cannot be overcome? Does it say that this is in reality how black people still exist, that disempowerment, prejudice or debt bondage keep them as slaves? Is it about the survival of Africans, their abilities to have endured and triumphed over the oppression of Atlantic slavery? Other images showed key buildings of cultural and institutional power thrust into the actual *Brookes* (see Figure 10.8). The miniature of the boat that Wilberforce had made in order to pass it around the House of Commons, to show politicians how many slaves could be legally packed into the *Brookes*, now takes on an extra cargo, the House of Commons or Buckingham Palace. These are complicated images, powerful photomontages, which place three-dimensional buildings on top of the boat, literally crushing the lifeless flat black bodies of the original plan, which Wilberforce then had cut out and pasted down. The final joke is surely that with these big pieces of iconic real estate on board the boat is going to go down, slaves, politicians, kings and queens sharing the same watery grave. The image also tells us to watch out in 2007 when the powers-that-be briefly want to 'celebrate' the abolition of slavery. They want a piece of the action, they want to climb on board, and here they have literally done so, but they do not fit, they do not belong.

Figure 10.8 Youth Bicentenary Project, 'PARLIAMENT-UPON-BROOKES', 15 October 2007. Author's own collection.

Visually the most complicated of all these images was an interpretation created by the young Ghanaian Ernest Gyasi simply carrying the interrogative title 'Identity' (see Figure 10.9). Here, the deck middle slave deck of the 'Description' is reproduced on the left. On the right it is reproduced again but the central section and the stern of the print have again had photomontage applied. Here a figure in a 'hoody' is repeated six times vertically down the centre and twice horizontally in the stern. The figure has clenched fists crossed over and pressed into its chest, like hard breasts. The space within the hood is black, and floating in front of it is a question mark. The question is not so easy to answer. We are challenged to say who lies within the hood, that black space might hold a white face, a male or a female chav. The irony, of course, is that these white youngsters have taken up the hoody from its origins in urban black street-wear because it is a good look; but are they being culturally re-colonised by black ghetto culture, or are they mimicking it because it is exciting to do so? I admire the graphic simplicity of the image, the way in which the repeated interlocking forms of the hoods suggest shackles. In the modesty of its scale and in the elegance of its layout it seems in tune with its source. These are not the stark crude chains on display in the cases of slavery museums

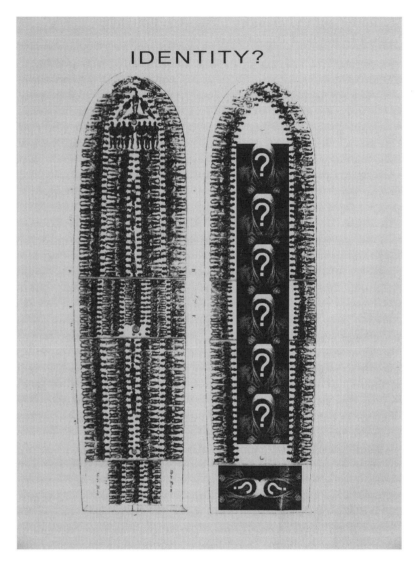

Figure 10.9 Ernest Gyasi, 'IDENTITY?' 15 October 2007. Reproduced by kind permission of Ernest Gyasi.

but the mind-forged manacles, which centuries of slavery imposed on the minds of blacks and whites alike. As a way of linking modern attitudes and modern life in the Diaspora with the memory of slavery as frozen in the stark formalism of the *Brookes* this image works for me.

Stamping out the memory of slavery: Philatelic appropriations of the *Brookes*

The *Brookes* also featured as an element within much of the official state-backed propaganda brought out for the Bicentennial. One of its most spectacular manifestations occurred within the context of philately, in Britain and in the Caribbean. The stamps and accompanying first day cover advertising materials produced by the Royal Mail in Britain, and by the Philatelic Bureau, of the General Post Office, Bridgetown, Barbados, recast the *Brookes* imagery in a number of ways. The marked differences with which the two cultures decided to re-appropriate the *Brookes* within a range of imagery dealing with slavery and memory reveal a lot about their respective agendas.

The decision to produce a full set of stamps in commemoration of the bicentenary of the abolition of the British slave trade situated the official British recollection of Atlantic slavery within a quite unique, and very carefully policed, popular graphic space. British commemorative stamps constitute a semiotic environment that has always been, and remains, heartily and unapologetically, celebratory. What these billions of little coloured pieces of paper celebrate, if they are viewed in their entirety, is a notion of nationhood, of what lies at the heart of 'Britishness'.[20]

Bearing this in mind, how perfect for the anniversary of 1807 and the official response to Britain and the abolition of the slave trade, that we should get a set of commemorative stamps celebrating British abolitionists. The Slave Trade series is part of a competitive market place that sells British culture and achievement with realism and confidence. The unremittingly positive nature of commemorative stamps sits strangely beside the memory of a national Shoah, until it is recognised that it is the myth of the abolition of the slave trade and not the trauma or guilt of this system of mass exploitation that the stamps are dedicated to. Because I want to keep the focus on the *Brookes* I will look at one stamp, and the envelope of the official first day cover, which used the image.

The stamp devoted to Thomas Clarkson shows him surrounded by prostrate slave bodies, contained in the prow of the *Brookes* (see Figure 10.10). Historically, there are solid reasons for linking Clarkson and this image. He was instrumental in gathering the information, which led to the construction of this famous 'Description'. He was also responsible for the mass distribution of the design, and personally gave out hundreds of copies in Revolutionary France, when he visited Paris in 1789.[21] Yet what this 'Description' now means is, as we have seen, not so easy to determine. It also forms the central design element in the

Figure 10.10 Royal Mail, Slave Trade Series, Thomas Clarkson, 2007. Reproduced by kind permission of Royal Mail Group Ltd.

special collectors' package in which the 'Mint' editions of the Abolition stamp set were sold (see Figure 10.11).[22] The front page of these display folders sets the six stamps on a chocolate brown background on the bottom half, while a long folding flap carries the image of the whole

Figure 10.11   Royal Mail, Slave Trade Series, Special Collectors' Pack, 2007. Reproduced by kind permission of Royal Mail Ltd.

length of the middle deck from the 'Plan' printed in light olive green, with the words 'Royal Mail Mint Stamps Abolition of the Slave Trade' printed over it in burnt sienna. Underneath, the word slave is a thick blood red rectangle, which blots out a block of slave bodies beneath. Is this supposed to be blood, the pain of memory, a sanguine under-lining, or merely an insensitive designer's caprice? The 'Description' consequently dominates the entire design, and the space in which all the stamps are read. It is a controlling symbol, which states implacably that the manner in which the slave body was packaged for abolition in 1788 remains unchanged in 2007. The effect of repeating a frag-ment of the design in a new colour behind Clarkson's head on his stamp enforces this message. Here, the tip of the middle deck edges across the stamp, like a bizarre yellow ochre turban, floating behind the round face of Clarkson. The tip of the prow of the boat nestles up against the small golden profile of Queen Elizabeth. There could be no clearer articulation of how the slave body, and the experience of slave suffering, exists literally as a backdrop framing the earnest reality of Clarksonian philanthropy. As ever, it is the face of abolition that has substance, personality, biography and a cultural presence, while the slave body remains anonymous and passive, a collective and nameless absent presence.

It appears to be the case that the agendas and creative attitudes at work in the postal systems of the Caribbean slave Diaspora may dif-fer from those of the Royal Mail, when it comes to the processes of

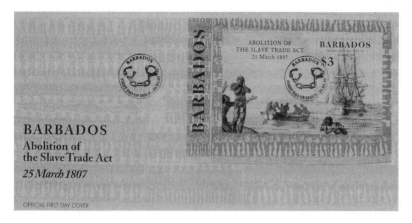

Figure 10.12 Philatelic Bureau, General Post Office, Barbados, First Day Cover, 'Abolition of the Slave Trade Act, 25 March 1807'.

commemorating the memory of slavery. The General Post Office in Bridgetown, Barbados, issued five stamps and two first day covers (FDCs). Both FDCs make extensive use of the slave figures from the central section of the *Brookes*. The first FDC was for the $3 stamp, printed as a souvenir sheet (see Figure 10.12). The stamp is a detail cut out from a nineteenth-century engraving showing slaves despairing as they are loaded into rowing boats and taken out to a slave ship. In the bottom left corner, and right foreground, a kneeling and standing slave respectively express their despair, theatrically clasping their heads and covering their faces with their hands. The design is framed by a series of margins that give fragmented sections of the slave bodies reproduced from the celebrated 'Description' of the *Brookes* printed in a soft indigo. The official envelopes for the FDCs also reproduce a section of the *Brookes*, the bodies this time printed slightly larger and in a faint grey. Floating above these designs are the circular cancellation stamps, which carry the image of an ankle shackle and chain open at one end. The FDC consequently integrates three quite distinct late eighteenth-century graphic styles: the detached power of the 'Description' of the *Brookes*, the emblematic imagery of the shackles, and the illustrational 'realism' of the elaborate copper engraving of the scene on the slave coast. The effect of the whole design is both elaborate and subdued, and cleverly extenuates the tendency of the originals to reduce human bodies into abstract geometrical configurations. The colour scheme is cold and mournful, the layers of slave bodies drifting

Figure 10.13   Philatelic Bureau, General Post Office, Barbados, First Day Cover, 'Abolition of the Slave Trade Act, 25 March 1807'.

in and out of each other in their shifting patterns of blues, purples and greys. The design looks intricate, fragile and as precious as a bank note, with the bodies of the *Brookes* stamped as merchandise.[23]

The second FDC, produced for the other four commemorative stamps, is also complicated in terms of the interventions it stages with the *Brookes* (see Figure 10.13). The envelope is identical to that used for the $3 stamp, but the four stamps carry radically different messages and take the imagery of the slave bodies from the *Brookes* out into a series of challenging graphic contexts. While the British commemorative stamps adopted a narrow focus, which exclusively prioritised individual abolitionists active in the late eighteenth century, the Barbados stamps attempt to place the slave trade in a much wider set of contexts. Only one of the stamps makes reference to a white abolitionist; this is the $1 stamp, which is very close in design to the British first-class Wilberforce stamp. A bust of Wilberforce, reproduced from a portrait engraving, dominates the design against a background that reproduces a section from the text of the Slave Trade Abolition Act. Yet this Barbadian Wilberforce does not sit easily at the head of a pantheon of other abolitionists. He is surrounded by stamps that are devoted to approaching 1807 through the memory and experience of the slaves.

The ten-cent stamp shows the agonistic figure of a slave raising his fists, which trail broken chains. The slave rises up out of a horizontal black bar at the bottom of the stamp. This compositional device of a lone figure rising out into the picture plane from a solid horizontal is adapted from Goya's wonderful etching of the colossus. The black figure consequently appears enormous and dominant. The slave figure has been taken from the central figure on the 1985 emancipation statue unveiled in Bridgetown, to commemorate the 1816 slave revolution in Barbados. The name 'Bussa' is printed below this figure on the stamp. Bussa was the legendary black guerrilla leader who led a force of four hundred slave revolutionaries against the British troops. He was killed in battle but his followers fought on to the death chanting his name. Although the statue was not specifically intended to be a portrait of Bussa, Barbadians call it the Bussa statue and the stamp has followed this popular appropriation. Bussa is a rather different abolitionist from Wilberforce. Like Zumbi, the legendary leader of the Palmares Quilombo in Brazil, Bussa lives beyond the confines of historiography, the archive and the database.[24] He is more an idea, an incarnation of the spirit of black resistance and autonomy, than a historical entity. Bussa stands over 1807 as a manifestation of the black will to resist enslavement, and of the desire actively to seize, rather than be gifted, freedom.

The $1.75 stamp constitutes a different but equally challenging approach to 1807. The horizontal design is a diptych made up of two photographs showing the interior in sepia, and an exterior, in black and white, of a slave hut. This stark reminder of the basic living conditions of the plantation slave operates in a different visual register. The style of documentary realism, the lack of humans in the pictures, and the stark juxtaposition of inside and outside space, give the image an air of anthropological detachment. 1807 and the slave trade are taken out of the hands of British abolition, and off the high seas, and into an intimate domestic space of deprivation. This work forces recognition of the fact that when the slave trade was finally abolished by Britain the damage had already been done and millions of Africans now lived in terrible conditions on foreign plantations. The image also forces confrontation with the reality that while the slave trade was abolished, at least on paper, slavery in the colonies was not. This thought leads naturally on to the $2 stamp, a pen and wash design showing ex-slaves celebrating abolition. The abolition they celebrate is not, however, that of the slave trade in 1807, or even colonial slavery in 1833, but the end of the coercive and hated apprentice system in 1838. Again, what this stamp insists upon is the complicated and compromised history that in reality surrounded the reluctant and flawed British approach to emancipation.

As a group, then, these stamps interrogate the stereotypes set up around the celebration of the abolition moment, and demand that slave agency, and slave labour, are integrated into the discussion. They consequently interact violently, as images, with the floating bodies of the slaves grafted in from the *Brookes* to act as a backdrop. Bussa, and the crowds celebrating the cessation of the apprentice system, deny the vision of the *Brookes*, and endow the slaves with life, liberty and the pursuit of happiness.

Finally, it needs to be emphasised that the confident and liberationist message of these stamps, in terms of the way they overturn the agenda of the *Brookes* imagery, found their counterpart in the British West Indian response to 2007. The YAA Carnival Village organised a wonderful parade on 6 October, which set out from Tothill Street, and went past the Houses of Parliament to Whitehall Place. The walk, or, in fact, carnival parade, was dedicated 'to the ancestors who died on the middle passage and to the Long Black presence in Britain since the beginning of the slave trade'. Many of the dancers wore vast carnival headdresses. And dressed in blue right at the centre of the parade was a woman who carried a huge boat on her head (see Figure 10.14). When I asked her what it meant she explained that it was both the *Brookes* and the *Windrush*, it

Figure 10.14   YAA Carnival Village Parade, 6 October 2007. Author's own collection.

was both sadness and a commitment to the triumphant survival of the descendants of slaves, and their arrival in Britain after the independence of the ex-slave colonies. The little black boat hanging over the side of her sculpture is both a literal lifeboat, and the *Brookes*, carried on, and carrying on, from the Caribbean into Britain. What a joyful reinvention of a very bleak image, what a complicated metaphor, what imagination.

It is attractive to believe, especially if you move in the intellectual circles of Atlantic studies, and Diaspora studies, that we have moved on, that big and difficult questions are being asked about the nature of white guilt, and white memory, as well as black trauma and black memory, and that there is a new emphasis on the world the slaves made, during and after the Middle Passage. But if you stand back and look at the bigger map of popular cultural responses to Atlantic slavery, I have serious doubts about the extent to which in Britain we have gone beyond, or desire to go beyond, the original myths in which the emancipation moment of 1807 was enshrined. The big memorial blocks, which were wheeled into place, for the most part remained, and remain, in place. The slaves are still iconically imprisoned within the visual rhetorics of disempowerment, stereotypification and passivity so brilliantly designed by British abolitionists in the late eighteenth century, in order to sell the abstracted emotional plight of 'our sable Brothers' to a sceptical but intensely sentimental British public. The rules they set up for the interpretational and cultural control of black bodies still maintain the tremendous power of a familiarity, which has become, as we see from the example of the *Brookes*, often invisible in its ubiquity.

Notes

1. Lola Young, 'The Truth in Chains: Two Centuries after Britain Began to Dismantle the Slave Trade the Whole Issue is Still Beset by Myths, Half-truths and Ignorance', *Guardian*, 15 March 2007, *G2* section, pp. 16–17.
2. Agbetu's intervention was recorded live on Radio 4 and on BBC 2 on 27 March 2007 between 12.22 and 12.35 pm. He then gained limited subsequent media coverage. See Toyin Agbetu, 'My Protest was Born of Anger not Madness', *Guardian*, 28 March 2007, and 'Protest at Slavery Service', *Independent*, 28 March 2007.
3. Agbetu, 'My Protest'.
4. All of these crucial visual elements are analysed in detail in Marcus Wood, *Blind Memory: Visual Representations of Slavery in England and America 1780–1865* (Manchester: Manchester University Press, 2000), pp. 16–36, 80–95, 218–30, 263–9.
5. For media treatments of the event, see Esther Addley and Hugh Mair, 'Marching to London to Hear a Single Word … Sorry', *Guardian*, 24 March

2007; Arifa Akbar, 'Wilberforce Family Marks Abolition of Slavery', *Independent*, 2 March 2007.

6. Jackie Kay, 'Missing Faces', *Saturday Guardian Review*, 24 March 2007. Despite the opportunistic use of imagery, the article is a timely and very well argued piece of polemic insisting that Scotland address its role in Atlantic slavery and the slave trade.

7. For the analysis of the iconography of this exhibition, see Marcus Wood, 'Packaging Liberty and Marketing the Gift of Freedom: 1807 and the legacy of Clarkson's Chest', in James Walvin, Melanie Unwin and Stephen Farrell, eds., *The British Slave Trade: Abolition Parliament and People* (Edinburgh: Edingburgh University Press, 2007), pp. 203–23. For the slave yoke, the model of the *Brookes* and the 'Description', see pp. 272–5, 278–9.

8. As MacGregor explained, 'La Bouche du Roi is a key acquisition for the British Museum collection and will form the centrepiece of a programme to mark the 200th anniversary of the Parliamentary abolition of the trans-atlantic slave trade. I am delighted that we are able to tour it to our partner venues across the country, thanks to the generosity of Arts Council England and the Dorset Foundation. It is important that this powerful work can be seen by as many people as possible in the UK, starting with the launch venue in Hull.' See http://www.wilberforce2007.com/index.php?/news/story/la_bouche_du_roi. Accessed 23 July 2009.

9. This detail and other subsequent reproductions of *La Bouche du Roi* are taken from the official British Museum publicity publications: *La Bouche du Roi, an Artwork by Romuald Hazoumé* (London: The British Museum, 2007); *Resistance and Remembrance 1807–2007* (London: The British Museum, 2007). There was, of course, a lot of a certain kind of remembrance in these publications, but nothing connected with resistance.

10. The work is on a myriad of websites for museums and newspapers, but it was on show at the following galleries between 2007–09, and each has web pages devoted to it (All accessed 1 January 2009): 22 March–13 May 2007, British Museum, http://www.thebritishmuseum.ac.uk/tradeandidentity; 2 June–15 July 2007, Ferens Art Gallery, Hull, http://www.hullcc.gov.uk/portal/page?pageid=221,93203; 4 August–2 September 2007, Merseyside Maritime Museum, Liverpool, http://www.merseysidemartimemuseum.org.uk/hazoumé; 15 September–28 October 2007, Bristol City Museums and Art Gallery, http://www.bristol.gov.uk/ccm/cms-service; 10 November 2007–2 February 2008, Laing Art Gallery, Tyne and Wear Museums, Newcastle, http://www.twmuseums.org.uk/search.php/hazoume; 5 December 2008–1 March 2009, Horniman Museum, London, http://www/horniman.ac.uk/exhbitions/archive.php. Following the end of the tour in March 2009 the work was returned to the British Museum where it is now in store.

11. Kevin Bales, 'Slavery Today', Purcell Room, South Bank Centre, 22 March 2007, 7.00–9.00 pm.

12. Material adapted from a tape recording of Sealey and Bales in dialogue, Purcell Room, South Bank Centre, 22 March, 8.03–8.07 pm. This exchange is recorded in full in the documentary, 'The Horrible Gift of Freedom' (Marcus Wood and Richard Misek, Bigslugsister Productions, 2008).

13. Paul Hope, 'Jam Packed Berth Space', mixed media on paper, 1996–2007.

14. Golliwogs are, of course, embedded within the folk culture of Anglo-America. Historically, their birth place is seen to lie in the 1890s in Florence Upton's illustrated children's books, but that is a convenient fiction, and these black male dolls in reality go back much further and are caught up in the history of Jim Crow, minstrelsy and those very early race satires on black male vanity and over-dressing. One thing about the golliwog, however, is that it constitutes a genuine example of black grotesque. *Webster's Dictionary* defines golliwog as 'a grotesque black doll, or a grotesque person'.

15. Hope was a Detective Sergeant in the Metropolitan Police and conducted motorway patrols and surveillance in the 1990s.

16. Thomas Clarkson, *Description of a Slave Ship* (London, 1789). This is the large woodcut broadside version of the London Abolition Committee version of the *Brookes*. It devotes almost precisely half of its space to the image, and half to the detailed accompanying text. This was the mass produced version. The wood engraved images of the slave decks could be set in the same form as the text, and printed with one pull on a large flat bed press.

17. For the use of human faeces in *La Bouche du Roi*, see Charlotte Higgins, 'Ship Shape Artwork Recalls Slave's Ordeal', *Guardian*, 22 March 2007. This aspect of the work is completely bypassed in all the official museum publicity distributed in London, Hull, Liverpool, Newcastle and Bristol.

18. For a detailed discussion of the work, including its relation to the 'Wonderful Tar Baby Story' of Joel Chandler Harris, see Marcus Wood, *High Tar Babies: Race, Hatred, Slavery, Love* (Manchester: Clinamen Press, 2001).

19. As far as I can gather from conversations with Ronnie Mosebach, the Project's education officer, the following works ironising the image of the *Brookes* were produced collaboratively during February and March of 2007: 'Southwark As *Brookes* (Slave Ship)' [photo-copy, photomontage]; 'Britain as *Brookes* (Slave Ship)' [photo-copy, photomontage]; 'BUCKINGHAM–UPON–BROOKES' [photo-copy, photomontage]; 'PARLIAMENT–UPON–BROOKES' [photo-copy, photomontage] The work 'IDENTITY?' was produced as part of the same student project, during the same time frame, by the Ghanaian student Ernest Gyasi, reproduced here as Figure 10.9.

20. There is little sophisticated work on the semiotic interpretation of stamps, and their relation to nationalist and imperial agendas. The best study by far in this area is David Scott, *European Stamp Design: A Semiotic Approach to Designing Messages* (London: Academy Editions, 1995). There has to date been no detailed work done on the treatment of slavery and the slave trade in postage stamps. The subject will be covered in depth and in global perspective in my forthcoming monograph, *The Horrible Gift of Freedom: Marketing the Emancipation Moment from 1807–2007* (Athens, GA: University of Georgia Press, 2009).

21. There have been several accounts of the genesis of the *Brookes* image and of its impact in Revolutionary France. The most recent, which draws heavily and rather exclusively on the work of Marcus Wood and John Oldfield, is Marcus Rediker, *The Slave Ship, A Human History* (London: Viking, 2007), pp. 329–31.

22. The marketing of the bicentenary via the Royal Mail and the Royal Mint have been neglected but fascinating processes. The actual stamps used in

daily circulation for a few months are only the tip of a philatelic iceberg that cannot be revealed here. Suffice it to say, there were postcards, posters and an enormous variety of elaborate and often surprising bespoke First Day Cover issues for collectors. The materials I deal with in this analysis are the mainstream productions of the Royal Mail, designed for purchase by the general public. These are the 50 pence stamp devoted to Clarkson and featuring the *Brookes*, the First Day Cover Royal Mail envelope featuring the stamps beneath the *Brookes*, and the 'ABOLITION OF THE SLAVE TRADE' presentation pack, featuring the *Brookes*. For the marketing of these, see the Royal Mail official web site http://www.royalmail.com/stamps/slavetradeaboliton (accessed 22 May 2008). An authoritative account of the design and distribution of these materials, and an illustrated account of all post marks issued across Great Britain on FDCs of the Abolition Bicentennial stamps, is the Norvic Philatelics website, http://www.norphil.co.uk/catalog/slavery(accessed 22 May 2008).

23. For the history of the design and for the technical details regarding this stamp, see http://www.bps.gov.bb; accessed 25 May 2008.

24. For the genesis of these stamps and the association of the figure in the statue with Bussa, see the anonymous illustrated pamphlet *Barbadoes 200th Anniversary of the Abolition of the Slave Trade from Africa* (Bridgetown: Barbados Philatelic Bureau, 2007).

Afterword: Britain 2007, Problematising Histories

Catherine Hall

2007, the bicentenary of the abolition of the slave trade, saw an unprecedented explosion of activities in Britain focused on the slave trade and
slavery, abolition and emancipation. This volume is one of the many
legacies of that year and bears witness to some of the critical thinking and scholarly work generated or encouraged by the bicentenary.
Drawing on British or American examples, authors have focused on
anti-slavery texts, neglected or re-read, on abolitionist identities across
and within the Atlantic world, on debates over the meanings of race, and
the challenges associated with 2007, in museums, the theatre and visual
culture. Writing as an historian, reflecting on the experiences of 2007
and the activities around it, I am struck above all by the multiplicity of
voices, of work of many kinds, and of the scale of the engagement that
took place on so many sites over the year. Prior to 2007, I would argue,
in so far as there was a collective memory in the United Kingdom on
issues of the slave trade and slavery, it was one of Britain's pride in having led the world, or so it was thought, in abolition and emancipation.
This version of abolition was established as early as 1808 when Thomas
Clarkson published his celebrated *The History of the Rise, Progress, and
Accomplishment of the Abolition of the African Slave Trade by the British
Parliament* in which he documented the growth of a white abolitionist
movement and its final triumph, the 'establishment of a Magna Charta
for Africa in Britain'.[1] It has been kept alive, in myriad ways, ever since.
Eric Williams's seminal text, *Capitalism and Slavery*, fundamentally challenged this view but it has remained extremely controversial, sidelined
from mainstream accounts.[2] The cornucopia of exhibitions, books, docu-
mentaries, theatrical productions and educational initiatives of 2007 has
put such an interpretation seriously in question. While understandings
of Britain's role in the slave trade and slavery are seriously contested,

191

the notion that it was the glorious achievement of white Christian men has, at the very least, been significantly challenged. What we saw in 2007 was an extraordinary public debate, at many different levels, on Britain's imperial history. Histories of the British Empire have been hotly contested in the last few years among academics. The key areas of debate have been about the legacies of empire; whether metropolitan society was significantly affected by Empire, whether British identities were constituted in part through constructions of colonised others, what kind of empire was that of the British?[3] The scale of the events around 2007, however, was something quite different, with a high level of engagement from many constituencies – community groups, schools and teachers, churches and chapels, politicians and the media. But there were also the conversations on the streets, in buses, even for me in the dentist's surgery, while a heated argument took place on a popular radio station. While the implications of all this are impossible to pin down it is undoubtedly the case that orthodox histories have been at least partially disrupted and new narratives of slavery and emancipation have achieved a much greater level of public visibility.

Nobody could have foreseen the ways in which the opportunity of the bicentenary would be taken up. Major new exhibitions were curated in Liverpool, Bristol, Hull, Birmingham, London's Museum in Docklands and the National Maritime Museum. Smaller exhibitions have been put on in innumerable local museums and galleries. A large number of special TV and radio productions were made, 30 hours of commissioned programmes from the BBC – from the award-winning 'Moira Stewart in search of Mr Wilberforce' to histories of racism, plays about the slave trade and Melvyn Bragg's paean of praise to William Wilberforce.[4] The film *Amazing Grace,* funded by evangelical Christian groups, represented the abolitionists as heroes but placed Olaudah Equino firmly in the frame, while Simon Scharma's *Rough Crossings,* the tale of black loyalists in Nova Scotia, London and Sierra Leone, was turned into a play and performed in London. At the local level churches and community groups set up innumerable activities, while local history societies, some with obvious links to the trade, such as Lancaster, others in apparently unlikely spots from Guernsey to St. Albans, explored the legacies of slavery. The Museum of Edinburgh mounted an exhibition – 'It didn't happen here' – challenging the national orthodoxy that it was the English who were responsible for slavery while the Scots led the way on anti-slavery. A primary school project in Yorkshire and East Lincolnshire focused on working with both teachers and pupils – making connections between past and present from the price of a pair of jeans to the

Morecombe Bay cockle pickers – its imperative to stimulate empathy and establish connections. Academic conferences, special issues of journals and new books – both academic and popular – have been produced in abundance. English Heritage and the National Trust, guardians of Britain's castles and country houses, have, for the first time, seen fit to investigate how some of the fruits of slavery were invested in properties 'at home'. And then there were the blogs – giving public voice to an enormous range of responses from violent racist diatribes about the wasting of public money to community groups challenging the whole enterprise. Perhaps most significant for the long term was the 'Understanding Slavery Initiative', which began in 2003, a government funded national education project linking five major museums and working 'to promote and support the effective teaching of the history and legacies of the transatlantic slave trade in schools and communities by producing resources that reflect the many historical and contemporary perspectives on this major part of world history'. A central aspect of this initiative, linked to the bicentenary programme, was the production of materials for Keystage 3 students, part of the national curriculum, focusing on the themes of Activism, Heritage, Identity and Routes, and a 'Big Conversation', a national competition drawing students into debate over the legacies of this complex history.[5]

So, what are we to make of all this? What is its significance both in terms of race politics and contestations over history? Marcus Wood in his contribution to this volume is pessimistic as to the impact of 2007 in terms of visual culture. 'Britain's participation in and domination of the Atlantic slave trade', he writes, 'have been registered ... in predominantly revisionist and unchallenging ways ... nothing has changed much in 200 years' (p. 163). Opinions have been very mixed from the beginning – some were deeply sceptical, challenging 'Wilberfarces' and 'Wilberfests', convinced that none of this would make any difference to black people living in Britain and experiencing everyday racism. Some have felt disillusioned in the aftermath: the year is over, the topic has disappeared, new issues now dominate the heritage agenda, what lasting effects has any of this had? Others are more cautiously optimistic – large numbers of people of every age, gender and ethnicity were involved; slavery was debated publicly in a way that had never happened before; surely this would mark some kind of change? Whatever conclusions can be drawn must still be speculative – we cannot judge at this stage whether any real break has occurred – yet I remain cautiously optimistic that the terrain has shifted somewhat, that some of the erasures associated with Britain's history in relation to its empire have been disturbed.

Just as Elizabeth Kowaleski Wallace argues in her contribution to this volume that the success of *Coram Boy* can only be fully understood as a specifically British phenomenon, so, I suggest, 2007 marked a very British moment, specific to the current conjuncture.[6]

So what was this moment? The plethora of representations of the slave trade and slavery that were on view in 2007 was made possible by the change in the nature of British society over the last half century. Without a significant black British population none of this would have happened. The re-thinking of Britain's historic role as an imperial power was impelled by the transformation of Britain into a different kind of multicultural society, no longer characterised by the mix of Saxons and Celts, with a modest Jewish and black presence – but now with a large population of people of colour, initially drawn primarily from the Caribbean and South Asia – the imperial subjects who 'came home' from the late 1940s. Those West Indian, Indian and Pakistani migrants have had to make a place for themselves in British society, against a long history of racisms and imperial hierarchies, while their own societies of origin have also gone through processes of transformation, including the writing of national histories. For West Indians in the UK the struggle for independence, the eruption of civil rights and black power, and the 'discovery' of Africa in the Caribbean have all impacted back on the construction of new black British identities with Bob Marley's 'Redemption Song' as an iconic rendition of the return to slavery as a constitutive element of blackness. The work of black artists since the 1950s, from film-makers, poets and novelists to those working with photographs or installations, has represented these experiences, making them available to wide audiences and providing a base from which to draw in 2007. At the same time the crisis of Englishness/Britishness associated with the end of empire, the loss of status as a world power and the realities of a multicultural society has inspired new historical work – a new interest in slavery and abolition, and a return to questions of empire from a variety of perspectives. The hunger for history – the roots and routes through which people have come to be where they are and who they are – is a striking feature of contemporary Britain. It is these processes spanning the last decades that provide the backdrop for the events of 2007.

More immediately there are the changes in patterns of migration since the 1990s, the phenomenon of large scale Eastern European entry into Britain, 9/11 and the 'war on terror', and the moral panics over refugees and asylum seekers fuelled in recent years by the tabloid press. The New Labour government, when it first came to power in 1997, made clear its commitment to a form of multiculturalism. The publication of the Runnymede Report on the future of Britain in 2000, however, marked the first government retreat – when it disassociated itself from the findings of that report, in particular its analysis of the historic associations between Englishness and forms of racial exclusion.[7] Since 9/11 and 7/7 the focus has been increasingly on how to create 'social cohesion' in the context of anxieties about 'the terrorists within' and a series of Nationality, Immigration and Asylum Acts have laid down new policies which recognise the need for managed migration (to allow for the required forms of skilled labour) alongside draconian restrictions on entry.[8] In the last two years there has been an explicit retreat from multiculturalism with Trevor Phillips, chair of the now defunct Commission for Racial Equality (CRE), arguing that what we need to talk about is how we reach an integrated society, one in which people are equal under the law, and where there are some common values. A historic policy of multiculturalism, he suggests, has led to a more polarised society with fears of segregated communities living in near ghetto conditions. Those values he cites are democracy, freedom of speech and equality – troubling terms given the deepening of inequalities and loss of civil liberties over the last ten years. He insists that the goal is integration, not assimilation. There must be a capacity for change on both sides, migrants should not have to give up their own cultures and accept that of the host community. Britishness, he argues, should be a civic not an ethnic identity.[9] Gordon Brown has long been eloquent on what he sees as the core British values – tolerance, respect, freedom of speech, justice, a 'shared British heritage'. A new emphasis is needed, he argues, on teaching citizenship, and you cannot be a citizen if you are not British.[10] Yet the values that are being lauded as British seem irredeemably monocultural and remarkably similar to those associated with the Whig vision of history as progress. Furthermore, the question of how this 'shared British heritage' is to represent 'our' imperial history has not been addressed.

This emphasis on 'social cohesion' has emerged in the context of concerns that multiculturalism has led to social fracturing and increasing separation, people living 'parallel lives', a retreat among South Asians especially into narrow ethnic and religious ties. The last CRE report *A Lot Done, A Lot to Do*, marking the end of its work, argued that Britain's diversity, which should be a source of strength, risked becoming one of division.[11] It is in this context that we can grasp what a contradictory moment 2007 was. AfroCaribbeans are now seen as 'old migrants' with long established communities. There are currently one million people of mixed race descent living in Britain, the vast majority the result of AfroCaribbean/white British relationships. Whereas it was once young black men who were the most stigmatised it is now young radical Islamists (or rather young Muslims since stereotyping destroys distinctions between one Muslim and another). AfroCaribbeans speak English as their first language, many of them are Christian, and they have become style, sport and music icons. At the same time Britain has seen the emergence of a black middle class as in the US – one of the legacies of the political struggles of the 1980s. Programmes for diversity have been initiated both in government departments and in business. All this was inaugurated when Tony Blair was Prime Minister: a man who sees himself as modern, would certainly think of himself as against racism, was proud of the Macpherson Report into the death of Stephen Lawrence naming the police as institutionally racist, and brought black ministers such as Valerie Amos and David Lammy, both of whom were very committed to the importance of commemorating the bi-centenary, into government.

At the same time there are very different indicators. The horrific numbers of killings of young black men and boys and the media coverage of this, focusing on gangs, drugs and guns, highlighting the anarchic situation in particular areas and the loss of control by the police, has provided an opportunity to revisit moral panics over black crime. It has also given an alarming insight to the deep inequalities and bleak prospects for large numbers of black Britons. The CRE report deals with the increasing inequalities in the society for the AfroCaribbean population – the unacceptably high level of mental health problems, the numbers of prosecutions and convictions, the numbers in prison, the poor performance in schools, the staggering number of exclusions of black children, the relatively low numbers in education and training at 16, the tiny numbers of black students in 'top' universities and the fact that black students only account for 5 per cent of the total student population, the lower levels of employment and the very small numbers in the most senior jobs – all of this amounts to a persistent pattern of inequality associated with blackness.

The memory work occasioned by the bicentenary has taken place in this extremely contradictory situation when black Britons are both more accepted and still excluded. Like the Irish in the nineteenth century they are characterised as both inside and outside the nation – still a 'problem' to be addressed. It is this that provided the context for the Blair government's initiative on the bicentenary, the stated intentions of which were tackling poverty and inequality in the Caribbean and Africa, racism in the UK and contemporary slavery in all its forms: an ambitious programme. The decision that the Heritage Lottery Fund would distribute £20 million (a strange after echo of the £20 million granted to owners of the enslaved in 1834 in compensation for the loss of 'their property?) to varied groups was critical, for it made many projects possible. The intention was also, I suggest, to promote a particular collective memory, with the logo 'reflecting on the past, looking to the future.' As Blair put it: 'it is vital that we reflect on the past and look to the future. The spirit of freedom, justice and equality that characterised the efforts of the abolitionists is the same spirit that drives our determination to fight injustice and inequality today'. He expressed his sorrow that the slave trade and slavery could ever have happened and invited us to 'rejoice at the different and better times we live in today'. 'It is hard to believe', he continued, 'that what would now be a crime against humanity was legal at the time'. He expressed his *regrets* that something bad had happened, but stopped short of the apology (which would have indicated responsibility and notions of restitution) that he had been pressed to make. He signed the Council of Europe Convention on Human Trafficking but evaded the historic responsibility of the imperial state in relation to the slave trade and slavery. In part this was, of course, to sidestep the question of reparations, which has been increasingly on the agenda, but it was symbolic too of a wider reluctance to confront an awkward history. Blair's statement pointed to the merchants as those responsible for the trade, erasing state complicity in the Royal Africa Company and the navy's protection of the trade, not to speak of imperial military conquest. He made his comments, he said, in the context of 'the enormous contribution today of black African and Caribbean communities to our nation'.[12] The government itself sponsored a commemorative coin and 6 stamps celebrating individual contributions to abolition including Equiano and Sancho as well as the more familiar figures of Wilberforce, Clarkson and Hannah More. An exhibition was mounted at Westminster focusing on the parliamentary history and a service of commemoration held in Westminster Abbey – memorably disrupted by Toyin Agbetu. All of this it might be said was to encourage a collective memory of pride in 'our' history, this 'shared legacy' – from the heroic efforts of the early abolitionists (now recognised as including one or two significant black figures) to the image of Britain that Blair attempted to promote, a nation that leads on humanitarian questions and that is not afraid to act, whether in Bosnia, Sierra Leone, Iraq or Afghanistan.

It is unlikely that such a perspective was shared by all those involved in the government committees set up. What is certain is that the money that was released encouraged and facilitated an enormous range of activities that were already being planned, building on the work of artists, writers and historians over the last decades, sometimes challenging orthodoxies and disrupting narratives, sometimes confirming a story of white heroism, sometimes exaggerating black resistance to the exclusion of all other factors, but always making space for public debate on questions of the slave trade and slavery. Melvyn Bragg, a leading radio and TV presenter and friend of New Labour, used his flagship programme 'In Our Time' to unequivocally celebrate William Wilberforce as one of the greatest Englishmen ever, the architect of the abolition of the trade. Rather than drawing on the extensive historiography that demonstrates the significance of black resistance to the destruction of the slave trade and slavery, or the equally extensive work exploring the relation between slavery and the development of capitalism, he chose as his leading historian the frontbench Tory, William Hague, whose admiring biography of Wilberforce was one of 2007's slew of new books.[13] Yet this programme has been the subject of extensive comment demonstrating the gap between the intentions of any presenter and audience reception. A very different picture was elaborated in another BBC effort (but seen by relatively small numbers) – a programme in which the well-known AfroCaribbean newsreader, Moira Stewart, went on a journey to West Africa and Jamaica, as well as Hull, London and Birmingham, to investigate how the trade was abolished and what the role of Wilberforce really was. This offered a very different narrative from that of the heroic white abolitionists – reminding viewers of the realities of the trade and slavery, commemorating enslaved rebels and focusing on the troubled voyage of discovery into her own past of one black woman.[14]

Voyages of discovery have not been confined to the descendants of slavery. Andrew Hawkins, of the line of Sir John Hawkins, one of the first Elizabethans to engage in the trade with the support of his queen, found out about his ancestor and became troubled by that legacy. He took part in a reconciliation festival in Gambia and apologised for the part his family had played in enslaving Africans. He was ridiculed in the *Daily Mail* and the *Daily Express*. Julia Elton, descendant of a major Bristol slave trading family with investment in ships and estates in Jamaica,

> thought the apology was absolutely nauseating. Talk about publicity-seeking! You could rationally say that the whole of Britain's modern wealth is based on the trade. What are we going to do? Tear down all our buildings? This is probably wildly politically incorrect – and

I'm not saying we didn't treat slaves disgustingly – but what would have happened to the Africans if they had stayed in Africa? If you had to choose between living in Darfur and living in America which would you choose? And actually you could argue that most working-class people in England in the eighteenth century lived in effectively slave-like conditions.[15]

Here what was striking was the continuities between eighteenth and nineteenth century pro-slavery discourse and the sentiments of this twenty-first century descendant of a plantation family.

Many of the initiatives in 2007 struggled to make connections between the past and the present, insisting that the past lives on in the present. Barnor Hesse argued in his analysis of Spielberg's *Amistad* that 'the legacy of slavery becomes the historical record of abolitionism, not the contemporary agenda of racism'.[16] Similarly the Haitian historian Michel-Rolphe Trouillot has commented on the ways in which slavery in the US ended long ago officially but continues in its institutional forms and in the cultural denigration of blackness.[17] Slavery does not haunt British culture in the same way as in the US, primarily because it happened at a distance. Nevertheless its legacies, and that of the empire more generally, are powerfully present in the racial hierarchies of contemporary Britain. The development of liberalism and democracy has been endlessly entangled with the colonial world. Race is still alive in people's lives and some of the exhibitions and events of 2007 sought to draw out the continuities without losing the historical specificities. None of this has been unproblematic. My own experience of working in a consultative group at the Museum in Docklands on their new gallery 'London, Sugar, and Slavery' made it clear how difficult it is for historians and curators to work effectively together when the demands of an exhibition are so different from that of academia, and demonstrated what huge variations of opinion and emphasis there are even across a group, all of whom were committed to exploring the *shared* history of the slave trade and slavery and the part it played in the making of modern London. Part of what mattered about that experience was the commitment to holding on, recognising the agonistic nature of the debate, being prepared to listen and hear, keeping minds open to difference.[18]

It will be a long time before we know what this all adds up to. But the floodgates have been opened and cannot now be shut. Toni Morrison famously wrote of the unrepresentability of the horrors of slavery: Beloved was forgotten 'like a bad dream, remembering seemed unwise'. What we saw in 2007 was a struggle to remember.

Notes

1. Thomas Clarkson, *The History of the Rise, Progress, and Accomplishment of the Abolition of the African Slave Trade by the British Parliament* (1808; rpt. London: Frank Cass, 1968), 2 vols, 2, p. 580. On Clarkson's famous map of the activities of white abolitionists, see Marcus Wood, *Blind Memory: Visual Representations of Slavery in England and America 1780–1865* (Manchester: Manchester University Press, 2000), pp. 1–6. On memories of slavery and abolition, see J. R. Oldfield, *'Chords of Freedom': Commemoration, Ritual and British Transatlantic Slavery* (Manchester: Manchester University Press, 2007).
2. See Anita Rupprecht, 'Excessive Memories: Slavery, Insurance and Resistance', *History Workshop Journal*, 64 (Autumn 2007), pp. 4–28.
3. For two opposing positions on this debate, see Bernard Porter, *The Absent-Minded Imperialists: Empire, Society and Culture in Britain* (Oxford: Oxford University Press, 2004) and Catherine Hall, *Civilising Subjects: Metropole and Colony in the English Imagination 1830–1867* (Cambridge: Polity, 2002).
4. Helen Weinstein has directed a research project at the University of York on the role of museums in 2007. Her own research on 'The Making of the 1807 Bicentenary in the Media: commissioning, production, and content' was presented at the conference 'Remembering Slave Trade Abolitions: Commemorations of the Abolitions of the Slave Trade in International Perspective', University of Newcastle, 23–24 November 2007. She concluded that the main effect of the BBC coverage, marked as it was by many internal disagreements, was to encourage forgetting rather than remembering.
5. For a brief account of the project, see *Unlocking Perceptions: Understanding Slavery's Approach to the History and Legacies of the Transatlantic Slave Trade.* http://www.understandingslavery.com (accessed 20 March 2007).
6. The international conference in Newcastle in November 2007 'Remembering Slave Trade Abolitions: Commemorations of the Abolition of the Slave Trade in International Perspective' clarified how very particular the British response was.
7. Parekh Report, *The Future of Multi-Ethnic Britain* (London: Profile, 2000); for a discussion of the responses, see Anne-Marie Fortier, 'Pride politics and multiculturalist citizenship', *Ethnic and Racial Studies* 28/3 (2005), pp. 559–78.
8. Gail Lewis and Sarah Neal, 'Introduction: contemporary political contexts, changing terrains and revisited discourses', *Ethnic and Racial Studies* 28/3, 2005 pp. 423–44.
9. 'Integration, multiculturalism and the CRE', http://www.cre.gov.uk/diversity/integration/index.html (accessed 22 September 2009).
10. See, for example, Gordon Brown, 'Annual British Council Lecture', *The Guardian*, 7 July 2004.
11. Commission for Racial Equality, *A Lot Done, A Lot to Do* (London: 2007).
12. Government Press Notice, 22 January 2007.
13. 'In Our Time', BBC Radio 4, 22 February 2007.
14. 'Moira Stewart in Search of Wilberforce', BBC 2, 16 March 2007.
15. Cited in Andy Beckett, 'Heirs to the Slavers', *The Guardian Weekend*, 2 December 2006.

16. Barnor Hesse, 'Forgotten like a Bad Dream: Atlantic Slavery and the Ethics of Postcolonial Memory', in David Theo Goldberg and Ata Quayson, eds., *Relocating Postcolonialism* (Oxford: Blackwell, 2002), pp. 143–73.

17. Michel-Rolphe Trouillot, *Silencing the Past: Power and the Production of History* (Boston: Beacon, 1995).

18. See the essay in this volume by Douglas Hamilton for a reflection on the experience at the National Maritime Museum. On the difficulties of museum and gallery commemorations, see Katherine Prior, 'Commemorating Slavery 2007: A Personal View from Inside the Museums', *History Workshop Journal*, 64/1 (Autumn 2007), pp. 200–11.

Index